The Long Game

The Long Game

Building Wealth with Patience and Discipline

Luca Reinhardt

Mindful Pages

Published in 2025

ISBN: 9789362924803 (PB)
ISBN: 9789371341615 (eBook)

Published by

Mindful Pages
Imprint of Alpha Editions LLC
312 W. 2nd St #1834
Casper, WY 82601, USA

Content

Introduction
Why the Long Game Matters

Wealth, as a concept, is often misrepresented—sometimes even romanticised. For many, it conjures images of windfalls and winning streaks, of overnight millionaires and turbo-charged trades. Contemporary culture, particularly in the age of social media, has a knack for spotlighting these dramatic success stories—stories that unfold with dizzying speed and vanish just as quickly. But behind this glamour lies a more enduring, less camera-ready reality: meaningful financial success is almost never immediate, and it's certainly not accidental. Rather, it is cultivated—deliberately, patiently, and with a quiet consistency. This book is an ode to that reality. It speaks not to those chasing the next financial spectacle, but to those ready to tend the slow-burning embers of long-term prosperity—a warmth earned over time, not snatched in haste.

What's most striking is that the foundations of sustainable wealth aren't hidden away in esoteric financial theory or locked behind velvet ropes of insider access. They're grounded in principles so straightforward they border on banal—yet mastering them is anything but easy. The temptation of rapid returns is potent, no doubt, but it often paves the way to rash decisions and recurring disappointment. This book stands as a counterweight to that impulse. It lays out a measured approach, aimed at those prepared to play the long game: one rooted in rationality, tested strategies, and a commitment to the future that remains unshaken by the noise of the present.

At the core of this philosophy is a shift in perspective: wealth is not solely a financial pursuit; it is, more deeply, a behavioural one. The chapters ahead go beyond charts and numbers. They explore the mental models, the habits, and yes—the emotional grit—that underpin genuine financial growth. To build wealth over time is not merely to accumulate knowledge; it's to cultivate temperament. It demands endurance during downturns, clarity in the face of hype, and a kind of internal ballast that keeps one steady when the crowd panics. Ultimately, this isn't just about acquiring wealth—it's about becoming the kind of person who can responsibly carry and grow it.

The opening chapter sets the stage with a psychological deep-dive. It tears down the myth of instant wealth, unpicking the fallacies that lure so many into chasing fast returns. Drawing on research and lived examples, it argues for patience—not out of virtue, but out of sheer advantage. Delayed gratification, often celebrated as a character trait, is here reframed as a smart strategy for compounding one's edge over time. The chapter also navigates the mental traps and emotional missteps that sabotage long-term thinking, offering ways to sidestep them in favour of steadier ground.

Then comes compounding: a phenomenon so quietly powerful it's often underestimated until it's too late. The second chapter explores this force not as a mathematical curiosity, but as the unsung engine of wealth creation. Through examples both modest and profound, it shows how small, sustained actions—when left to work their magic over decades—can eclipse the most daring bets or market timing attempts. Often called "the eighth wonder of the world", compounding doesn't shout. But given time, it roars.

With that foundation, the book shifts to asset allocation—arguably the most important yet frequently overlooked decision in investing. Chapter Three challenges the obsession with individual stocks or market-timing wizardry. It argues that long-term outcomes hinge far more on how one allocates capital across different asset classes than on any single trade. Here, readers are guided through building a diversified portfolio, one that reflects their risk tolerance and long-term objectives. Rebalancing, far from a bureaucratic chore, is presented as a vital act of self-discipline—one that keeps ambition in check and strategy on track.

Chapter Four takes a more practical turn, surveying the various investment vehicles available: equities, bonds, funds, real estate, and others. It also ventures into the more controversial waters of alternative investments—cryptocurrencies, gold, private equity—not with hype or alarm, but with a sober eye. The point is not to endorse any one route, but to equip readers with the discernment to evaluate these options through a long-term lens.

Next, the focus turns to risk—not in its pop culture sense, but in its financial reality. Chapter Five invites readers to rethink risk not as something to fear or chase, but to manage. It categorises the different types—market volatility, inflation, liquidity shortfalls, and the more insidious sequence-of-return risk—and offers a toolkit for addressing each. Risk, as this chapter argues, isn't binary. It's complex, malleable, and—if understood—controllable.

Markets, as any seasoned investor knows, are not obliging creatures. They lurch, they slide, they soar, and they stumble. Chapter Six peels back the curtain on these cycles, explaining how economic rhythms affect both behaviour and outcome. It's a chapter that cautions against the seduction of market timing and instead advocates for strategic calm—a kind of stoicism in the face of uncertainty. Historical case studies anchor these ideas in reality, showing that those who endure often come out ahead, not in spite of downturns, but because they stayed the course through them.

But even more than markets, the human mind is the real battlefield. Chapter Seven delves into behavioural finance, making a compelling case that our greatest enemy is often ourselves. Emotional missteps, cognitive blind spots, and irrational impulses can dismantle even the most carefully constructed financial plans. The chapter doesn't merely warn against these pitfalls; it offers practical defences—automation, structured decision-making, and increased self-awareness—to help keep intentions aligned with action.

Passive investing, the focus of Chapter Eight, brings these insights into tangible form. Here, simplicity becomes strategy. Instead of attempting to outguess the market, passive investing aims to ride its long-term trajectory. This chapter makes the case for indexing, low fees, and minimal interference—not as concessions, but as active choices that yield powerful results over time. It's a roadmap for those more interested in building a life than obsessing over a portfolio.

Closely related is the subject of Chapter Nine: automation. When harnessed correctly, automation isn't lazy; it's wise. By setting up automatic contributions, regular rebalancing, and systematic investing practices, individuals remove friction and avoid the trap of constant decision-making. The chapter walks through tools like robo-advisors and employer retirement schemes, and outlines techniques like dollar-cost averaging—all designed to ensure that wealth-building continues steadily in the background of life.

All of this theory and structure coalesces in Chapter Ten, where readers are invited to create a tailored financial plan. This is the moment where abstract strategy becomes lived reality. The plan is not meant to be rigid—quite the opposite. It's built to flex, to adapt to shifting goals, changing incomes, and evolving priorities. The chapter also flags common stumbling blocks and distils lessons from those who've navigated the path before, sometimes imperfectly, but always instructively.

The book concludes not with a simple recap, but with a broader meditation on what it means to "play the long game". Wealth, in this context, is recast as a vehicle for autonomy, for purposeful living, for shaping a life that reflects one's values. It calls on readers to think beyond spreadsheets and stock tickers, and to consider legacy—not in a grandiose sense, but as the quiet imprint of a life lived with patience, clarity, and integrity.

No promises of secrets here. No breathless formulas or clickbait wisdom. Instead, what this book offers is a philosophy—a steady, thoughtful way of approaching wealth and life alike. It invites readers to slow down, to think carefully, to act deliberately. And for those who do, it offers something deeper than riches: a durable peace of mind, and the quiet power of knowing they've built something that lasts.

Wealth, in the end, is not the destination. It's what accumulates when one walks the path with care, foresight, and purpose. What lies ahead is not just instruction—it's an invitation to reimagine the journey.

Chapter 1
The Long-Term Mindset - Why Patience Wins

In today's frenzied financial culture, wealth is too often equated with speed. We are inundated with stories of crypto millionaires, influencers striking gold on social media, and day traders making fortunes with a few swipes of an app. These tales are catchy, no doubt—they shimmer with possibility—but they are also deeply misleading. Anecdotes are paraded as trends, outliers mistaken for norms. In truth, such success stories represent exceptions, not the rule, and in mistaking them for blueprints, many are led astray. This chapter begins by gently dismantling the illusion of instant riches, then methodically builds the case for a slower, more deliberate path—one grounded in sound principles and behavioural awareness.

The appeal of quick money is easy to understand—but it's not just a harmless fantasy. It's a seductive lie, and a dangerous one at that. When people begin to believe that financial security can be achieved through sheer luck or high-stakes wagers, they're far more likely to make reckless decisions. The 2021 meme-stock frenzy offers a striking example: spurred on by social media and the promise of easy returns, thousands plunged their savings into highly speculative bets like GameStop and Dogecoin. A few emerged victorious, yes—but the majority did not. Their losses, though largely absent from headlines, were no less real: wiped-out savings, mounting debts, dreams quietly abandoned. And worse, the psychological scars—shame, disillusionment, fear—often linger long after the financial damage is done.

This, then, is the fatal flaw of the quick-wealth mindset: it confuses luck with skill, hype with wisdom. It mistakes noise for signal. Speculation, by its nature, is emotionally charged and short-sighted. It thrives on urgency. Strategy, on the other hand—true wealth-building strategy—requires patience, long-range vision, and the discipline to act even when the rewards aren't immediate. And while it may lack the glamour of a windfall, it's far more consistent.

Genuine wealth tends to grow quietly, almost invisibly, over time. It gathers strength like a slow tide, not a sudden wave.

Which brings us to a concept as old as prudence itself: delayed gratification. In a world designed to deliver everything now—next-day delivery, real-time updates, instant streaming—the idea of waiting for a greater reward later can feel almost quaint. But make no mistake, it remains one of the most powerful principles underpinning lasting success, financial or otherwise. Whether you're training for a marathon, writing a novel, or building a nest egg, the pattern is the same: short-term sacrifice for long-term gain. To invest rather than spend, to plan rather than improvise, to endure discomfort in the present so as to flourish in the future—these are not heroic acts, but habitual ones. And over time, they compound into something formidable.

You might recall the famous "marshmallow test," conducted in the 1960s by psychologist Walter Mischel. Children were offered a single marshmallow immediately or two if they could wait a short while. The results, tracked over decades, suggested a clear correlation between the ability to delay gratification and long-term success in various life domains. The study has its critics today, of course—what long-standing psychological experiment doesn't?—but its central insight still holds weight. In financial terms, this capacity to wait, to resist the itch of now, can make the difference between fleeting comfort and lasting wealth.

Still, there's more to it than willpower. Understanding the time value of money—an essential, if often misunderstood, concept—is key. Quite simply, money today is worth more than the same amount tomorrow, because it can be put to work. It can earn. And those earnings can themselves earn. This is compounding, the quietly miraculous engine that drives so much of wealth creation. It's not a get-rich-quick scheme; it's a get-rich-eventually certainty—if given time.

Consider two savers. One begins investing £200 per month at the age of 25 and stops after ten years. The other waits until 35 to begin, and then contributes the same monthly amount until they reach 65. At a 7% annual return, the first investor—the one who stopped contributing after just a decade—will likely end up with more. The reason? Time. The earlier the start, the more time there is for compounding to work its exponential magic. It's not just about how much you invest, but how long it's left to grow.

And yet, despite its reliability, long-term investing often goes neglected. Why? Because human beings are not rational creatures—not in matters of money, at least. Our financial lives are shaped less by spreadsheets and more by emotion. Greed, fear, envy, self-doubt—these inner forces have torpedoed more retirement plans than any market crash ever could. We are wired for survival, not for investing. And so we react to dips with panic, chase fads with reckless hope, and sabotage our own strategies with stunning regularity.

This is not a personal failing—it's human nature. Greed surges when the markets rise; fear takes over when they fall. Impatience tells us we're moving too slowly. Envy, amplified by social media's highlight reels, convinces us that everyone else is getting richer, faster. The challenge is not to rid ourselves of these impulses—no one can—but to put systems in place that help us resist their pull. Automatic investing, routine portfolio reviews, clearly defined goals rooted in personal values—these are not just tactics. They're anchors.

Financial literacy, too, plays a critical role. Understanding how markets behave over time, how different assets perform, and how risk is managed—all of this builds a mental buffer against rash decisions. History reminds us that markets have survived wars, pandemics, political turmoil. They fall, they recover, they grow. The variable isn't the crisis; it's how we respond to it.

Ultimately, developing a wealth-building mindset requires more than adjusting one's strategy. It demands an evolution of identity. The best investors don't think of themselves as speculators, but as caretakers of capital. They approach the process much like a gardener approaches an orchard. Early on, the work feels slow, perhaps even unrewarding. But with time and consistency, the fruits become impossible to ignore. Not just for the planter—but often for those who follow.

Discipline is the great equaliser. A basic strategy, executed consistently, often trumps a sophisticated one applied sporadically. The quiet act of making monthly contributions to a retirement account, regardless of market noise, might appear dull—but it's this very dullness that proves effective. In the end, it's not about cleverness, but commitment.

None of this comes naturally. The long-term view must be cultivated. It requires regular reflection, self-honesty, and no small amount of humility. But it also frees us—from the tyranny of the urgent, from the pressure to outperform, from the noise. Investing, once reframed, becomes less a game of prediction and more an expression of values. It allows room for mistakes. It absorbs shocks. And it rewards, patiently, those who persevere.

This chapter is a stake in the ground. It's the psychological and philosophical spine of what follows. It challenges you not merely to reconsider your tactics, but to shift your perspective. To zoom out. To pause before reacting. To exchange illusion for insight. Because wealth built over time doesn't just last—it means more. And patience, far from being passive, is one of the most active and enduring forms of wisdom we can wield.

The Myth of Quick Wealth

Few ideas have proved as enduringly seductive as the belief in fast money. From lottery tickets to cryptocurrency surges, high-frequency trading to speculative property flipping, modern culture is saturated with narratives that suggest wealth can be amassed swiftly, dramatically, and with minimal effort. The myth of quick wealth is not only persistent—it's increasingly glamorised. Yet, this illusion comes at a steep cost, both financially and psychologically. It distorts expectations, fuels risky behaviour, and undermines the principles that truly build enduring prosperity. To dismantle this myth, we must examine its origins, understand its appeal, and confront its consequences with clear-eyed analysis.

At the heart of this illusion lies a cognitive bias: our tendency to give disproportionate attention to outlier events. Stories of individuals who turn modest sums into millions through timely investments or risky ventures occupy headlines and dominate social discourse. Consider the speculative mania surrounding Bitcoin during its meteoric rise in 2017 and again in 2020–2021. Those who bought early and sold near the peak achieved spectacular returns. These success stories were widely shared, creating an impression that similar gains were accessible to anyone with a smartphone and a trading app. What remains less visible are the countless individuals who entered late, sold in panic, or lost money entirely. These stories lack the drama of overnight riches and, as such, are conveniently excluded from the cultural narrative.

The allure of fast wealth is further amplified by media portrayals that romanticise risk-taking. Films like *The Wolf of Wall Street*, *Boiler Room*, or *Wall Street* elevate high-stakes trading to a form of heroism. Characters who outwit the system, bend rules, and reap outsized rewards are portrayed not as cautionary figures, but as aspirational. Social media compounds the effect, offering curated glimpses into lifestyles supposedly funded by effortless success—luxury cars, exotic holidays, and designer wardrobes—often with little transparency about the source or sustainability of that income. This spectacle fuels unrealistic expectations, especially among younger generations who may not have seen the hard-won gains of disciplined investing modelled by those around them.

Yet behind every apparent success built on fast money is a rarely told tale of volatility, stress, and fragility. Day trading, for example, is often touted as a legitimate alternative to long-term investing. However, multiple studies, including those by financial researchers at institutions such as the University of California, Berkeley, and the Brazilian stock exchange, show that the overwhelming majority of day traders lose money over time. Even among those who initially succeed, few can maintain profits consistently. This is not merely a question of skill but one of structural disadvantage. Markets are influenced by vast, complex forces—many beyond the reach of individual investors—and short-term movements are notoriously difficult to predict with accuracy.

Moreover, the psychological toll of chasing quick wealth is frequently underestimated. Fast-money strategies often demand constant monitoring, rapid decision-making, and a high tolerance for uncertainty. For most individuals, these demands produce stress, fatigue, and impulsivity—conditions that degrade judgement and increase the likelihood of poor decisions. One becomes reactive rather than reflective, more attuned to short-term fluctuations than to long-term fundamentals. It is a state of mind more akin to gambling than to investing. The line between speculation and addiction can be alarmingly thin, and the consequences—financial, emotional, even relational—are rarely confined to the individual.

There is also an ethical dimension to consider. Many fast-wealth schemes rely on hype, misinformation, or unsustainable business models. Multi-level marketing schemes, pump-and-dump stock groups, and certain high-leverage trading platforms prey on the financially uninitiated, offering promises of easy riches while extracting fees, data, or credibility. These operations thrive on the myth of fast success, often wrapping themselves in the language of empowerment and entrepreneurship. In reality, they perpetuate cycles of disillusionment and debt.

It is important here to distinguish between legitimate entrepreneurship or innovation and the cult of quick wealth. Building a successful business can certainly produce substantial financial returns, sometimes rapidly. However, even in the world of startups, the overnight success story is largely mythical. Most so-called "overnight" successes are years in the making, built through long hours, repeated failures, and strategic reinvestment. For every founder whose app is acquired for millions, there are hundreds whose ventures folded, often taking personal savings, mental health, and hard-earned reputations with them.

Why, then, does the myth of quick wealth persist with such tenacity? Partly, it reflects a human tendency to seek shortcuts. Delayed gratification, though intellectually appealing, is emotionally taxing. It requires resisting temptation, deferring consumption, and accepting uncertainty over long timeframes. Fast money offers the opposite: immediate excitement, the fantasy of control, and the dopamine rush of potential reward. These are powerful motivators, especially when combined with the peer pressure and performance anxiety engendered by social comparison.

Yet perhaps the most insidious feature of the quick-wealth narrative is its distortion of the concept of wealth itself. True wealth is not merely the possession of large sums. It is stability, freedom, the capacity to make choices without fear or constraint. It is health, time, security, and the peace of mind that comes from knowing one's future is not contingent on luck or timing. Fast money rarely delivers these qualities. It is often volatile, unsustainable, and built on illusions. Long-term wealth, by contrast, is cultivated through habits—saving, investing, learning, adjusting. It may lack the drama of speculative wins, but it possesses something far more valuable: durability.

The financial principles that generate lasting prosperity are not mysterious. They include diversification, consistent contributions, prudent spending, and the intelligent use of time and compounding. They demand patience, to be sure, but they also reward it. Consider the long-term returns of broad-market index funds, which have historically outperformed most active strategies over multi-decade periods. Or reflect on the power of reinvested dividends, which quietly and steadily increase returns in ways that short-term traders often overlook. These are not the tactics of the impatient. They are the choices of those playing the long game.

Real-world examples reinforce this truth. Take the case of Ronald Read, a Vermont janitor and gas station attendant who lived modestly, avoided debt, and invested consistently in blue-chip stocks over decades. When he died in 2014, he left behind a fortune of over $8 million, most of which was donated to local institutions. He made no headlines during his lifetime. He had no viral moment. Yet his story is arguably more instructive than that of any hedge fund manager or tech prodigy. It demonstrates that wealth is not about brilliance or boldness, but about behaviour.

Similarly, legendary investor Warren Buffett amassed more than 90 percent of his wealth after the age of 60—not because he suddenly became smarter or luckier, but because compounding needs time to reach full strength. Buffett began investing as a child, stayed invested, and allowed time to magnify his returns. His success, often celebrated as genius, is just as much a testament to patience.

These stories challenge the dominant script and offer a more grounded, accessible template for wealth building. They remind us that financial success is not a race, but a process. A slow process, at times, but one that is robust, repeatable, and inclusive. It is not reserved for the extraordinarily talented or the exceptionally fortunate. It is available to those willing to think in decades, not days; to focus on principles, not predictions.

To reject the myth of quick wealth is not to reject ambition. It is to redefine it. It is to embrace the idea that wealth worth having is wealth worth waiting for. It is to find satisfaction not in sudden windfalls, but in the quiet confidence that comes from a well-constructed plan, faithfully executed. It is to understand that financial freedom is not won in a single transaction, but earned through thousands of small, deliberate acts.

As we move through this book, you will encounter strategies, tools, and mental models designed to support this philosophy. But at the outset, one lesson must be made unequivocally clear: shortcuts in wealth often become detours into disappointment. Patience is not only a virtue—it is a financial strategy, a competitive advantage, and the foundation upon which real wealth is built. Discarding the myth of fast success is the first step toward building a financial future that is not only rich in capital, but rich in confidence, clarity, and peace of mind.

The Power of Delayed Gratification

Among the many virtues required to build wealth, few are as underestimated—or as quietly potent—as the ability to delay gratification. In a world designed for immediacy, resisting short-term temptation in favour of long-term gain can seem both counterintuitive and burdensome. Yet the evidence is overwhelming: those who consistently choose to forgo short-term pleasures in exchange for long-term rewards achieve not only superior financial outcomes, but often richer, more meaningful lives. Delayed gratification is not simply a character trait; it is a learned behaviour, a cognitive skill, and a cornerstone of sustainable wealth-building.

The psychological underpinnings of delayed gratification are rooted in behavioural science. One of the most famous studies exploring this concept is the Stanford marshmallow experiment, conducted by psychologist Walter Mischel in the 1960s. Children were given a choice: eat one marshmallow now, or wait and receive two later. Decades later, researchers found that those who delayed gratification tended to perform better across a variety of life domains, from academic achievement to emotional regulation. While the study's findings have been subject to reinterpretation and debate, its central insight remains powerful: the ability to pause, to resist the pull of the immediate, is a predictor of future success.

In financial terms, this principle plays out in myriad ways. Consider the choice between spending discretionary income on luxuries today versus investing it in a compounding asset. The former delivers an immediate dopamine hit—a new gadget, a designer item, an indulgent experience. The latter offers nothing tangible now, yet quietly accumulates value over time. When repeated consistently, these small, seemingly mundane choices produce radically different outcomes over the span of a decade or more. The individual who invests consistently from their twenties will, by middle age, likely have built a financial cushion that offers freedom, security, and options. Meanwhile, their counterpart who consistently opted for present gratification may find themselves underprepared, reliant on credit, or locked into work they cannot afford to leave.

This distinction is not just theoretical. Real-world case studies illustrate its power. Take the example of Grace Groner, a secretary who lived modestly, wore second-hand clothes, and never married. She purchased $180 worth of shares in Abbott Laboratories in 1935 and held them for decades, reinvesting dividends without touching her growing nest egg. Upon her death in 2010, she left over $7 million to a foundation supporting students at Lake Forest College. Her wealth was not the result of a high income or sophisticated trading—it was the compound product of simplicity, consistency, and the deliberate deferral of consumption.

Compare this with the all-too-common story of lottery winners who find themselves bankrupt within a few years. A 2016 study published by the National Bureau of Economic Research found that nearly one-third of lottery winners file for bankruptcy within five years. Despite a sudden influx of wealth, the absence of financial discipline and an ingrained preference for immediate gratification often lead to poor decisions, unsustainable lifestyles, and eventual financial ruin. These examples illustrate a fundamental truth: wealth creation is less about how much one has, and more about how one manages what one has over time.

The power of delayed gratification also extends beyond saving and investing—it plays a crucial role in reducing financial stress and cultivating contentment. When individuals learn to wait for what they want, they often discover that they no longer want it as urgently. The impulse to buy fades, replaced by a growing satisfaction in the control exercised. This restraint creates space for intentional living, where spending is aligned with values rather than emotion or impulse. It transforms money from a source of anxiety into a tool for meaning.

Of course, delaying gratification is not without challenge. The modern economy is engineered to erode patience. We live in a culture of instant downloads, one-click purchases, and perpetual advertising. Every platform we engage with is designed to capture attention and convert desire into action with as little friction as possible. Delayed gratification, by contrast, requires the deliberate creation of friction. It involves pausing, reflecting, and often saying no—not just to others, but to ourselves. This resistance is not natural. It must be cultivated through systems, habits, and mental frameworks that make long-term thinking easier and more rewarding.

One effective strategy is to frame financial decisions within the context of long-term goals. Rather than viewing money as a means to acquire, reframe it as a means to enable: what kind of life do I want to build? What freedoms do I value? What responsibilities do I want to honour? This shift in perspective transforms financial choices from acts of denial into acts of affirmation. Skipping a frivolous purchase is not merely about saving—it is about moving closer to financial independence, early retirement, or the ability to support a loved one. It turns "I can't" into "I choose not to—for something greater."

Another tool is automation. By setting up regular transfers into investment accounts or savings vehicles, individuals can bypass the moment of decision altogether. What is automatic is often invisible, and what is invisible is less tempting to disrupt. This reduces the cognitive load associated with financial discipline and reinforces consistency. Automation does not eliminate the need for intention, but it strengthens it by removing temptation from the point of contact.

Technology, when used thoughtfully, can further support the practice of delayed gratification. Budgeting apps, financial trackers, and goal-setting platforms offer real-time feedback on progress, turning abstract goals into tangible benchmarks. Seeing a retirement fund grow, a debt balance shrink, or an emergency fund accumulate can be more motivating than any single purchase. It provides the emotional reinforcement necessary to sustain long-term behaviour in a short-term world.

Importantly, delayed gratification does not imply deprivation. It is not an argument against enjoyment, comfort, or quality of life. Rather, it is a strategic recalibration—an alignment of spending with purpose. It invites us to distinguish between impulse and intention, between transient pleasure and enduring value. It asks not, "Can I afford this now?" but "Will this support the life I'm building?"

This principle has deep historical roots. Many philosophical and religious traditions emphasise restraint, temperance, and future-oriented thinking. The Stoics spoke of mastering desire to achieve inner freedom. The teachings of many Eastern philosophies advocate detachment from craving as a path to peace. In financial life, these same principles find modern expression in budgeting, investing, and long-term planning. They are not constraints on freedom; they are its foundations.

The intergenerational impact of delayed gratification is also significant. Parents who model restraint and future-thinking instil these values in their children, setting the stage for financial literacy and stability across generations. Family wealth is often less about inheritance and more about mindset—habits passed on through example, conversations, and attitudes towards money. A household that values patience, planning, and discipline is one that fosters resilience and adaptability, qualities that outlast even the most generous trust fund.

Ultimately, the power of delayed gratification lies in its quiet compounding. Like financial interest, its effects are subtle at first, then transformative. The individual who practices it may not draw attention in the short term, but over years, they find themselves with options others do not—freedom from debt, freedom to leave toxic environments, freedom to give generously, to take risks, or to retire early. This is not the dramatic success of windfalls or viral stories, but the solid, lasting success of those who chose the long road—and walked it with purpose.

The temptation of immediacy will always be present. But so too is the opportunity to choose differently. To choose to wait, to invest, to plan—not because one must, but because one understands what's at stake. Delayed gratification is not about denial. It is about design. It is about shaping a life that reflects our deepest values, rather than our shallowest impulses. And in the world of finance, as in life, those who master it wield a quiet power: the power to build something that lasts.

Understanding the Time Value of Money

One of the most fundamental principles in finance, and arguably the most misunderstood by novice investors, is the time value of money. At its core, the concept is simple: a pound today is worth more than a pound tomorrow, because the pound today can be invested and earn a return. Yet this deceptively straightforward idea carries profound implications. It underpins nearly every financial decision, from saving and investing to borrowing and retirement planning. To grasp the time value of money is to unlock a new understanding of how wealth grows—not just through effort or earnings, but through time itself.

The notion that money changes in value over time may seem abstract, particularly when inflation is low or interest rates are stagnant. But money is not static. It possesses potential—potential that increases the longer it is allowed to work. This is the principle that fuels compounding, the force Albert Einstein reportedly described as the most powerful in the universe. When you invest, your money earns a return. If you reinvest those earnings, they begin to earn returns as well. Over time, this self-reinforcing cycle accelerates, creating exponential growth from what began as modest contributions.

To illustrate, imagine two individuals: Alice and Ben. Alice begins investing £3,000 annually at age 20 and stops at age 30. She invests for just ten years. Ben, on the other hand, delays. He starts at 30 and continues investing £3,000 every year until age 60—thirty years of disciplined contributions. Assuming both achieve an average annual return of 7%, who ends up with more money at age 60? Remarkably, Alice does. Despite investing a third of what Ben did, her early start gave her a decisive advantage. Her money had more time to grow, to compound upon itself, and to generate gains from gains. This example, often used in financial education, is not hypothetical. It reflects real-world outcomes shaped by time, not talent or timing.

The implications are significant. Starting early not only maximises wealth accumulation—it reduces the pressure to contribute large amounts later. It transforms financial security from a herculean task into a series of manageable, consistent actions. Yet despite this, many delay investing, believing that small sums are inconsequential or that they can 'catch up' later with higher earnings. This delay is costly. Every year postponed is a year of lost growth, and those cannot be recovered. Time, once passed, is the one asset no amount of money can reclaim.

But the power of the time value of money goes beyond retirement planning. It also influences everyday decisions, such as taking on debt. When you borrow, you're essentially working against the time value of money—paying interest over time rather than earning it. Credit card debt, for example, can accrue at rates of 20% or more annually. Inversely, this is compounding in reverse. What begins as a manageable balance can quickly balloon, as interest is charged not only on the principal but on previously accrued interest. Understanding this dynamic equips individuals to make smarter borrowing decisions, distinguishing between constructive debt—

such as a mortgage or student loan—and high-interest liabilities that erode wealth.

The time value of money also plays a crucial role in evaluating financial opportunities. When comparing investment options or business ventures, it is not enough to consider absolute returns. One must account for the timing of those returns. Receiving £10,000 today is more valuable than receiving £10,000 five years from now, even if the nominal figure is the same. This is why financial analysts use tools like Net Present Value (NPV) and Internal Rate of Return (IRR)—they adjust for the value of money over time, providing a more accurate picture of an investment's true worth.

Yet, despite its importance, this concept is often underemphasised in mainstream financial discourse. Personal finance advice tends to focus on budgeting, debt reduction, or income generation—all important elements, but insufficient without an understanding of how time influences value. Schools rarely teach compounding with the seriousness it deserves, and many adults only encounter the concept when planning for retirement—often too late to benefit fully from its effects.

Part of the issue is psychological. Human beings are wired to focus on the immediate. We discount the future, a bias known as hyperbolic discounting, and overvalue short-term gratification. This makes the benefits of early investing seem abstract, while the rewards of spending now feel tangible. Overcoming this bias requires a shift in perspective—a reframing of time as an asset, not merely a backdrop. It means seeing your future self as a real person, someone whose quality of life depends directly on the decisions you make today.

Technology can assist in making this shift. Online calculators, investment simulations, and retirement planning tools can vividly demonstrate the impact of early and consistent investing. Seeing how a monthly contribution of £250, begun at age 25, can grow into a seven-figure retirement fund by 65—even at modest rates of return—has a clarifying effect. It transforms financial planning from an abstract obligation into an empowering exercise in foresight.

Real-world examples offer further validation. Consider Warren Buffett, widely regarded as one of the most successful investors in history. While his skill and business acumen are undeniable, much of his wealth is attributable to the time his money has been invested. Buffett made his first stock purchase at age 11 and didn't stop. Today, over 90% of his net worth was accumulated after he turned 60. His fortune is not just the product of high returns, but of consistency, reinvestment, and, above all, time.

This lesson holds true even for those of modest means. The power of compounding is not reserved for the rich or the financially sophisticated. It is accessible to anyone with the patience to let their money grow. And the earlier one begins, the less one needs to contribute to achieve significant results. This is financial freedom not as a distant dream, but as a measurable, achievable outcome—one that is built day by day, pound by pound.

But the benefits of respecting the time value of money extend beyond personal gain. They also foster societal stability. Individuals who understand and apply these principles are less likely to become burdens on public systems, more likely to contribute to charitable causes, and better equipped to support future generations. Financial literacy, particularly with regard to time and compounding, has ripple effects that extend into families, communities, and national economies. It encourages self-reliance, long-term thinking, and responsible stewardship.

To fully embrace the time value of money is to reject the cultural fixation on immediacy. It is to resist the pressure to consume now, and to instead cultivate a vision of the future that is rich in possibility. It is to trust in a process that rewards patience over panic, consistency over cleverness. It requires no exotic strategies, no perfect timing, no insider knowledge—only the will to begin, and the discipline to continue.

Those who do so reap not only financial rewards, but psychological ones as well. Knowing that your money is working—even while you sleep, rest, or holiday—creates a sense of security that no salary alone can provide. It shifts the relationship with time from one of scarcity to one of opportunity. Time is no longer an enemy, ticking down towards retirement or old age. It becomes a partner, compounding your efforts and magnifying your intentions.

In a world that increasingly demands immediate results, understanding the time value of money is a radical act of foresight. It is a commitment to future self, a strategy that transcends trends, and a discipline that rewards those who begin early and persist with purpose. By recognising and applying this principle, individuals can transform their financial trajectories—not through dramatic action, but through the quiet power of time, patiently and faithfully applied.

Psychological Barriers to Long-Term Investing

Building wealth through long-term investing is, in theory, a straightforward process. The basic formula—save consistently, invest in diversified assets, and allow time to compound returns—has proven effective across generations, geographies, and economic cycles. Yet, despite this clarity, many individuals fail to act on these principles, or abandon them prematurely. The discrepancy lies not in a lack of information, but in the complexity of human behaviour. The greatest obstacles to long-term investing are not found in market volatility, inflation, or geopolitical uncertainty, but within the mind itself. Fear, greed, and short-term thinking quietly sabotage even the most well-intentioned plans.

To understand these psychological barriers, one must begin with fear—a powerful emotion that has evolved to protect us from harm but often misfires in the financial context. Fear of loss, also known as loss aversion, is a well-documented cognitive bias whereby people experience the pain of losing money more acutely than the pleasure of gaining it. Studies in behavioural economics, particularly those by Daniel Kahneman and Amos Tversky, have demonstrated that individuals are more likely to make irrational decisions to avoid losses than to achieve equivalent gains. In investing, this translates into a tendency to sell at the worst possible times—during market downturns—driven by panic rather than prudence.

The 2008 financial crisis offers a stark illustration. Amid the global sell-off, many investors liquidated their portfolios at steep losses, fearing a complete collapse of the system. While such anxiety was understandable, those who sold missed the subsequent market recovery, which began in March 2009 and continued for over a decade. The cost of acting on fear was not only immediate—it was compounded over time by missed growth. By contrast, investors who held their positions, or even added to them during the downturn, were richly rewarded. This divergence in outcomes was not due to superior market knowledge, but to emotional restraint.

Greed, fear's counterpart, presents a more subtle but equally dangerous threat. It lures investors into speculative bubbles, high-risk trades, and strategies that promise outsized returns with minimal effort. The cryptocurrency frenzy of the 2010s and 2020s is a case in point. Stories of massive gains in Bitcoin, Ethereum, and lesser-known tokens triggered widespread FOMO—fear of missing out—and led many to invest without due diligence. While some profited handsomely, many more were left holding rapidly depreciating assets when the speculative fever cooled. Greed not only clouds judgement; it inflates expectations and fosters a mentality of gambling rather than investing.

One of the challenges with greed is that it often disguises itself as ambition or confidence. It persuades investors that they are smarter than the market, that they can time the highs and lows, or that they deserve higher returns because they've read the right books or followed the right influencers. This overconfidence can lead to concentrated bets, frequent trading, and a lack of diversification—all of which erode long-term performance. Academic research consistently shows that active traders, on average, underperform passive investors, largely due to transaction costs and poor timing. Greed fuels activity, but it rarely enhances results.

Short-term thinking, though less dramatic than fear or greed, may be the most pervasive psychological barrier of all. It is woven into the fabric of contemporary life. From social media feeds to quarterly earnings reports, from twenty-four-hour news cycles to instant gratification technologies, modern society conditions us to think in days and weeks rather than years and decades. This mindset is fundamentally at odds with the nature of long-term investing, which requires patience, consistency, and a tolerance for delayed results.

The tendency to fixate on short-term outcomes can lead to counterproductive behaviour. Investors may obsessively monitor daily portfolio fluctuations, misinterpreting normal volatility as evidence of failure. They may abandon well-constructed strategies after a few months of underperformance, forgetting that markets are inherently cyclical and that no single period reflects the full picture. Short-termism also breeds emotional whiplash—euphoria when prices rise, despair when they fall—which encourages reactive decision-making. Over time, these habits compound not only financially, but psychologically, fostering anxiety and undermining confidence.

Countering these psychological barriers requires a shift in both mindset and method. One powerful approach is to reframe investing not as a series of tactical decisions, but as a long-term discipline akin to physical fitness. Just as health is built through regular exercise and balanced nutrition over years, wealth is built through regular contributions and strategic diversification over time. There will be setbacks, plateaus, and external shocks—but consistency matters more than perfection. The investor's role is not to predict the market, but to remain engaged with a system designed for resilience.

Developing such discipline is easier with the right behavioural tools. Automation is one of the most effective. By setting up automatic transfers into investment accounts, individuals remove the need to make constant decisions, thus reducing the emotional noise that often leads to poor choices. Automating investing not only encourages consistency, but also reinforces a savings habit that becomes self-sustaining over time. When contributions are regular and decisions are fewer, investing becomes part of life rather than an occasional dilemma.

Another key strategy is establishing clear, values-based financial goals. When investment decisions are linked to meaningful outcomes—retiring comfortably, educating children, buying a home—they acquire emotional significance that can counteract the pull of short-term volatility. Abstract numbers on a screen are easier to abandon than a vision of future security or freedom. Visualising these goals, whether through journaling, digital planning tools, or discussions with loved ones, strengthens emotional commitment and reduces the sway of market fluctuations.

Historical context also offers valuable perspective. Looking back over a century of market data reveals that downturns, corrections, and recessions are not anomalies—they are features of the system. Yet over time, markets have consistently trended upwards, reflecting human innovation, population growth, and economic expansion. By anchoring expectations to this long-term trajectory rather than short-term performance, investors can reduce the emotional whiplash of daily news and focus on what matters: staying invested and allowing time to do its work.

Financial education is a crucial component in this behavioural transformation. The more one understands about asset classes, diversification, inflation, taxation, and risk, the less likely one is to be swayed by emotional reactions or sensational headlines. Knowledge creates psychological distance—it allows for detachment, perspective, and rational analysis. It doesn't eliminate emotion, but it creates a buffer against impulsivity. This is why financial literacy must be a lifelong pursuit, not a one-off event.

Support systems also matter. Accountability partners, whether financial advisers, mentors, or investment communities, can provide external perspective when internal biases threaten to take control. The simple act of discussing fears, doubts, or temptations with someone else can deflate their power. Moreover, being part of a network of like-minded investors encourages discipline through social reinforcement. When others are staying the course, one is more likely to do the same.

Ultimately, overcoming psychological barriers to long-term investing is not about suppressing emotion—it is about understanding it. Fear and greed are not flaws to be eradicated, but signals to be interpreted. They tell us about our values, our vulnerabilities, and our worldview. The goal is not to become emotionless, but emotionally intelligent—to recognise when an impulse arises, to question its origin, and to respond with intention rather than instinct.

This emotional maturity lies at the heart of successful investing. It allows individuals to weather storms, resist fads, and trust in a process whose results unfold over years rather than moments. It enables a shift from reactive to proactive behaviour, from anxiety to agency. And most importantly, it aligns financial actions with long-term aspirations rather than fleeting impulses.

The market will always test patience. Headlines will always stir fear. Opportunities will always tempt with the promise of rapid gains. But those who can manage their inner world—who can see beyond the now—will find themselves not only better off financially, but more grounded, more focused, and more free. Investing, in the end, is not merely a technical endeavour. It is a psychological practice. And like all such practices, it rewards those who commit not just with their minds, but with their habits, values, and vision.

Developing a Wealth-Building Mentality

Wealth is often perceived as the result of fortunate circumstances—inheritance, high income, or market timing. While these factors can indeed accelerate financial growth, they are not the primary determinants of lasting prosperity. What truly separates those who build enduring wealth from those who struggle to maintain it is mindset. More than a set of financial strategies, wealth-building is a mentality: a way of thinking, deciding, and acting over time. This mentality is cultivated—not inherited—and its core ingredients are discipline, consistency, and a clear understanding of how small habits compound into substantial outcomes.

At its essence, a wealth-building mentality begins with the ability to delay gratification and prioritise future benefit over present comfort. This idea, explored in depth in behavioural science, is more than a psychological curiosity. It is the foundation for virtually every financial behaviour that leads to long-term success. The individual who saves regularly, invests with discipline, avoids high-interest debt, and lives within their means is not necessarily more intelligent or better educated than their peers. More often, they are simply more consistent in applying sound principles, and more emotionally anchored to their long-term objectives.

The creation of wealth, much like the cultivation of health or mastery of a craft, hinges on routine. Financial decisions are not isolated events—they are embedded in daily life. The decision to cook at home rather than dine out, to buy a reliable used car rather than lease a new one, or to increase one's retirement contributions by a few percentage points each year may seem trivial in isolation. But repeated across years, these habits shape financial trajectories in profound ways. The key insight here is that wealth is not built in dramatic moments, but in the quiet repetition of wise choices.

Discipline is at the heart of this process. It is what transforms intention into action, and action into outcome. But discipline is not a fixed trait—it is a practice, one that must be nurtured with intention and context. Behavioural design plays a critical role here. Those who build wealth consistently tend to structure their environments to support good decisions. They automate savings, limit exposure to temptation, track spending patterns, and set reminders for financial check-ins. Rather than rely on willpower alone, they reduce the cognitive load of discipline by building systems around themselves.

Consider the practice of paying oneself first—a principle long championed by personal finance educators. By treating saving as a non-negotiable line item rather than a residual activity, individuals prioritise their future well-being. This habit, when automated, ensures that saving happens regardless of market noise, personal distraction, or competing short-term desires. Over time, it creates a cushion of capital, a sense of control, and a trajectory towards financial freedom that would otherwise be difficult to sustain through sporadic effort.

Another aspect of the wealth-building mentality is strategic patience. The modern world prizes speed—fast returns, instant gratification, rapid results. But wealth grows slowly, especially in its early stages. This slow pace can be discouraging, particularly for those just beginning their financial lives. The temptation to chase quick wins, to speculate on hot tips, or to abandon a long-term plan in favour of something more exciting can be powerful. Here, the wealth-building mentality asserts itself not with bravado, but with quiet persistence. It recognises that compounding does not yield impressive results immediately—but once it gathers momentum, it becomes a force of immense power.

The story of Anne Scheiber exemplifies this perfectly. A former IRS auditor who retired in 1944 with modest savings and a small pension, she began investing in quality stocks with a long-term focus. She never married, lived frugally, and continued to reinvest her dividends. When she passed away in 1995, she left a portfolio worth over $22 million—all built from disciplined investing over half a century. Her wealth was not the product of extraordinary income or insider knowledge. It was the result of sustained commitment to a strategy, deep frugality, and a mindset oriented around growth over decades.

Adopting such a mentality requires more than intellectual understanding—it demands emotional maturity. One must learn to be comfortable with delayed results, to resist the pull of social comparison, and to stay the course through periods of uncertainty. This is particularly difficult in a digital age where the highlight reels of others' financial lives are constantly on display. The appearance of sudden success can erode confidence, even in a well-crafted plan. Developing a wealth-building mindset therefore includes cultivating a sense of internal grounding—an ability to define success on one's own terms rather than through external validation.

Part of this grounding comes from setting meaningful goals. Financial targets, when abstract, do little to inspire sustained effort. But when linked to personal values—a secure retirement, the ability to support children through university, the freedom to travel or volunteer—financial decisions gain emotional resonance. They become expressions of identity and purpose rather than exercises in self-denial. This alignment of money with meaning is one of the most powerful motivators available to the long-term investor.

Education also plays a critical role. Understanding how markets work, how different asset classes behave, and how fees and taxes impact returns demystifies the process and reduces anxiety. Knowledge builds confidence, and confidence fosters discipline. When an investor understands that volatility is normal, that downturns are expected, and that long-term returns are historically positive, they are less likely to panic or abandon their plan at the worst possible time. Financial literacy is not simply a toolkit—it is a shield against poor decisions and an enabler of sound ones.

Mentorship and social reinforcement further strengthen the wealth-building mentality. Individuals who engage in regular financial discussions—whether with partners, advisers, or peer groups—tend to exhibit greater financial responsibility and resilience. These conversations normalise long-term thinking, provide accountability, and create a shared language around money that transcends superficial consumerism. In this way, building wealth becomes not only a personal goal, but a relational practice—one embedded in community and supported by shared values.

Of course, discipline does not mean rigidity. A mature wealth-building mentality allows for flexibility, enjoyment, and adaptation. Life is unpredictable, and a plan too tightly drawn can lead to frustration or burnout. The key is to balance structure with responsiveness—to build habits strong enough to endure pressure, but flexible enough to evolve with changing circumstances. The best investors are those who review their strategies periodically, adapt when necessary, and maintain focus without becoming dogmatic.

It is also important to acknowledge that building wealth does not occur in a vacuum. Systemic factors such as education, healthcare, housing, and employment all influence individual financial capacity. A wealth-building mentality, while powerful, must be supported by policies and environments that allow it to flourish. Nevertheless, within the constraints of one's circumstances, cultivating the right mindset can significantly enhance financial outcomes. It is not about perfection, but about progress. Not about guarantees, but about probabilities made more favourable through preparation and discipline.

Ultimately, developing a wealth-building mentality is not merely about acquiring money—it is about acquiring mastery. It is about learning to think across decades, to act with intention, and to align daily behaviours with future aspirations. It is about transforming money from a source of stress or scarcity into a tool for empowerment and freedom. And it is about realising that the most important investment one can make is not in markets, but in mindset.

By shaping habits that prioritise consistency over drama, discipline over impulse, and values over trends, individuals can lay a foundation for financial well-being that endures across life stages and market cycles. The wealth-building mentality is not a secret—it is a choice. A choice to think long, act wisely, and trust that the compounding effect of good decisions, repeated over time, will deliver not only financial success but a life lived with greater agency and meaning.

Chapter 2
Compounding - The Most Powerful Wealth-Building Tool

If there's a single, enduring principle at the heart of wealth creation, it's compounding. Often lionised as the "eighth wonder of the world", it operates not through magic but through mathematical inevitability—though its results can feel nothing short of miraculous. Compounding doesn't shout for attention; it works quietly in the background, rewarding patience and constancy while quietly transforming the ordinary into the extraordinary. Despite the media's fondness for stories of overnight success, it is this unassuming mechanism that sits behind most lasting fortunes. And yet, its power is often underestimated—misunderstood, even. To take compounding seriously is to take long-term financial growth seriously.

Strip it to its essence and compounding is the snowball effect of money earning returns—and those returns earning returns themselves. What starts as a gentle incline eventually becomes a steep curve. Not because one is adding more, but because growth is feeding upon itself. This isn't linear arithmetic; it's exponential growth. And like most things that change the game, it takes time to reveal its teeth. At first, progress is sluggish, almost frustratingly so. Then, seemingly all at once, momentum takes hold—and the numbers begin to climb with startling speed. There's a certain elegance in the simplicity of it.

A story often shared in finance circles—precisely because it makes the point so well—involves two fictional savers: Sarah and Tom. Sarah begins investing £200 per month at age 25 and stops at 35. Tom, on the other hand, waits until he's 35 and invests the same monthly amount all the way to 65. At retirement, Sarah ends up with more money, despite investing for a third as long. The reason? She gave her money more time to work. This isn't just a fable with a moral—it's cold, clear mathematics. Compounding, given enough time, makes the early mover a formidable force.

Let's get into the arithmetic for a moment. Say you invest £10,000 and it earns 7% a year. After one year, you've got £10,700. After ten, you're looking at nearly £20,000. Fast forward to twenty years and the total climbs above £38,000. Stick with it for thirty years and you'll find yourself north of £76,000. The numbers don't just increase—they accelerate. The longer the money stays invested, the more disproportionate the later gains become. That's the genius of compounding: it saves its most generous rewards for those who wait.

This is precisely why hesitation, when it comes to investing, can be so costly. Too many people put off investing, thinking small sums now are inconsequential or that they'll have more capacity to invest later. But here's the catch: time is the variable you can't retrieve. A 25-year-old investing £5,000 once and walking away could see it grow to over £160,000 by 65 (assuming an 8% return). A 45-year-old hoping to match that would need to cough up more than £25,000. Time does the lion's share of the work—but only if you give it the reins early on.

Another often-overlooked element in this process is the reinvestment of dividends and interest. Investors are frequently caught up in capital gains—buy low, sell high—but overlook the immense power of income left alone to grow. Reinvested dividends, for example, buy more shares, which themselves produce more dividends, feeding a loop that's astonishing in its impact. Interest, similarly, compounds when rolled over. Those who treat passive income as expendable, to be spent or skimmed, are cutting short one of compounding's most potent levers. The aim isn't merely to generate returns—it's to let those returns keep working, year after year.

In fact, long-term data tells us that a substantial slice of historical market returns comes from reinvested dividends. Not from price appreciation alone. Portfolios that consistently reinvest income tend to outpace those where earnings are withdrawn or left idle. Savvy investors grasp this—and they shift their focus from today's yield to tomorrow's total return. It's a subtle shift, but it's the kind of shift that accumulates millions.

That said, the whole edifice of compounding can be undone—quickly and often irreparably—by one simple action: cashing out too soon. Whether it's a bout of panic during a downturn or the lure of a tempting purchase, withdrawing funds breaks the chain of growth. And when that chain is broken, it doesn't just pause growth—it forfeits the future growth those gains would have generated. That's not just a lost opportunity—it's compounding in reverse.

Let's say someone pulls £50,000 out of their investments at age 40 to fund, say, a luxury holiday home. At 7% annual growth, that amount would've become almost £200,000 by age 65. The actual cost, then, isn't £50,000—it's the £200,000 they'll never see. This is the shadow world of investing: the invisible toll of opportunity cost. And it's why wise investors think in decades, not in immediate pleasures.

Of course, resisting the temptation to withdraw isn't merely a matter of cold logic. Human emotion plays a messy, persistent role. Fear, euphoria, insecurity—they all conspire to make us act against our own long-term interests. That's why we need defences. Automation helps—regular, set-it-and-forget-it contributions that don't rely on daily discipline. Psychological framing helps too: seeing investment accounts as untouchable, as sacred even, can reduce the temptation to meddle. And then there's perspective. Markets wobble. That's what they do. Staying the course through those fluctuations is what separates the consistent from the erratic.

And if you're still wondering whether this works in the real world, look no further than Ronald Read. He was a janitor in Vermont. Never earned much. But he died with more than $8 million, built not on windfalls or clever trades, but on consistent investing and reinvested dividends. His story isn't an outlier—it's a blueprint. It shows that wealth doesn't require brilliance. It requires time, habits, and restraint.

There's also something deeper at work here—a life lesson, not just a financial one. Compounding mirrors the arc of everything worthwhile. Whether it's career mastery, meaningful relationships, or personal growth, the most rewarding outcomes arrive not in sudden leaps but in slow, layered accumulation. Financial compounding teaches patience, yes—but also faith. Faith that consistent effort, applied over time, yields results worth waiting for.

This principle also invites us to think generationally. Wealth, when allowed to grow uninterrupted across decades, can support not only one life but many. It can educate children, create opportunities for grandchildren, or sustain charitable causes long after we're gone. Families that understand this often pass down not just capital, but the wisdom and values that sustain it. Compounding, in that light, becomes a philosophy of stewardship.

And it bears mentioning—because it's too often forgotten—that compounding doesn't belong solely to finance. It applies just as much to learning, health, habits, and relationships. A few pages of reading each day, ten minutes of movement, a regular phone call with a friend—these small acts, done consistently, reshape lives over time. To see compounding only in financial terms is to miss its broader, human truth.

Unlocking the full potential of compounding doesn't require complex tools or insider knowledge. It requires clarity, discipline, and the willingness to start. Early. And then to keep going, even when results seem small or progress feels slow. There are no shortcuts—but there are accelerators: reinvesting earnings, ignoring noise, staying the course. It's the long way around, yes—but it's the surest path there is.

This chapter will delve further into the mechanics, the mindset, and the practices that make compounding work. But more than that, it aims to shift how you think about time, money, and progress itself. Because when compounding is allowed to do what it does best—uninterrupted—it not only alters your net worth. It alters your future. Quietly, steadily, and with unrelenting force.

How Compounding Works

Compounding is the quiet architect of wealth. It operates not through drama or complexity, but through the unrelenting application of time and growth. At first glance, the mechanics of compounding seem unremarkable—your money earns returns, and those returns begin to earn returns of their own. Yet when this process is allowed to unfold over years, even decades, its power becomes transformative. It is exponential in nature, not linear, and therein lies its magic. To understand compounding is to understand how ordinary people, using modest sums and patient discipline, can build extraordinary financial outcomes.

The essence of compounding lies in reinvestment. Rather than pocketing earnings or spending dividends, the investor allows them to remain within the investment vehicle, where they continue to generate returns. This means that the next cycle of growth is calculated not just on the initial capital, but on an increasingly larger base. As each period passes, the value of the portfolio grows at an accelerating rate—not because the rate of return increases, but because the base to which that rate is applied becomes larger. This is what distinguishes compounding from simple interest or static savings. It is not merely accumulation—it is acceleration.

To visualise this, imagine a snowball rolling down a hill. At first, it picks up only a few flakes, but as it gains momentum, it collects more and more snow. By the time it reaches the bottom, its size bears little resemblance to where it started. Compounding functions in a similar way. The early years feel slow, even insignificant. Progress can seem negligible. But these early stages are foundational, not because they impress with size, but because they plant the seeds for exponential expansion later on. The investor who recognises this understands that patience is not just a virtue—it is a strategy.

Consider the case of a twenty-five-year-old who invests £5,000 in a fund earning 7% annually. After one year, the investment grows to £5,350. After ten years, it reaches roughly £9,835. This is respectable, but hardly life-changing. However, if left untouched for thirty years, the same investment grows to nearly £38,000. At forty years, it surpasses £74,000. The difference between year ten and year forty is not driven by additional contributions or higher returns—it is driven purely by time. This is the compounding curve in action. It begins slowly, almost imperceptibly, and then steepens dramatically. Those who quit too soon never reach the steepest part of the curve, where wealth growth becomes truly powerful.

The full potential of compounding is perhaps best illustrated through historical case studies. Warren Buffett, often cited as one of the greatest investors of all time, accumulated the vast majority of his wealth after the age of sixty. While his returns were strong, they were not unusually high by hedge fund standards—what made the difference was how long he allowed compounding to work. He began investing as a child and never stopped. His net worth didn't just rise—it exploded—because of decades of uninterrupted compounding. Buffett's fortune is as much a tribute to consistency and time as it is to skill.

What makes compounding unique among wealth-building tools is its accessibility. It does not require a six-figure salary, a finance degree, or insider knowledge. What it does require is early engagement and long-term perspective. Many individuals hesitate to invest because they believe they do not have enough money to make it worthwhile. But compounding is not about how much you start with—it is about when you start and whether you remain consistent. A person investing £100 per month from age twenty-five to sixty-five will likely amass more than someone investing £300 per month from age forty-five, despite contributing less overall. Time is the great multiplier.

The emotional challenge of compounding lies in its delayed gratification. The early years often feel thankless. Returns appear modest, even underwhelming. It is tempting to wonder whether it is worth continuing—especially when others appear to be getting rich faster through speculation, entrepreneurship, or inheritance. But compounding does not cater to the impatient. Its rewards are back-loaded. The investor who perseveres through these slow beginnings eventually finds themselves in a position that others, who chased quick success, can only envy.

A powerful aspect of compounding is that it rewards not only time, but behaviour. Investors who contribute consistently, reinvest earnings, avoid panic selling, and maintain a diversified portfolio are the ones who benefit most. These behaviours are not complex, yet they are difficult to sustain in a world of constant noise and distraction. Markets fluctuate. Media sensationalises. Friends boast of sudden wins. In this context, the long-term compounding investor must cultivate emotional discipline. They must understand that the volatility of markets is a feature, not a flaw—that the compounding machine keeps working, quietly, even when prices dip.

One of the most overlooked facets of compounding is the reinvestment of dividends. Many investors view dividends as income to be spent, but when reinvested, they become a powerful engine of growth. Consider an investment in a dividend-paying stock or fund. If dividends are reinvested, they purchase more shares. These additional shares then generate their own dividends, which buy even more shares. Over time, this feedback loop leads to significant increases in both share count and total value. Numerous studies of market indices over long periods demonstrate that reinvested dividends often account for the majority of total return. Ignoring this is akin to building a car but leaving the engine out.

Tax-efficient reinvestment can further amplify this effect. Utilising accounts such as ISAs or pensions, where gains and dividends grow free of tax or deferred until withdrawal, ensures that compounding is not interrupted by unnecessary friction. Taxes, while necessary, act as speed bumps in the compounding process. Smart investors structure their portfolios to minimise these interruptions, allowing the compounding effect to proceed with maximum efficiency.

Despite all this, the temptation to interrupt compounding is ever-present. The urge to cash out early, especially after seeing substantial gains, is natural. But doing so is akin to harvesting a crop before it is ripe. The principal is reduced, future earnings are diminished, and the compounding curve is flattened. This is not merely a matter of lost gains—it is a strategic error with long-term consequences. Those who resist the impulse to spend or reallocate for short-term benefit often find themselves with exponentially greater freedom later.

This restraint is not about asceticism or denial. It is about alignment—choosing future freedom over present gratification, purpose over impulse. Financial goals such as early retirement, philanthropy, or generational wealth require long-term thinking. Compounding is the bridge between those aspirations and reality. It is the tool that allows small, disciplined acts to become transformative outcomes.

Understanding compounding also shifts one's mindset around risk. Many fear market volatility, imagining that a downturn will wipe out years of progress. Yet the investor who has embraced compounding sees these downturns differently. They understand that lower prices allow reinvested dividends to buy more shares, that continued contributions during bear markets accelerate long-term gains, and that the true measure of success is not month-to-month performance, but growth across decades.

The philosophy of compounding extends beyond finance. It applies to personal growth, relationships, learning, and health. Just as money compounds, so too do habits, knowledge, and discipline. The person who reads daily, exercises regularly, or builds positive routines benefits from the same exponential effect. Small actions, repeated consistently, yield disproportionate outcomes. Compounding is not merely a financial strategy—it is a universal principle of growth.

Those who embrace it position themselves not only for financial success, but for a life shaped by foresight and discipline. They learn to see time not as a constraint, but as an asset. They recognise that greatness is often built slowly, invisibly, and that the most powerful rewards are those which unfold over time. Compounding teaches humility, patience, and confidence in process—qualities that serve not just the investor, but the human being.

To fully leverage compounding, one must start early, remain invested, reinvest returns, and avoid interruptions. These are simple actions, yet their power is anything but. The magic of compounding is not magic at all. It is mathematics, applied with consistency. It is the quiet accumulation of advantage over time. And for those with the patience to understand it and the discipline to apply it, it is nothing short of transformative.

The Mathematics of Growth

Understanding wealth accumulation through compounding requires more than belief—it demands clarity. While the concept of compounding may seem intuitive, its full impact is best appreciated through numbers. The mathematics of growth reveal how consistent, modest investments—when given time—produce outcomes far greater than instinct might suggest. Unlike gambling, speculation, or sudden windfalls, compounding is grounded in logic. Its rewards are not arbitrary, but predictable. Once internalised, this logic changes not only how people view money but how they behave around it.

The first principle to grasp is that compounding magnifies over time. The effect is not linear, but exponential. This means that while initial progress may appear slow, each passing year adds disproportionately more to the final total. Most people intuitively understand addition, but our brains are less equipped to intuitively grasp exponential functions. We think in straight lines, not curves that suddenly shoot upwards. Compounding growth defies this linear expectation.

Let's begin with a straightforward example. Imagine an individual, Mark, who invests £200 per month into a broad-based equity index fund yielding an average annual return of 7%. Over the course of a single year, this amounts to £2,400 in contributions. With growth, that might increase to approximately £2,572. After five years, the value of his portfolio will reach around £14,300. But the most illuminating effects occur as the time horizon extends. After twenty years, his contributions—totalling £48,000—grow to roughly £104,000. And if Mark continues investing the same amount for forty years, his total contributions of £96,000 result in a portfolio worth over £500,000. Nothing about the investment strategy changed. The monthly contribution stayed constant. What changed was the effect of time applied to a regular process.

This example highlights two vital truths. First, consistent action—however modest—yields dramatic results when multiplied by time. Second, the late-stage years are disproportionately productive. In the first decade, growth barely outpaces contributions. In the final decade, growth outpaces contributions many times over. That is the compounding curve: slow, then sudden.

It's tempting to assume that higher income is the primary lever for wealth. But the mathematics of compounding suggest otherwise. Consider two individuals: Clara, who begins investing £100 per month at age 20, and Sam, who waits until 35 to begin, contributing

£300 per month. Assuming the same return of 7%, Clara contributes £54,000 over 45 years, while Sam contributes £108,000 over 30 years—twice as much. Yet, by retirement age, Clara's portfolio is worth more. Her early start, even at a lower amount, allows her capital to benefit from an additional 15 years of compounding. Sam's larger contributions cannot fully compensate for the lost time. This illustrates why starting early often trumps contributing more later.

Compound growth, when viewed numerically, also debunks a common misconception—that investing is only worthwhile with large sums. Many individuals delay investing because they assume their savings are too small to make a difference. But the data tell a different story. A teenager investing part-time job income into a simple index fund can accumulate six-figure sums over several decades with no financial wizardry, only consistency. The difference between starting at age 18 versus 28 is not ten years' worth of returns—it can be hundreds of thousands of pounds.

These figures are not merely interesting—they are transformative. They shift the narrative away from windfalls and timing, and towards habits and horizons. They also help people move past financial fatalism. The belief that one must already be wealthy to build wealth is a myth dismantled by compounding mathematics.

Another powerful example can be drawn from historical stock market returns. The S&P 500, one of the most commonly referenced indices, has produced average annualised returns of around 7–8% after inflation over the long term. While there are fluctuations and crises along the way—the Great Depression, the dot-com bust, the global financial crisis, and the COVID-19 pandemic—the general trajectory remains upward over multi-decade periods. This historical resilience supports the idea that even when markets are volatile, compounding continues to work—as long as the investor remains committed.

Take the period between 1980 and 2020. An individual who invested £10,000 in a low-cost S&P 500 index fund at the beginning of this window and reinvested dividends would have seen that investment grow to over £700,000 by 2020. That growth includes the crashes of 1987, 2000, and 2008. The lesson is not that markets are smooth, but that patience pays. The underlying mathematics, driven by consistent growth and reinvestment, rewards those who hold on.

Of course, compounding also works against you if you are on the wrong side of it. Credit card debt, often carrying interest rates upwards of 20%, illustrates reverse compounding. A balance of £5,000 accruing interest monthly at 20% grows rapidly if left unpaid. What seemed like a manageable amount quickly spirals into a financial burden. This duality reinforces the importance of understanding compounding not only as a tool for growth but as a risk factor when ignored.

Practical application of compounding means more than investing early—it means investing often. Regular, automated contributions help smooth out market volatility and maintain forward momentum. This is the philosophy behind dollar-cost averaging, where fixed amounts are invested at regular intervals regardless of market conditions. Over time, this reduces the average cost per unit and ensures continued participation in the compounding process, even during downturns.

It also requires resisting the temptation to interrupt the process. Early withdrawals, lifestyle inflation, and reactive selling during market declines all diminish the power of compounding. These behaviours not only reduce capital but truncate the exponential growth phase just as it begins to accelerate. The mathematics of compounding are indifferent to motive. Once the cycle is broken, it cannot be retroactively restored.

The simplicity of the compounding formula—FV = P(1 + r)^n, where FV is future value, P is principal, r is the rate of return, and n is the number of periods—belies its profundity. The exponent, n, representing time, has an outsized influence. Doubling the time horizon does not double the return; it can multiply it severalfold. The difference between twenty and forty years in the market is not additive, it's explosive.

Even small changes in the rate of return make a significant difference over time. At 5% annual growth, £10,000 becomes £70,000 in forty years. At 8%, it grows to over £217,000. This highlights the value of reducing investment fees, improving asset allocation, and maintaining tax efficiency—all of which can enhance net returns and thus strengthen the compounding effect.

But perhaps the most remarkable insight from the mathematics of growth is this: it places financial success within reach of the average person. Building wealth is not reserved for financial professionals, entrepreneurs, or the naturally gifted. It is available to those who understand the basic arithmetic of time, patience, and persistence. It shifts the emphasis from income to behaviour—from what you earn to what you consistently do with what you earn.

This democratising power of compounding has profound implications. It empowers young people to take control of their financial future. It encourages households to prioritise saving over spending. It offers hope to those with modest incomes. And it challenges the cultural obsession with speed by showing that the most powerful financial outcomes are built slowly, predictably, and logically.

To internalise the mathematics of growth is to reorient one's approach to time. It replaces the need for heroic financial acts with the discipline of small, repeated steps. It inspires confidence not through speculation, but through certainty. And it reveals that the most potent force in wealth creation is not luck, leverage, or timing—but the mathematical elegance of compounding, applied consistently across the arc of a life well planned.

Why Starting Early Matters

In the architecture of wealth-building, time is the most critical and yet most undervalued material. While investing prowess, asset allocation, and discipline are undeniably important, it is the length of time money is allowed to compound that makes the greatest difference. Beginning early in one's financial life creates a multiplier effect that no other variable can replicate. The difference that even a single decade can make in long-term wealth accumulation is startling—not because time alone generates returns, but because it enables compounding to work in full force.

To appreciate the impact of starting early, one must first understand the concept of compounding not just as a mathematical mechanism, but as a strategic advantage. When returns are reinvested and allowed to generate further returns, growth accelerates. This compounding is most potent when applied over long time horizons. Early investing doesn't simply yield more returns—it yields exponentially more because each additional year adds another layer to the compounding process. Missing out on these early years is not just a matter of lost opportunity—it is a structural disadvantage that becomes harder to overcome with time.

Consider two individuals, Anna and Michael, both of whom aim to retire at 65. Anna begins investing at 25, contributing £300 per month into a portfolio that yields an average annual return of 7%. She continues this for 15 years and then stops at 40, having invested £54,000. Michael, on the other hand, starts at 40 and contributes the same £300 monthly until 65, totalling £90,000 in contributions. Despite contributing less and stopping after 15 years, Anna ends up with a larger retirement fund than Michael—often by a wide margin. The reason is not a better return, but a longer timeline for compounding to work. This is the asymmetry of early action. Once the compounding curve takes hold, it rewards time more than capital.

These outcomes are not financial anomalies. They are entirely predictable and repeatable. Yet, many individuals delay investing until later in life, often citing low income, lack of knowledge, or competing priorities. While these are understandable concerns, they also reflect a cultural misconception: that wealth-building is something reserved for later stages of life, when income is higher and circumstances feel more stable. This mindset overlooks the extraordinary advantage held by those who start early, even with small amounts. A person who invests £1,000 at 20 will likely end up with more wealth than someone who invests £5,000 at 40, assuming similar returns. Time outperforms size in the long run.

The psychological hurdle, however, is real. Young investors often struggle to connect with their future selves. Retirement feels distant, abstract, and less urgent than present needs. This disconnect, known in behavioural science as temporal discounting, leads many to prioritise immediate gratification over long-term planning. But by reframing early investing as a gift to your future self—not just financially, but emotionally and strategically—one can begin to appreciate its deeper significance. It is not just about building wealth; it is about buying options, reducing stress, and creating autonomy over future decisions.

One illustrative real-world example is that of Ronald Read, a janitor and gas station attendant in Vermont. Despite his modest earnings, he began investing early and consistently, mostly in dividend-paying stocks. He lived frugally and allowed his investments to grow for decades. By the time of his death in 2014, he had accumulated over $8 million, much of which he donated to charity. Read's story is a powerful reminder that investing success is less about income level and more about behaviour, timing, and consistency. His wealth was not inherited, nor was it the product of financial wizardry. It was simply the fruit of early, uninterrupted compounding.

The benefit of starting early extends beyond monetary value. It also allows for greater risk tolerance. Younger investors can afford to invest in growth-oriented assets like equities because they have time to recover from market downturns. This enables them to pursue higher long-term returns without compromising financial stability. Older investors, closer to retirement, must often shift towards more conservative portfolios, which—while safer—typically yield lower returns. Starting early provides the luxury of both growth and resilience.

Moreover, early investing helps to normalise positive financial behaviours. It builds discipline, establishes healthy savings habits, and cultivates a mindset geared towards future planning. These habits often spill over into other areas of life, from budgeting and debt management to career planning and life satisfaction. By embedding financial planning into the fabric of daily life early on, individuals develop a sense of control and confidence that compounds along with their investments.

It also acts as a hedge against unpredictability. Life is seldom linear. Careers shift, health fluctuates, and economic conditions evolve. Starting early provides a buffer—a margin of safety that allows one to adapt to unexpected challenges without derailing long-term goals. Those who begin late must invest more aggressively, save at higher rates, or work longer to reach the same financial milestones. Early starters, by contrast, have flexibility. They can pause contributions during lean years, pursue career changes, or take sabbaticals—all without compromising their long-term financial well-being.

There is also a significant educational component. Investing early provides a hands-on learning experience. One begins to understand the mechanics of markets, the importance of diversification, the psychology of volatility, and the impact of fees and taxation. Mistakes made early—when portfolios are smaller—become valuable lessons that inform better decisions as the stakes grow. Those who wait until middle age to start often enter the market with more capital but less experience, which can lead to costly errors at the most critical time.

Financial tools and platforms today make early investing more accessible than ever. Low-cost index funds, fractional shares, and automated investing services have democratised access to markets. It is now possible to begin investing with as little as £10 a month, and to do so in a diversified, tax-efficient manner. These innovations eliminate many of the traditional barriers to entry and leave behavioural inertia as the main obstacle. Knowledge and technology are no longer gatekeepers—only mindset is.

The broader economic implications of early investing are also worth noting. When individuals take responsibility for their long-term financial futures, they reduce pressure on public welfare systems, contribute to capital formation, and build intergenerational wealth. The compounding process doesn't end with one person's retirement—it can continue into the next generation through inheritance, education, or philanthropy. Starting early is not just an individual advantage—it is a societal asset.

Yet the message must be carefully framed. The goal is not to create fear of missing out or to pressure people into perfect financial behaviour. Rather, it is to illustrate a truth that is both empowering and actionable: that small, early decisions carry extraordinary weight. A single choice, made decades in advance, can change the course of a financial life. It can provide peace of mind in retirement, options in midlife, and confidence throughout.

Starting early is not a panacea. It does not eliminate the need for strategic planning, adaptability, or emotional intelligence. But it provides a foundation upon which all other financial decisions are strengthened. It gives space to learn, room to recover, and time to grow. In an investment landscape dominated by noise, short-termism, and speculative hype, the power of beginning early offers a refreshing and enduring truth.

Ultimately, starting early matters because time is the one variable we cannot manufacture. It cannot be borrowed, accelerated, or replaced. Once gone, it is irretrievable. But when used wisely, it becomes the most powerful financial asset of all. It transforms modest means into meaningful outcomes. It shifts the focus from short-term gains to long-term security. And it turns the act of investing from a chore into a form of self-respect. Those who understand this act not out of fear, but from a quiet confidence in the arithmetic of patience.

Reinvesting Dividends and Interest

One of the most underestimated yet profoundly effective strategies in long-term wealth accumulation is the reinvestment of dividends and interest. While much attention is given to the selection of high-growth assets, market timing, or tactical asset allocation, the role of reinvested income often remains underappreciated. Yet it is this steady, almost unglamorous practice that silently magnifies portfolio growth. When understood and applied with discipline, reinvesting dividends and interest is not merely a prudent strategy—it becomes a key driver of exponential financial compounding.

Dividends and interest represent the passive income generated by investments. Dividends are typically paid out by shares in profitable companies, offering investors a portion of the firm's earnings. Interest, on the other hand, is earned through fixed income instruments such as bonds, savings accounts, or money market funds. While these distributions can be taken as cash and used for consumption or held separately, reinvesting them directly into the investment vehicle allows them to generate returns of their own. This subtle distinction—between withdrawing and reinvesting—has significant implications over time.

The real power of reinvestment lies in its cumulative effect. When income is reinvested, it increases the capital base. This larger base then earns more income, which is again reinvested, further enlarging the base. Over successive cycles, this creates a self-reinforcing loop of growth. What begins as a modest income stream can, over time, evolve into a significant portion of the total return. It is through this quiet, continuous layering of growth that wealth scales beyond what most would expect from principal returns alone.

To appreciate this impact numerically, consider an investor who places £10,000 into a dividend-paying index fund yielding 4% annually. If dividends are withdrawn each year, the investment grows only through capital appreciation—say, at an average of 5% per annum. After twenty years, assuming static yields and returns, the capital might double to £20,000, and the investor would have received around £8,000 in income over that period. However, if those dividends are reinvested, total returns can exceed £33,000, with the additional gains fuelled not by the market alone, but by the compounding of reinvested income.

The compounding effect is especially pronounced in equity markets, where dividends form a surprisingly large part of long-term returns. Historical data from developed markets, including the United Kingdom and the United States, shows that reinvested dividends have accounted for as much as 40–60% of total equity returns over multi-decade horizons. This is not because the yields are extraordinarily high—most hover between 2% and 4%—but because reinvestment harnesses the mechanics of exponential growth.

Reinvesting interest operates under the same logic, though it tends to be more relevant in bond-heavy or income-focused portfolios. While bonds generally offer lower long-term returns compared to equities, their predictability makes them a staple in conservative or retirement portfolios. By reinvesting bond coupons rather than withdrawing them, investors can maintain a more stable growth trajectory and extend the longevity of their capital—especially important in a low-yield environment where every basis point of return matters.

Real-world examples make this principle tangible. Take the story of Grace Groner, a former secretary who invested $180 in three shares of Abbott Laboratories in 1935 and opted to reinvest every dividend. She lived modestly and never withdrew from the investment. By the time of her death in 2010, her shares—thanks to growth and reinvested dividends—were worth over $7 million. She bequeathed the entire sum to a scholarship fund, showing not only the power of compounding but the enduring legacy that reinvested income can create. Her success was not built on timing markets or aggressive speculation, but on patience and a systematic reinvestment approach.

From a behavioural standpoint, reinvesting passive income also serves a psychological benefit: it reduces the temptation to spend. When dividends and interest are paid out in cash, they present an invitation to consume—to treat the proceeds as a reward or discretionary bonus. While this may be appropriate in retirement or in certain cash flow-focused strategies, for those still building wealth, this approach undermines future potential. Automatically reinvesting income removes the friction of decision-making, ensuring that discipline triumphs over impulse.

Many investment platforms and retirement schemes now offer automatic dividend reinvestment options (often referred to as DRIPs—Dividend Reinvestment Plans), making it easier for investors to keep their money working without manual intervention. These tools help to systematise the reinvestment process, reduce trading costs, and ensure that newly acquired shares begin contributing to future income immediately. Over time, these small additions compound, often unnoticed, until their cumulative impact becomes substantial.

Another overlooked benefit of reinvestment is the effect on diversification and risk distribution. When dividends are reinvested in a fund or index, they are typically allocated proportionally across the underlying assets. This can help maintain or rebalance portfolio diversification automatically, especially in passive investment vehicles. Rather than selectively purchasing new securities, the reinvested income flows back into the broader mix, reinforcing the original allocation strategy.

However, it is worth noting that reinvestment is not always the optimal strategy in every circumstance. In taxable accounts, reinvested dividends and interest may still trigger tax liabilities, even if the cash was not received. This creates a situation where the investor pays tax on income they didn't spend—a consideration that must be managed carefully, particularly in higher tax brackets. Tax-advantaged accounts such as ISAs, pensions, and other sheltered investment vehicles are ideal for reinvestment, as they allow returns to compound tax-free or tax-deferred.

Another scenario where reinvestment might be re-evaluated is in late-stage retirement, where the investor's primary need is income rather than growth. In this phase, withdrawals may be more appropriate, provided they are managed in alignment with sustainable drawdown strategies. Even so, reinvestment during the accumulation years ensures a larger pool of capital from which income can later be drawn, making early reinvestment a foundational strategy regardless of future income needs.

For younger investors or those in the accumulation phase of their financial lives, the message is clear: reinvestment should be the default posture unless there is a compelling reason to do otherwise. The earlier reinvestment begins, the more time it has to amplify returns. And even for those who begin later, reinvesting income remains a powerful way to catch up, reinforce discipline, and maximise portfolio efficiency.

Perhaps most importantly, the practice of reinvesting passive income embodies a philosophy that transcends finance. It reflects a commitment to future over present, to building rather than consuming, and to allowing small, regular actions to produce extraordinary outcomes. It demonstrates how wealth is not merely a function of what we earn, but of what we retain and reinvest.

Investing, at its best, is not about reacting to markets or chasing trends—it is about building structures that grow and endure. Reinvesting dividends and interest may lack the glamour of speculative wins or headline trades, but it possesses something far more valuable: reliability. It is the silent engine behind most financial success stories, quietly converting income into growth, and growth into freedom.

In a financial world often captivated by novelty and noise, the reinvestment of passive income offers a timeless reminder: the most powerful tools are often the simplest. By putting earnings back to work, investors create a compounding effect that expands not only their wealth but their sense of financial security and independence. Through this discipline, what begins as modest income evolves into a powerful force—a legacy not of consumption, but of deliberate, sustained growth.

Avoiding the Temptation to Cash Out

One of the greatest threats to long-term wealth accumulation is not market volatility, poor investment selection, or even economic downturns—it is premature withdrawal. The compounding effect, often hailed as the engine of long-term growth, requires uninterrupted time to operate at full capacity. When an investor withdraws early from a portfolio—particularly during the accumulation phase—they do not simply reduce their holdings. They disrupt the exponential growth that their capital was poised to achieve in the future. The cost of cashing out is therefore not only measured in what is taken out today, but in what is no longer allowed to grow tomorrow.

The appeal of early withdrawals is understandable. Life presents urgent needs, tempting opportunities, and emotional reactions to market fluctuations. A financial windfall—especially one that appears paper-based—can feel detached from immediate priorities. Whether it's the down payment on a home, a dream holiday, debt repayment, or simply fear during a market dip, the impulse to liquidate investments can be strong. Yet this decision, while emotionally satisfying in the short term, can carry long-term consequences that are often difficult to reverse.

The mathematics of compounding reveal just how detrimental early withdrawals can be. Consider an investor who has accumulated £50,000 by age 35 in a portfolio growing at an average of 7% per year. If they leave this untouched until age 65, it would grow to approximately £381,000. However, if they withdraw just £20,000 at 35 and let the remaining £30,000 continue compounding, the final amount falls to around £228,000. That £20,000 withdrawal today doesn't merely reduce the portfolio by 40%—it effectively halves the final value. This stark contrast illustrates the hidden cost: the lost compounding on both the principal and the returns that principal would have generated.

This effect is further exacerbated when the withdrawal occurs during a market downturn. Selling during a low point crystallises losses that, given time, might have reversed or even rebounded significantly. Historical data across multiple global markets has shown that downturns are often followed by periods of strong recovery. Investors who hold firm during bear markets typically emerge with stronger portfolios than those who exit and attempt to re-enter later. Timing the market—especially during emotionally charged periods—is notoriously difficult, even for professional fund managers. The better strategy, supported by decades of behavioural finance research, is simply to remain invested.

There is also a psychological cost to early withdrawals. Once the precedent is set—once an individual has liquidated a portion of their investments for non-retirement purposes—they are more likely to do it again. This behavioural pattern weakens the mental boundaries around long-term savings and turns what was intended to be untouchable into a ready source of liquidity. This erosion of financial discipline is not always visible at first, but it undermines the long-term structure and purpose of the investment plan.

Real-world examples illustrate this vividly. During the global financial crisis of 2008–2009, many individual investors panicked and withdrew substantial portions of their portfolios. In doing so, they missed the subsequent recovery, which saw markets not only regain lost ground but reach new all-time highs within a few years. Those who cashed out often did so at significant losses, locking in declines that would have otherwise been temporary. Meanwhile, those who held their positions—or even increased their contributions during the downturn—benefited handsomely as markets rebounded. The lesson was clear: staying invested pays off, even when emotions suggest otherwise.

This lesson became even more apparent during the rapid COVID-19 market crash of March 2020. Equity markets plunged by over 30% in a matter of weeks. Yet, within just a few months, they had fully recovered. Investors who panicked and cashed out during the crash missed one of the fastest recoveries in financial history. Those who remained invested, or who viewed the dip as an opportunity to buy rather than sell, saw substantial gains. These episodes reveal a consistent pattern: markets are volatile in the short term but resilient over the long term. The temptation to react emotionally—to protect capital by withdrawing it—often results in permanent losses that could have been avoided.

Avoiding early withdrawals is not merely a matter of financial logic—it requires intentional strategy and emotional discipline. One approach is to create clear distinctions between short-term savings and long-term investments. Emergency funds, held in easily accessible and low-volatility accounts, serve as a buffer against financial shocks. These funds are designed to absorb life's immediate expenses, so that long-term investment portfolios can remain untouched. By separating liquidity needs from long-term growth strategies, individuals reduce the psychological pressure to raid their investments when unexpected costs arise.

Another tactic involves mentally reframing long-term investments as 'locked away' assets. Just as one would not consider selling a piece of property every time they need extra cash, long-term portfolios should be viewed as untouchable until a predefined point—typically retirement. This mental separation, while artificial, is remarkably effective in reinforcing discipline. Investment accounts held in pensions or ISAs with withdrawal restrictions also help enforce this boundary by making it more difficult or tax-disadvantaged to access funds prematurely.

Automated investing strategies can also reduce the temptation to withdraw. When contributions are made automatically and portfolios are rebalanced without manual intervention, the investor is removed from frequent decision-making. This reduces the influence of emotion, impulse, or reactionary thinking. The less friction there is in maintaining an investment plan, the less likely an individual is to interfere with it during periods of uncertainty.

It is also vital to understand that early withdrawals don't just affect the individual—they can affect future generations. A portfolio that compounds uninterrupted can become a source of legacy wealth, supporting education, healthcare, charitable giving, or multigenerational security. Interrupting that growth prematurely diminishes not only personal outcomes but the broader impact that wealth could have. Long-term investing is, in this sense, a moral and generational decision as much as a financial one.

Even when life circumstances make a withdrawal feel necessary, the decision should be weighed carefully against alternatives. Could a loan, a temporary budget adjustment, or a delay in spending achieve the same outcome without disrupting long-term capital? Sometimes the answer will be no. But often, with a clear understanding of the future costs involved, a better solution can be found. The key is to make decisions from a place of clarity rather than stress, with a full view of what is being sacrificed.

One of the most compelling insights about early withdrawals is this: the cost is invisible until it's too late. Unlike a direct loss, which is immediate and painful, the loss of future returns is abstract. It doesn't show up on a statement, and no one reminds you of what could have been. But compounding does not forget. The years that capital was not invested continue to echo across decades. This is what makes the decision to stay invested both powerful and profound—it is a commitment to a future that may be distant, but is no less real.

Ultimately, the temptation to cash out is not simply a financial challenge—it is a behavioural one. It is a test of priorities, patience, and vision. It asks whether we are willing to forego immediate comfort for lasting freedom. Whether we can remain steadfast in the face of uncertainty. Whether we truly understand that the rewards of long-term investing are reserved for those who do not interrupt the process.

By internalising the cost of early withdrawals—not just in numbers, but in opportunity and momentum—investors can arm themselves with the conviction to stay the course. Because the true power of investing is not found in the amount of capital deployed, nor even in the returns achieved. It is found in the discipline to let capital remain undisturbed, to allow growth to beget more growth, and to trust that time, more than anything else, is the most faithful ally in wealth creation.

Chapter 3
Strategic Asset Allocation - Building a Balanced Portfolio

When it comes to building wealth that lasts, what you invest in certainly matters—but how you distribute those investments can be even more crucial. Asset allocation, the process of spreading your money across different asset categories such as equities, bonds, cash, and alternatives, might sound like a technical chore best left to specialists. Yet, in truth, it forms the very backbone of any sound investment approach. It shapes not just the composition of your portfolio but how it responds to the ever-shifting rhythms of the market, how robust it remains amid turmoil, and how well it reflects your personal aims and temperament over the long haul.

At its heart, asset allocation is an exercise in balance and realism. No single asset class behaves reliably under every economic condition. Shares might rally when the economy is booming, but bonds tend to offer shelter during tougher times. Real estate often provides a hedge against inflation, while cash cushions against sudden shocks and preserves liquidity. Then there are alternative investments—commodities, private equity, hedge funds—that add another layer of diversification, albeit with their own quirks and risks. By spreading investments across these varied categories, one avoids the peril of putting all eggs in one basket, thereby mitigating risk without necessarily sacrificing returns. This isn't about watering down gains; it's about managing risk in a manner consistent with your individual financial objectives.

A persistent myth in investing is that success hinges on picking the "right" stocks or timing the market's next move perfectly. Yet, rigorous studies from respected firms like Vanguard and Morningstar repeatedly demonstrate something far more profound: asset allocation accounts for the lion's share of a portfolio's long-term returns. In other words, deciding how much to allocate between stocks and bonds, or growth versus income assets, often makes a far greater difference than attempting to identify the next big winner. This insight shifts the paradigm of investing away from guesswork towards thoughtful design: the question is not, "Which asset will perform best next year?" but rather, "What combination of investments will help me achieve my goals in a way I can stick with?"

Grasping the distinct traits of each asset class is where the journey begins. Equities represent partial ownership of companies and typically offer the highest returns over extended periods—but also come with notable volatility. Bonds, essentially loans to governments or corporations, generally yield steadier, if lower, income streams and act as a stabilising force. Alternatives, including property, commodities, and hedge funds, bring further diversity, though with complexities like illiquidity and variable risk profiles. Each plays a unique role, and understanding these characteristics is vital before making allocation decisions.

Determining how to divide your capital is a matter not just of market knowledge but of personal reflection. Two key considerations are your risk tolerance and your investment horizon. Risk tolerance—how much volatility you can emotionally and financially endure—varies widely. Some might remain calm through a 20% portfolio drop, while others feel uneasy after a 5% dip. This tolerance is dynamic, shifting with age, experience, and life changes, and must be evaluated honestly. Overreaching beyond what you can comfortably bear often leads to rash decisions exactly when steadiness is required.

Time horizon refers to the length of time your funds can remain invested before you'll need access to them. A person saving for a house in five years has very different needs from someone building a retirement nest egg over three decades. Generally, a longer horizon allows for greater risk-taking, since there is time to ride out the market's inevitable storms. This explains why younger investors often lean heavily into equities, while those approaching retirement typically favour safer, income-generating investments.

When these elements—asset traits, risk appetite, and timeframe—are combined, they produce a portfolio tailored to the individual rather than a one-size-fits-all solution. Yet, even the best-laid plans require upkeep. Different asset classes will appreciate or decline at varying rates, causing your allocation to drift. In a strong bull market, for example, equities might surge ahead and become a disproportionately large slice of your holdings, pushing your portfolio out of alignment with your original risk profile.

This is where rebalancing comes in. It's the practice of selling some of the overperforming assets and redirecting the proceeds into those that have lagged, thus returning your portfolio to its target allocation. While it may seem counterintuitive to trim your winners, rebalancing enforces discipline and keeps your risk in check. It isn't about trying to predict what's next; it's about maintaining the structure that suits your goals. Many investors find a yearly or semi-annual schedule practical, while others prefer to rebalance when allocations deviate beyond set thresholds. Crucially, this process encourages a "buy low, sell high" mindset, one of the rare behaviours that can enhance returns over time.

Yet asset allocation is not without its traps. One common error is chasing after past performance—overweighting asset classes that have recently flourished while neglecting those that have stumbled. This reactive approach almost guarantees buying high and selling low, the opposite of prudent investing. Another frequent misstep is failing to diversify adequately, concentrating holdings in a particular sector, country, or style, thereby exposing the portfolio to avoidable risk. Diversification is less about maximising returns in any given year and more about ensuring resilience over the long haul.

There is also the temptation to overcomplicate matters. Some investors pile into dozens of holdings, equating complexity with sophistication. In reality, a well-diversified portfolio can be constructed with just a handful of broad, globally focused funds. What truly matters is not the quantity of holdings, but how each contributes to the portfolio's overall risk-return profile and interacts with others under various market conditions.

Emotions too frequently undermine sound asset allocation. Fear can prompt a rush to cash in volatile markets, while greed tempts overexposure during speculative frenzies. Remaining faithful to your allocation throughout the inevitable market ups and downs demands not just knowledge, but psychological fortitude. For many, crafting a written investment policy that spells out their objectives and risk tolerance provides a vital anchor when markets turn choppy.

Technology has eased some of these challenges. Robo-advisers, automatic rebalancing features, and sophisticated tracking tools make it simpler than ever to maintain allocations and respond wisely to changes. While no algorithm replaces human judgment, these tools reduce the friction of decision-making and help investors steer clear of impulsive, emotion-driven mistakes.

At its essence, strategic asset allocation is about aligning your financial resources with your broader life goals. It acknowledges that while markets are beyond anyone's control, you do retain control over your exposure to them. This transforms investing from a game of chance into a deliberate, evidence-based plan—shaped by your needs and adapted over time.

As we delve deeper into each aspect of asset allocation, this chapter will blend theory with practical advice. Whether you're assembling your first portfolio or refining a seasoned one, these principles will assist you in crafting a strategy both resilient and rewarding. Because when investments are thoughtfully diversified, grounded in your personal goals, and maintained with discipline, they become far more than mere financial instruments—they become the bedrock of lasting stability and freedom.

What is Asset Allocation?

At the core of every successful investment strategy lies a deceptively simple concept: asset allocation. While novice investors may focus on picking the "right" stocks or timing the market to perfection, seasoned professionals know that these pursuits are, more often than not, distractions. It is the strategic distribution of investments across different asset classes that determines the majority of long-term returns and risk exposure. Asset allocation is not just a technical procedure—it is a reflection of one's financial goals, time horizon, and tolerance for uncertainty. It is both an art and a science, combining statistical logic with personal insight.

To understand asset allocation, we must first understand its function. The purpose is to build a portfolio that is diversified across various categories of investments, each of which behaves differently under different market conditions. The rationale behind this is simple: no single asset class performs best all the time. Equities may surge during periods of economic expansion, but falter in recessions. Bonds might offer stability during downturns but provide limited growth. Cash and short-term instruments preserve capital but erode in value due to inflation. Alternatives, such as real estate, commodities, or private equity, add another layer of diversification, each with unique performance patterns and risk characteristics. By combining these assets thoughtfully, investors can reduce volatility and improve the consistency of returns.

The underlying principle here is correlation—or more precisely, the lack thereof. Different asset classes do not move in perfect sync. When one declines, another might rise, or at least remain stable. This interaction between asset classes is what gives asset allocation its power. Diversification does not eliminate risk, but it mitigates the impact of any single poor-performing investment. It transforms a collection of assets into a cohesive, resilient strategy.

Consider a real-world example. Suppose an investor places their entire retirement portfolio in shares during a bull market. For a time, they may enjoy impressive gains. But when the market inevitably corrects or crashes, their portfolio suffers significantly. If, instead, the portfolio had included a mix of shares, bonds, and perhaps some exposure to commodities or property, the decline might have been cushioned. Bonds often perform well when shares are falling, providing a stabilising force. The result is a portfolio that is less exposed to market swings and more aligned with the investor's long-term goals.

Asset allocation also serves as a psychological anchor. Investing is not just about numbers—it's about behaviour. Market volatility can provoke anxiety, leading to reactive decisions that erode returns. A well-structured asset allocation plan helps investors stay grounded. By setting clear expectations about how much risk they're taking and why, it becomes easier to endure downturns without abandoning the strategy. This behavioural benefit is as valuable as any statistical advantage.

The specific allocation that is right for one person may be wholly inappropriate for another. A young professional with a 40-year horizon and a strong appetite for risk might hold a portfolio heavily weighted in equities. Conversely, a retiree who depends on their investments for income might prioritise bonds, dividend-paying stocks, or income-generating real estate. The key is to match the asset mix with personal circumstances—taking into account age, financial goals, income needs, tax considerations, and risk appetite. This alignment transforms investing from speculation into financial planning.

One of the most compelling aspects of asset allocation is its proven impact on investment outcomes. Numerous academic studies, including the seminal research by Brinson, Hood, and Beebower, have demonstrated that the vast majority of portfolio returns—upwards of 90% in some cases—can be attributed to the overall asset allocation, not to individual stock selection or market timing. While the exact percentage varies depending on methodology, the central message is unequivocal: it is the structure of the portfolio, not the brilliance of the stock picks, that drives success over time.

Asset allocation also supports adaptability. Markets and personal situations change. A well-designed allocation strategy is not static—it evolves. As people move through different life stages, their investment objectives shift. A person saving for a house in three years needs a different asset mix than someone planning for retirement in thirty. Rebalancing—adjusting the portfolio periodically to maintain the intended allocation—ensures that the risk level remains consistent with changing goals. This ongoing process is not just maintenance; it is strategic calibration.

Practical implementation of asset allocation has never been easier. Today's investors have access to a wide array of tools and investment vehicles—index funds, exchange-traded funds (ETFs), managed portfolios—that allow for precise, low-cost exposure to various asset classes. With a few well-chosen funds, one can build a globally diversified portfolio that reflects the principles of modern portfolio theory. And for those seeking further refinement, there are even target-date funds and robo-advisers that automatically adjust allocations over time, offering a passive yet intelligent approach to portfolio management.

Yet, despite the availability of these tools, many investors fall into common traps. One frequent error is over-concentration—placing too much capital in one type of investment, often because it has recently performed well. This behaviour, driven by recency bias, can expose the portfolio to unnecessary risk. Another error is neglecting to rebalance. Over time, a portfolio can drift from its intended allocation, becoming riskier or more conservative than originally planned. Regular rebalancing—whether calendar-based or threshold-based—helps correct this drift and preserves the strategic intent of the portfolio.

Asset allocation also provides a framework for thoughtful risk management. Rather than avoiding risk altogether—a strategy that often leads to stagnation—investors can take measured risks in proportion to their goals and needs. For example, a portfolio might include a small allocation to emerging markets or high-yield bonds to enhance return potential, while maintaining a core of diversified equities and investment-grade bonds to ensure stability. This balance of risk and return, calibrated to personal preference, is the essence of effective asset allocation.

Crucially, asset allocation does not require perfection. No one can predict which asset class will lead in a given year. But that is precisely the point: asset allocation assumes uncertainty and builds around it. It provides a plan that works not by guessing correctly, but by preparing intelligently. It empowers investors to participate in market growth while protecting against its inevitable downturns. It shifts the focus from speculation to strategy, from emotion to discipline.

In a financial world filled with complexity and noise, asset allocation offers clarity. It distils the investment process into a structured, customisable, and research-backed approach. It does not promise excitement or immediate gratification. Instead, it delivers something far more valuable—resilience, predictability, and long-term progress.

It is the investment strategy for those who understand that wealth is not built by racing toward returns, but by constructing a portfolio that will weather decades of change.

For anyone serious about financial independence, understanding asset allocation is essential. It is not merely a technique—it is a mindset. It reflects a willingness to think strategically, act consistently, and remain focused on what truly matters. Through diversification, personal alignment, and disciplined execution, asset allocation transforms the abstract ambition of wealth into a concrete, achievable reality. It is not the most glamorous part of investing, but it is, undoubtedly, the most important.

Stocks, Bonds, and Alternatives

To build a resilient investment portfolio, one must first grasp the fundamental building blocks that make it up. While the broader framework of asset allocation defines how a portfolio is structured, the choice of specific asset types determines its behaviour under different market conditions. Among the most widely used components are stocks, bonds, and alternative investments. Each offers distinct characteristics in terms of risk, return potential, and role within a diversified portfolio. Understanding how these instruments function—both individually and in combination—is essential for any investor seeking long-term stability and growth.

Stocks, or equities, represent ownership in a company. When you purchase a share, you are buying a slice of a business, with a proportional claim on its assets and earnings. This ownership structure aligns the investor's fortunes with the performance of the underlying company. If the company grows and becomes more profitable, its stock price typically rises, delivering capital gains. In some cases, companies also return profits to shareholders through dividends, which can be reinvested to fuel compounding returns. Stocks are often the engine of growth in a portfolio, delivering higher returns over time than most other asset classes.

However, this potential comes with significant volatility. Stock prices are influenced by a wide array of factors: company earnings, industry trends, macroeconomic indicators, geopolitical events, and investor sentiment. These variables introduce a level of unpredictability that can unsettle even experienced investors. A company's fundamentals might remain sound while its stock declines due to broader market anxiety. Conversely, a weak company might see its share price inflated during periods of speculative exuberance. For this reason, equities require a long-term perspective and the emotional fortitude to endure market swings.

Within the equity universe, there is considerable variation. Large-cap stocks, typically representing established companies, tend to offer more stability but slower growth. Small-cap stocks, reflecting newer or niche businesses, can deliver outsized returns but with greater risk. International equities expose investors to foreign economies and currencies, expanding diversification but also adding layers of geopolitical and regulatory complexity. Sector-specific stocks—such as technology, healthcare, or energy—can be used to capitalise on particular trends, but they introduce concentration risk if not managed carefully. Thus, even within equities, diversification remains a guiding principle.

Bonds, by contrast, serve a very different function. When you invest in a bond, you are effectively lending money to a government, corporation, or municipality in exchange for regular interest payments and the promise of your capital back at maturity. Bonds are typically less volatile than stocks and provide predictable income, making them an attractive option for conservative investors or those nearing retirement. They also act as a counterbalance to equities. Historically, when stock markets decline, bond prices often rise or remain stable, helping to stabilise the overall portfolio.

Yet bonds are not risk-free. Interest rate changes are a key factor affecting bond prices. When rates rise, existing bonds with lower yields become less attractive, causing their prices to fall. Credit risk is another concern, particularly with corporate bonds. If the issuing entity faces financial distress, it may default on its payments. To manage this, bonds are categorised by credit rating. Government bonds, especially from developed nations, are considered low-risk, while high-yield—or "junk"—bonds offer higher returns but carry greater default risk. Duration risk also matters: longer-term bonds are more sensitive to interest rate movements and can experience significant price swings even when their credit quality is stable.

While stocks and bonds form the traditional backbone of most portfolios, alternative investments introduce a broader set of tools to enhance diversification, hedge against specific risks, or pursue higher returns. These alternatives include real estate, commodities, hedge funds, private equity, infrastructure, and even emerging areas like cryptocurrency. Each carries its own risk-return profile, liquidity characteristics, and role within an allocation strategy.

Real estate is among the most widely held alternatives, both directly through property ownership and indirectly through real estate investment trusts (REITs). Property often appreciates in value over time and provides rental income, making it attractive for income-focused investors. It also tends to perform well during inflationary periods, as rents and property values can rise with the general price level. However, real estate is less liquid than stocks or bonds, and direct ownership involves maintenance costs, tenant risks, and market-specific exposure.

Commodities, such as gold, oil, and agricultural products, serve a different purpose. They are often seen as a hedge against inflation and geopolitical instability. Gold, in particular, has historically acted as a store of value during economic turmoil. However, commodities are volatile and driven by supply-demand dynamics that can be difficult to predict. They typically do not produce income and are best used as a small diversifying element rather than a core holding.

Hedge funds and private equity are more complex alternatives, generally accessible only to high-net-worth individuals or institutional investors due to their regulatory structures. Hedge funds use sophisticated strategies, including leverage, short selling, and derivatives, to pursue absolute returns regardless of market direction. While some hedge funds have delivered exceptional performance, many have underperformed benchmarks after fees. Private equity involves investing in companies that are not publicly listed, often with the aim of improving their operations and eventually selling them at a profit. These investments can offer high returns but are illiquid and carry high execution risk.

In recent years, cryptocurrencies have emerged as a new alternative asset class. While they remain speculative and highly volatile, their proponents view them as digital stores of value or decentralised financial infrastructure. As with all emerging asset classes, the role of cryptocurrencies in a diversified portfolio is still being defined. For most investors, if included at all, exposure should be minimal and approached with caution.

Each asset class, whether traditional or alternative, contributes something unique to a portfolio. Equities offer growth. Bonds provide income and stability. Alternatives expand diversification and may hedge against specific risks. The key is not to view these options in isolation, but to understand how they interact with one another within the broader context of your financial goals, risk tolerance, and time horizon.

Real-world portfolio construction reflects this integration. A 30-year-old investor saving for retirement may hold 80% in equities, 15% in bonds, and 5% in alternatives, aiming for maximum growth with some diversification. A 60-year-old nearing retirement may flip this, with a heavier weighting in bonds and income-generating assets, and a reduced equity exposure to mitigate volatility. These ratios are not static—they evolve with age, economic conditions, and life priorities.

It is also important to note that risk is not inherently bad. Risk, in investing, is the price we pay for the possibility of return. The goal is not to eliminate risk, but to align it with what you need and can emotionally withstand. Some investors can handle the highs and lows of an equity-heavy portfolio. Others find peace of mind in stable, income-oriented strategies. The mix of stocks, bonds, and alternatives must reflect not only market realities but personal psychology.

The real challenge is not in understanding the mechanics of each asset class—it is in resisting the temptation to chase performance. Investors often pour money into what has recently performed best, only to suffer when trends reverse. Equally damaging is the tendency to abandon a diversified strategy during short-term market stress. A strong allocation plan, grounded in a clear understanding of each asset class, provides the structure to navigate through such behavioural pitfalls.

Ultimately, building a successful portfolio is about thoughtful design. It is about knowing that no single asset class will serve all needs or thrive under all conditions. It is about blending growth and stability, liquidity and long-term potential, risk and reward. And it is about trusting in a strategy that reflects both the numbers and the individual behind them. When investors move beyond the headlines and begin to truly understand the instruments at their disposal, they equip themselves not only with knowledge, but with the tools to build something lasting.

Risk Tolerance and Time Horizon

Every successful investment strategy begins with clarity—not just about markets and returns, but about the individual making the investment. At the centre of this clarity lies a delicate alignment between risk tolerance and time horizon. These two concepts form the emotional and temporal backbone of a financial plan. Together, they shape not only the structure of a portfolio but the investor's experience of owning it. They determine how much volatility one can withstand and how long one can remain invested. More importantly, they define how effectively one's investments can serve their life goals.

Risk tolerance is often misunderstood as a fixed personality trait, but it is far more nuanced. At its most basic level, it refers to the degree of variability in investment returns that an individual is comfortable accepting. However, risk tolerance encompasses more than just comfort with market fluctuations—it also includes financial capacity, psychological disposition, life stage, and past experiences with money. An investor's ability to endure a 20% drawdown on paper is one thing; their willingness to hold firm when it actually occurs is quite another.

This distinction between theoretical and real-world tolerance has critical implications. Many investors believe they have high risk tolerance during bull markets, only to discover otherwise during downturns. This mismatch often leads to poorly timed decisions—such as selling during a crash—resulting in real losses that could have been avoided with a more accurate assessment of risk capacity. True risk tolerance is not tested when markets are soaring; it is revealed when they are falling. Knowing your limits before those limits are tested is a hallmark of good planning.

Risk tolerance also changes. A 25-year-old with few financial obligations might embrace aggressive strategies, riding out market swings in exchange for higher long-term returns. That same individual, now 50 with dependants and a mortgage, may no longer find the same level of volatility tolerable. Conversely, some investors grow more comfortable with risk over time as they gain experience and perspective. They learn to separate market noise from structural shifts and develop the discipline to stay invested through cycles. Understanding where you sit on this evolving spectrum is not just useful—it's essential.

Time horizon, meanwhile, acts as a natural moderator of risk. It defines how long you expect your money to remain invested before you need to access it. The longer the time horizon, the more risk you can afford to take, because you have time to recover from short-term volatility. This is why a pension plan decades away from maturity can hold a large proportion of equities, while a university savings fund for a child entering school in two years should favour lower-volatility assets like bonds or cash equivalents.

However, time horizon is not simply about dates on a calendar—it's about purpose. Money intended for a house deposit, an emergency fund, or retirement income all has different timelines and liquidity needs. A well-structured portfolio aligns each of these goals with the appropriate level of risk and return. For instance, an investor might maintain a core retirement account invested for the long term, alongside shorter-term allocations that are more conservative and accessible. This is often referred to as a "bucket" approach—assigning portions of the portfolio to different timeframes and tailoring each to its objective.

Matching risk tolerance and time horizon to investment choices is as much an exercise in self-awareness as it is in financial acumen.

Consider an investor who wants to retire in 30 years and is comfortable with risk. They might build a portfolio heavily weighted in global equities, knowing that short-term volatility is outweighed by long-term growth potential. Now consider another investor of the same age but with low risk tolerance, perhaps due to past negative experiences or a preference for capital preservation. For them, a more balanced mix—perhaps a combination of equities and bonds—would be more appropriate, even if it means accepting lower long-term returns.

This highlights a crucial principle: the best investment strategy is not necessarily the one with the highest projected return. It is the one an investor can stick with through all market conditions. Consistency beats brilliance when it comes to building wealth. A theoretically optimal portfolio that an investor abandons during a downturn is far less effective than a less aggressive strategy that allows them to stay invested.

The consequences of ignoring risk tolerance and time horizon can be profound. Many investors overestimate their appetite for risk, especially during extended bull markets. They chase performance, piling into high-growth sectors or speculative assets, only to suffer significant losses when markets inevitably correct. The emotional toll of these losses often leads to panic selling, missed recoveries, and long-term underperformance. On the other end, some investors are so risk-averse that they avoid equities altogether, leaving their portfolios overly reliant on low-yield instruments that struggle to keep pace with inflation. Both extremes illustrate the perils of misalignment.

A particularly illustrative case is that of investors during the dot-com bubble. In the late 1990s, technology stocks were delivering extraordinary returns. Many retail investors, swept up by media enthusiasm and peer influence, shifted heavily into tech-heavy portfolios. But when the bubble burst in 2000, the Nasdaq index lost nearly 80% of its value over two years. Those who had invested beyond their true risk capacity suffered heavy losses—and many sold out at or near the bottom, locking in those losses permanently. Meanwhile, diversified investors with clearer risk frameworks and longer time horizons were better positioned to weather the storm and eventually recover.

Similarly, the 2008 global financial crisis exposed mismatches between investor expectations and portfolio construction. Many portfolios that appeared diversified were heavily tilted toward equities or correlated assets. Investors with short time horizons or low risk tolerance discovered too late that their asset mix was not aligned with their needs. Those who had built more resilient portfolios—balancing asset classes according to their goals and psychological comfort—fared better, both financially and emotionally.

To align investments with personal goals, it is helpful to segment them into short-, medium-, and long-term categories. Short-term goals—typically within one to three years—require capital preservation and liquidity. These are best served by cash, money market funds, or short-duration bonds. Medium-term goals, ranging from three to ten years, can tolerate modest volatility and might include a balanced mix of bonds and equities. Long-term goals, particularly those over ten years away, can shoulder more risk and thus benefit from a higher allocation to equities and growth-oriented assets. This framework allows for a nuanced approach that reflects the complex nature of real lives and evolving priorities.

Financial advisers often use questionnaires and simulations to assess risk tolerance, but the most revealing insights often come from honest reflection. How did you feel during the last market downturn? What action did you take, and why? Do fluctuations in your portfolio cause you stress, or can you remain detached? These questions provide a more accurate measure than a risk score on a form. Risk tolerance is not simply a number—it is a psychological profile informed by life experience, temperament, and context.

Time horizon, too, deserves thoughtful consideration. It is easy to default to assumptions—"I'll retire in 30 years"—without considering the nuances. Will you need to draw income immediately upon retirement? Do you have other sources of income or assets? Are there milestones along the way—such as purchasing property, funding education, or supporting family members—that require liquidity? A single time horizon rarely captures the full financial picture. A robust investment plan will address multiple timeframes, each with its own strategy.

Ultimately, aligning investments with personal goals requires more than matching assets to timelines. It requires coherence between what you say you want, what you can emotionally endure, and how your portfolio is structured to serve both. It is about designing a plan that reflects not just markets, but humanity—the unpredictability of life, the variability of emotions, and the evolving nature of dreams.

The value of getting this right cannot be overstated. When risk tolerance and time horizon are properly understood and integrated, investing becomes less reactive and more purposeful. It reduces stress, enhances resilience, and builds confidence. More importantly, it transforms investing from a source of anxiety into a source of empowerment. For those willing to do the work of honest self-assessment, the reward is a portfolio that not only grows, but supports the life it was designed to serve.

Rebalancing Your Portfolio

Building a thoughtful portfolio is an essential first step in any long-term investment strategy, but maintaining that portfolio over time is just as critical. Rebalancing is the process by which investors realign their asset allocations to ensure they remain consistent with their financial objectives and risk tolerance. While it may sound like a purely technical task, rebalancing is in fact a vital behavioural and strategic discipline. It serves as a safeguard against the quiet drift that markets inevitably introduce—ensuring that your investments continue to reflect your intended strategy rather than being shaped passively by market movements.

At its core, rebalancing is about staying aligned. When an investor designs a portfolio, they typically begin with a strategic allocation across different asset classes—say, 60 percent equities and 40 percent bonds. This mix reflects their time horizon, risk appetite, and income needs. But as markets fluctuate, these proportions naturally shift. In a strong bull market, equities may outperform bonds significantly, resulting in a portfolio that is now, perhaps, 70 percent equities and 30 percent bonds. The investor has not made any active changes, but the risk profile of their portfolio has materially increased. Left unaddressed, this silent drift can expose them to more volatility than they originally intended.

Rebalancing counteracts this drift. It involves trimming the outperforming assets and reallocating the proceeds into underperforming or lagging ones. On the surface, this appears counterintuitive—why sell what's done well and buy what hasn't? Yet that very logic embodies the fundamental discipline of investing: buying low and selling high. It is an exercise in rationality over emotion, structure over instinct. Rebalancing forces the investor to correct course when market trends begin to pull them away from their original objectives.

The practical execution of rebalancing can vary. Some investors rebalance at regular intervals—annually, semi-annually, or quarterly—regardless of how much their allocations have shifted. This calendar-based approach simplifies decision-making and encourages routine oversight. Others prefer a threshold-based method, where rebalancing is triggered only when an asset class deviates by a predetermined percentage—say, 5 or 10 percent—from its target weight. Both approaches have their merits, and the choice between them often comes down to preference, trading costs, and the nature of the investments involved.

Rebalancing also brings important behavioural benefits. One of the most common mistakes investors make is allowing recent performance to dictate future decisions. They chase returns by overweighting asset classes or sectors that have recently surged, often arriving late to the rally and suffering when the cycle reverses. Rebalancing disciplines investors to systematically resist this impulse. It imposes a counter-cyclical framework—taking profits in hot markets and reinforcing positions in lagging areas. Over time, this can smooth returns and reduce volatility, which is particularly valuable for investors relying on their portfolios for income or those with medium-term spending goals.

Consider the experience of the post-2008 recovery. Equity markets rebounded strongly in the years following the financial crisis, particularly in the United States. Investors who had rebalanced during the downturn—buying equities at depressed prices and trimming bonds that had held their value—were well positioned to benefit from the ensuing rally. By contrast, those who avoided equities due to fear or who allowed their bond-heavy allocations to persist missed a significant portion of the recovery. Rebalancing, in this context, acted as both a strategic and emotional corrective.

There are, however, challenges associated with rebalancing that must be thoughtfully managed. Tax implications are a prime consideration, particularly in taxable accounts. Selling appreciated assets can trigger capital gains taxes, potentially eroding the benefits of rebalancing. For this reason, many investors prioritise rebalancing within tax-advantaged accounts—such as ISAs, pensions, or retirement schemes—where gains are sheltered. Others use new contributions or dividend reinvestments to adjust allocations without triggering sales. This technique, known as cash-flow rebalancing, is particularly efficient and minimises the cost of maintaining alignment.

Transaction fees are another practical concern. Frequent rebalancing, especially in accounts with brokerage charges, can generate costs that outweigh the benefits. Here, the principle of materiality applies: small drifts may not warrant immediate action. A certain level of flexibility allows the investor to avoid unnecessary churn while still preserving the integrity of their strategy over time. The goal is not precision for its own sake, but meaningful control over risk and allocation.

Rebalancing also becomes more complex as portfolios increase in size and sophistication. High-net-worth investors may hold dozens of securities across various accounts, asset classes, and geographies. In such cases, rebalancing requires coordinated oversight, often with the aid of software or professional advisers. However, the underlying principle remains unchanged: to periodically assess whether the current structure still reflects the investor's goals, and to adjust as needed.

Psychologically, rebalancing can be uncomfortable. Selling winners feels wrong, particularly when their momentum seems unstoppable. Buying underperforming assets feels contrarian, especially when headlines are dominated by negativity. Yet history has repeatedly shown that market leadership rotates. Sectors and styles fall in and out of favour. What is despised today may outperform tomorrow. Rebalancing does not attempt to predict these shifts—it merely ensures the investor is not overexposed when they occur.

An illustrative example is the early 2000s. Following the tech bubble, technology stocks dramatically underperformed while traditional sectors like financials and energy came back into favour. Investors who had rebalanced away from tech at the peak—however painful that may have seemed—avoided severe losses. Similarly, those who added to underweighted sectors found themselves well positioned for the rotation. Rebalancing, in these instances, was not merely a safeguard—it was a source of opportunity.

Importantly, rebalancing should always be viewed through the lens of financial objectives. The purpose is not to maximise returns in every period, but to maintain a consistent strategy that reflects the investor's values, constraints, and time horizon. For example, an investor saving for a retirement two decades away may tolerate larger equity swings than a retiree drawing down their portfolio. The former may rebalance infrequently, allowing equities to drift upwards over time, while the latter may rebalance more often to ensure sufficient liquidity and risk control.

This objective-driven approach extends to life changes. A new job, the birth of a child, the sale of a business, or nearing retirement may all warrant a reassessment of allocation targets. Rebalancing, in this context, becomes part of a broader financial planning process. It prompts questions such as: Are my goals still the same? Has my risk tolerance changed? Am I still on track? In this way, the mechanics of rebalancing support not only portfolio health but holistic financial clarity.

In today's investment environment—characterised by low interest rates, elevated valuations, and global uncertainty—discipline matters more than ever. Rebalancing is one of the few tools that consistently encourages disciplined, rational action. It creates a system for staying focused in an age of distraction, grounded in principle amid the noise of prediction.

For the thoughtful investor, rebalancing is not an afterthought or an optional add-on. It is a core component of the investment process. It embodies the recognition that markets move, but goals endure. That performance fluctuates, but purpose should not. And that the real work of investing is not only in building a portfolio, but in tending to it with care and consistency over time.

By keeping your investments aligned with your financial objectives through regular, purposeful rebalancing, you give your portfolio the best chance to perform not just in any one year, but across decades. It is this quiet, structured discipline that transforms good intentions into enduring outcomes—and that ultimately distinguishes the investor who merely starts strong from the one who finishes well.

Common Mistakes in Asset Allocation

Asset allocation sits at the very heart of investment strategy. It defines how an investor's capital is distributed across various asset classes—typically equities, bonds, cash, and alternatives—and plays a decisive role in determining both risk and return over time. When done well, it aligns with an investor's financial goals, personal risk tolerance, and time horizon. However, despite its foundational importance, asset allocation is frequently misunderstood or misapplied. Even experienced investors can fall prey to seemingly minor errors that, when compounded over years, erode returns, increase volatility, or steer portfolios away from their intended purpose.

One of the most common mistakes is chasing performance. Investors often look to the recent past as a guide to future success, directing funds toward the best-performing asset classes or sectors with the expectation that the trend will continue. This behaviour is grounded in a cognitive bias known as recency effect—the tendency to give undue weight to recent events. For example, during the late 1990s, technology stocks experienced extraordinary gains, prompting many to shift their allocations heavily into tech. When the dot-com bubble burst, those portfolios suffered severe losses, not because the strategy was inherently flawed, but because it had become dangerously unbalanced due to reactive allocation decisions.

Another widespread error is neglecting to diversify adequately. Some investors mistakenly believe that owning multiple funds or stocks equates to diversification, when in reality, those holdings may be highly correlated. A portfolio consisting entirely of technology stocks, even across different companies or regions, is still exposed to the same sectoral risks. True diversification spans not only sectors but asset classes, geographies, and investment styles. Failing to diversify leaves portfolios vulnerable to specific downturns, as evidenced by the financial crisis of 2008, when many investors discovered that their supposedly diversified portfolios were, in fact, heavily weighted towards equities and lacked exposure to defensive assets.

A related issue is over-concentration, where investors place too much faith—and too much capital—into a single stock, asset class, or market segment. This often arises from personal familiarity or strong conviction. A business owner, for instance, may invest heavily in their own industry, believing that their insight gives them an edge. Yet this concentration amplifies risk, particularly when the business and the investment portfolio are exposed to the same economic forces. Similarly, employees who hold large portions of their retirement savings in company stock expose themselves to double jeopardy: if the company falters, they may suffer both professionally and financially.

Misjudging risk tolerance is another significant pitfall. Risk tolerance is not just a theoretical concept—it's a reflection of how much volatility an investor can endure without abandoning their strategy. Many people overestimate their comfort with risk during bull markets, only to panic and sell when markets decline. This emotional mismatch between expected and actual behaviour often leads to poor timing decisions—buying high and selling low. To avoid this, investors must take a realistic view of their psychological and financial ability to weather downturns and adjust their asset mix accordingly. A portfolio that looks ideal on paper but induces anxiety in practice is unlikely to deliver long-term success.

Time horizon is also frequently misunderstood or ignored. Investors may allocate assets based on current market conditions rather than their actual financial objectives. For example, someone saving for retirement in thirty years may shift to bonds due to short-term fears about stock market volatility, undermining their ability to generate the long-term growth needed. Conversely, someone with a short-term goal—such as a home purchase in two years—may take on unnecessary risk by allocating heavily to equities. A misaligned time horizon leads to volatility where stability is needed, or stagnation where growth is required. Aligning asset allocation with the timing of financial needs is not optional—it is foundational.

Overcomplicating the portfolio is another subtle but damaging mistake. In pursuit of optimisation, some investors build portfolios with dozens of funds or individual securities, including overlapping strategies and redundant exposures. While complexity can offer nuance, it often becomes a barrier to clarity. Managing such portfolios can be time-consuming, expensive, and psychologically taxing. More importantly, it increases the likelihood of misallocation and hinders effective rebalancing. Simplicity, when rooted in thoughtful design, often outperforms complexity precisely because it is easier to manage, understand, and adjust.

Failure to rebalance is equally problematic. As markets shift, the relative weightings of asset classes change. Without rebalancing, a portfolio may become overly aggressive or too conservative, drifting away from its original intent. For instance, after a prolonged equity rally, a portfolio initially designed with 60 percent equities and 40 percent bonds may have tilted to 75 percent equities. This increases the portfolio's risk without the investor making a conscious decision to do so. Regular rebalancing, whether calendar-based or threshold-based, is essential to maintain the integrity of an asset allocation strategy.

Ignoring tax implications is another area where investors stumble. Asset allocation decisions must take into account the tax treatment of different accounts and assets. Holding income-generating investments such as bonds in tax-advantaged accounts and placing capital gain-oriented assets in taxable accounts can improve after-tax returns. Neglecting to structure the portfolio tax-efficiently can lead to unnecessary liabilities that chip away at net gains. While tax considerations should not override sound investment strategy, they must be factored into how and where assets are allocated.

Investors also err by failing to evolve their asset allocation as life circumstances change. What works at age 30 may no longer be appropriate at 55. Marriage, children, career changes, inheritance, or retirement all alter the financial landscape and require adjustments to the asset mix. Yet many investors continue with default allocations established years earlier, either out of inertia or lack of awareness. A dynamic approach—one that incorporates periodic reviews and adapts to shifting goals—is critical to keeping the portfolio relevant and effective.

A particularly modern mistake is being seduced by thematic investing without context. The rise of ETFs and increased media coverage has made it easy to invest in specific trends—clean energy, artificial intelligence, blockchain, or biotechnology. While these themes may offer compelling narratives and long-term potential, they can also lead to overly concentrated, trend-driven allocations that lack the balance needed for resilience. Theme-based investing should complement, not dominate, a strategic asset allocation. Otherwise, the investor risks turning their portfolio into a collection of speculative bets rather than a cohesive, goal-oriented strategy.

Perhaps the most overarching mistake is failing to connect asset allocation to purpose. Investing is not about beating benchmarks or chasing returns for their own sake. It is about achieving goals—whether that means funding retirement, paying for education, supporting family, or leaving a legacy. When asset allocation becomes disconnected from these purposes, it loses its guiding logic. Investors may find themselves making decisions based on market noise, peer comparisons, or fear of missing out, rather than on what is genuinely aligned with their lives.

Avoiding these mistakes requires not perfection, but awareness. It requires a willingness to engage with your finances beyond the superficial level—to ask hard questions, revisit assumptions, and course-correct when necessary. It demands an investment strategy that is not static, but responsive; not reactive, but intentional.

Financial markets will always surprise us. Economies will shift, crises will emerge, and innovations will change the investment landscape. What keeps investors grounded through these fluctuations is not their ability to predict them, but the strength of the structure they've built. Asset allocation, when done correctly, offers that structure. It provides the scaffolding that supports all other investment decisions. But like any structure, it must be built wisely and maintained thoughtfully.

By learning from common errors—rather than repeating them—investors can transform asset allocation from a theoretical exercise into a living, responsive framework. One that not only reflects who they are today but is capable of growing with them over time. And that is the essence of long-term financial success: not avoiding risk, but managing it with intelligence, humility, and clarity of purpose.

Chapter 4
Understanding Investment Vehicles - Where to Put Your Money

Every sound investment strategy rests firmly on two intertwined pillars: how your assets are allocated and the vehicles through which those assets are held. While asset allocation sketches the broad contours of risk and reward within a portfolio, the choice of investment vehicles is what brings that framework to life, translating abstract strategy into tangible outcomes. This chapter turns the lens onto the instruments investors use to deploy capital—whether traditional stocks and bonds, mutual funds, ETFs, property, or the more esoteric realms of gold and cryptocurrencies—each with its distinct purpose and inevitable trade-offs.

At first glance, the notion of an investment vehicle seems quite straightforward: it is simply any financial instrument used to access an asset class or generate returns. Yet, beneath this apparent simplicity lies a sophisticated web, where market mechanics intertwine with human psychology, regulatory frameworks, tax consequences, and strategic intent. Selecting the right vehicle is far from a one-off choice; it demands continual reassessment as your personal objectives, risk appetite, and the economic landscape evolve.

Perhaps the most familiar and widely held vehicle is the equity—shares representing fractional ownership in publicly traded companies. Equities tend to be the growth engines of portfolios, promising the highest potential returns over the long term. By purchasing a stock, you are buying into a company's fortunes, its successes and failures alike. Historically, equities have outpaced inflation substantially, delivering real returns that outstrip those of other asset classes. For anyone with a horizon measured in decades, equities are virtually indispensable to outpace the rising cost of living.

That said, equities are hardly without their ups and downs. Subject to corporate performance, investor sentiment, economic cycles, and geopolitical events, stocks are inherently volatile. This volatility is the price one pays for superior long-term gains. In the short term, prices can plunge sharply, but over the long haul, such fluctuations tend to smooth out, revealing a steady climb upwards. Consequently, equities suit those with extended time horizons—retirement savers and those planning wealth transfers, for instance—since longer investment periods tend to reward patience.

To soften the sharp edges of equity swings, many investors incorporate bonds and fixed income instruments into their portfolios. In essence, bonds are loans to governments, corporations, or other borrowers, with the investor receiving periodic interest payments plus the return of principal at maturity. These securities serve as ballast: stabilising a portfolio, reducing overall risk, and providing a predictable income stream. When markets wobble or economic conditions sour, bonds often play a counterbalancing role to declining equities, helping to protect capital and smooth returns.

The importance of fixed income grows especially apparent as investors age or when the preservation of capital takes precedence. Someone approaching retirement, for example, might increase their bond holdings to safeguard accumulated wealth and ensure a reliable income source. However, bonds are not monolithic. Government bonds from highly rated countries typically offer low risk but modest yields, while corporate bonds promise higher returns at the expense of greater credit risk. Furthermore, a bond's duration—its maturity timeline—influences its sensitivity to interest rate shifts. These subtleties require careful navigation to ensure fixed income allocations bolster rather than compromise your overarching objectives.

While direct investment in individual stocks and bonds remains common, pooled investment vehicles—mutual funds and exchange-traded funds (ETFs)—offer alternative routes to diversification. These funds enable investors to buy into a broad basket of securities with a single purchase, whether focused on equities, bonds, or a mix of assets. Mutual funds tend to be actively managed, with professional managers making selections based on research and market outlooks. ETFs, on the other hand, usually follow a passive strategy, tracking specific indices and thereby offering lower fees.

Choosing between mutual funds and ETFs often boils down to considerations of cost, accessibility, and investment philosophy. Active management might add value in less efficient markets or during turbulent times but comes with higher expenses and a risk of underperformance. Passive investing—championed by visionaries like John Bogle, founder of Vanguard—asserts that low-cost index tracking generally beats most active managers over the long term. For many investors, particularly those with limited budgets and long horizons, ETFs provide a transparent, cost-effective gateway to broad market exposure.

Real estate, one of the oldest and most tangible investment vehicles, has long been a mainstay of wealth creation. Property offers the dual allure of rental income and capital appreciation, while also acting as an inflation hedge. Unlike stocks or bonds, real estate is a physical asset—something you can see, touch, and improve—which appeals strongly to those who prize direct control and ownership.

However, real estate is far from a perfect solution. It lacks liquidity, meaning it cannot be quickly sold without potential losses. Moreover, owning property requires active management, involves maintenance costs, and exposes investors to localised market risks. For those unwilling or unable to manage property directly, real estate investment trusts (REITs) offer an attractive alternative. REITs are publicly traded entities that own or finance income-generating properties and distribute the bulk of their earnings as dividends, marrying the benefits of property investment with the liquidity and diversification of a fund.

Venturing beyond traditional classes, alternative investments broaden the horizon further but bring their own complexities. Gold, for instance, has been revered as a store of value and a haven during economic turmoil for centuries. Though it does not produce income, gold's worth lies in its ability to hedge against inflation or currency depreciation. Its role is less about generating spectacular returns and more about diversification and psychological reassurance when other assets falter.

Cryptocurrencies, meanwhile, remain a hotly debated frontier. Proponents herald digital assets like Bitcoin as the future of decentralised finance and a hedge against fiat currency erosion. Critics warn of their speculative nature, lack of regulation, and wild price swings. For most investors, crypto should be treated with caution, reserved for a small, speculative portion of a well-diversified portfolio. While the underlying technology may prove revolutionary, the investment merits remain uncertain and subject to evolving regulation and market acceptance.

Private equity and hedge funds represent further alternative options, typically accessible only to institutional or high-net-worth investors due to their complexity, illiquidity, and high entry thresholds. These vehicles pursue niche strategies—leveraging, arbitrage, distressed assets—in search of outsized returns but carry substantial risks and limited transparency. Although unsuitable for most retail investors, they play a significant role for endowments and pension funds seeking diversification and enhanced yields.

When it comes down to placing your money, the crucial question is rarely "Which vehicle is hot right now?" but rather, "Which combination aligns with my purpose?" Investment choices must flow from your goals, not fleeting market fads. A well-considered portfolio frequently blends these various vehicles, each fulfilling a role in a coherent strategy aimed at growing and preserving wealth over time.

A young investor just embarking on their financial journey might lean heavily on equities and ETFs for growth and simplicity. Someone juggling family commitments or business ventures could favour real estate and fixed income for stability and tangible returns. Meanwhile, those nearing retirement or managing inheritances might diversify into bonds, mutual funds, and selected alternatives to generate income and reduce downside exposure.

Understanding investment vehicles isn't about mastering every option or predicting future outperformers. It's about knowing what you hold, why you hold it, and how each piece fits within your broader financial plan. The most successful investors aren't those juggling the most complicated portfolios, but those whose holdings clearly reflect their values, ambitions, and risk tolerance.

In the chapters ahead, we will delve deeper into each of these vehicles, exploring their mechanics, strengths, weaknesses, and ideal uses. By journey's end, you will not only understand where to put your money but also how to ensure every pound invested serves a purpose you can confidently define, defend, and, ultimately, realise.

Stocks and Equities

Equities occupy a foundational position in the architecture of long-term wealth creation. Among all asset classes, they have historically delivered the highest real returns—outpacing inflation and building value over time. Investing in stocks is not merely a financial tactic; it is a direct participation in the enterprise economy. When an investor purchases a share, they acquire ownership in a company, sharing in its profits, growth, and future prospects. This unique combination of ownership and return potential makes equities an essential component of any portfolio designed to grow capital meaningfully over decades.

The rationale for investing in stocks extends far beyond speculation. Equities represent claims on productive enterprise. Unlike fixed income securities, which offer predetermined interest payments, stocks provide uncapped upside potential. A well-run company that expands its market share, innovates, and increases profitability can deliver compounded returns for years. While the price of a stock may fluctuate on a daily basis, its intrinsic value is tied to the underlying performance of the business. Over long periods, stock prices tend to follow earnings growth. This linkage is what makes equities such a powerful engine for wealth accumulation.

Take the historical perspective. Over the past century, equity markets in developed countries have produced average annual returns of roughly 7 to 9 percent after adjusting for inflation. By contrast, bonds have delivered around 2 to 3 percent, and cash has barely kept pace with inflation. The compounding impact of this difference over time is dramatic. For instance, an investment of

£10,000 in equities growing at 7 percent annually becomes nearly £150,000 in 40 years. The same investment in bonds growing at 3 percent would yield only £32,000. This disparity is not incidental—it is structural. It reflects the inherent dynamism of equity markets.

Despite this compelling long-term advantage, many investors remain wary of equities, especially when confronted with short-term volatility. The global financial crisis of 2008, the dot-com crash of the early 2000s, and the COVID-19 market panic of 2020 have all served as vivid reminders of the market's capacity for sudden declines. However, volatility should not be confused with risk. While stocks can and do fall sharply, long-term investors who remain invested typically recover their losses—and more. Markets have demonstrated a remarkable ability to rebound, reflecting the resilience of human enterprise and the adaptability of businesses to changing environments.

This is not to downplay the psychological difficulty of investing through downturns. Watching the value of a portfolio decline can be deeply unsettling, and it requires discipline to stay the course. Yet the most successful investors are those who understand the difference between temporary price movements and permanent capital loss. Equities, when held across a diversified portfolio and over a sufficient time frame, tend to recover from downturns and go on to reach new highs. The cost of avoiding equities—opting instead for the perceived safety of cash or low-yield bonds—is often the slow erosion of purchasing power and missed opportunities for growth.

One of the most powerful features of equities is the potential for reinvested dividends to accelerate compounding. Many companies distribute a portion of their profits as dividends, offering investors a steady income stream. When these dividends are reinvested to purchase additional shares, they generate further income and capital growth. Over time, this reinvestment effect becomes substantial. Historical studies show that dividends have accounted for a significant portion of total stock market returns, particularly in markets outside the United States where payout ratios are traditionally higher. For the long-term investor, this passive reinvestment can be an invaluable wealth-building mechanism.

Moreover, equities provide exposure to innovation and economic growth in a way that few other assets can. By investing in stocks, one taps into the ingenuity of entrepreneurs, the expansion of industries, and the shifting dynamics of global trade. The companies that dominate today's markets—Amazon, Apple, Unilever, Nestlé—were once small enterprises with uncertain futures. Investors who recognised their potential and stayed invested through their periods of volatility have been rewarded handsomely. While not every stock becomes a star performer, a diversified portfolio ensures exposure to those that do, cushioning the impact of those that falter.

Investors can access equities in a variety of forms. Direct ownership of individual stocks allows for targeted exposure, giving investors the opportunity to research, select, and build a portfolio based on specific convictions. However, this approach requires time, expertise, and emotional resilience. A more accessible alternative is equity mutual funds or exchange-traded funds (ETFs), which pool capital from many investors to buy a broad basket of stocks. These funds provide instant diversification, reducing company-specific risk and simplifying portfolio construction. Index-tracking funds, in particular, offer a cost-effective way to gain exposure to the broader market, often outperforming actively managed funds over the long term due to their low fees and consistency.

Equities are also categorised by region, size, and style, each offering different risk-return profiles. Large-cap stocks, representing established companies, tend to be more stable but offer slower growth. Small-cap stocks, while more volatile, often deliver higher returns over time due to their growth potential. International equities diversify exposure beyond one's home market and introduce currency and geopolitical dynamics. Style-based investing—such as growth versus value—adds further dimensions, allowing investors to tailor their exposure based on prevailing market conditions or personal philosophy.

The globalisation of equity markets has further expanded the range of opportunities available. Emerging market stocks offer access to the growth of developing economies, often accompanied by higher volatility but also higher return potential. The inclusion of international equities in a portfolio not only enhances diversification but also mitigates the risk of economic stagnation in any one country. For British investors, for example, exposure to the US, European, and Asian markets provides a hedge against domestic market fluctuations and opens up broader investment horizons.

Yet, equities are not without structural risks. Companies can underperform, industries can be disrupted, and market bubbles can distort valuations. The key to managing these risks lies in diversification and disciplined investing. Owning a broad mix of companies across sectors, geographies, and market capitalisations reduces the impact of any single failure. Equally important is maintaining a long-term perspective—resisting the urge to chase trends or panic in the face of temporary setbacks.

Another common mistake is attempting to time the market—buying in anticipation of gains and selling in anticipation of declines. Numerous studies have shown that even missing just a handful of the best-performing days in the market can significantly reduce long-term returns. Timing is notoriously difficult to get right, and even professional investors frequently underperform benchmarks when attempting to do so. The more reliable strategy is to remain consistently invested, allowing time and compounding to do the heavy lifting.

Equities also offer an element of liquidity and transparency that other asset classes often lack. Shares can be bought and sold quickly, with prices available in real time. This liquidity allows for flexibility in managing portfolios, rebalancing allocations, or accessing capital when needed. Listed companies are also subject to regulatory oversight and reporting requirements, providing investors with a degree of transparency and accountability.

For those committed to long-term financial growth—whether saving for retirement, funding a child's education, or building intergenerational wealth—equities are not optional. They are essential. They offer unmatched potential for capital appreciation, exposure to the growth of the global economy, and an efficient way to harness the power of compounding. Their volatility is not a flaw to be avoided, but a feature to be managed—one that creates opportunities for those with the discipline to stay the course.

Investing in equities is not a guaranteed path to wealth, but it is the closest thing the financial markets offer to a long-term strategy with consistent success. It rewards patience, consistency, and rational decision-making. In an investment landscape crowded with complexity and short-term noise, equities provide a simple but powerful proposition: own a piece of the world's most productive enterprises and allow time to do its work. For those who can embrace this principle with clarity and commitment, the rewards are both profound and enduring.

Bonds and Fixed Income

While equities are often celebrated as the driving force of long-term capital growth, bonds and fixed income instruments provide a quieter but equally vital role within a well-structured portfolio. They are the financial counterweights to the more volatile nature of stocks—offering predictability, preserving capital, and creating stability during times of market stress. For investors seeking a measured approach to building and protecting wealth, understanding the role of bonds is indispensable. Far from being static or conservative by default, fixed income strategies can be highly nuanced, responsive to economic cycles, and adaptable to the evolving needs of individual investors.

At its core, a bond is a loan. When an investor purchases a bond, they are effectively lending money to a government, corporation, or other institution in exchange for periodic interest payments—known as coupons—and the promise of repayment of the principal at a predetermined maturity date. This contractual nature of bonds gives them a distinct characteristic within the investment universe: their cash flows are relatively predictable. Unlike equities, which offer no assurance of return and whose dividends may be reduced or eliminated entirely, bonds establish a clear payment structure from the outset. This certainty makes them a foundational component for investors prioritising income or risk mitigation.

The stabilising role of bonds becomes especially evident during periods of equity market downturns. Historically, high-quality bonds—such as government securities—have demonstrated a negative or low correlation with equities. When stock prices fall, investors often seek refuge in safer assets, driving bond prices higher. This inverse relationship can act as a natural shock absorber, softening portfolio losses and preserving overall value. It is this dynamic that underscores the importance of including fixed income in a diversified portfolio: not to maximise returns, but to enhance resilience.

For example, during the global financial crisis of 2008, equity markets suffered catastrophic declines, with some indices falling by over 40 percent. Yet government bonds, particularly those issued by stable economies like the United Kingdom, the United States, and Germany, experienced strong demand, pushing their prices up and yields down. Investors who held a balanced mix of equities and bonds saw smaller losses than those who were entirely exposed to equities. Similarly, during the early months of the COVID-19 pandemic, when markets reacted with extreme volatility, high-quality fixed income assets provided a cushion against the sell-off in riskier securities.

Beyond their defensive characteristics, bonds offer flexibility across a wide spectrum of investment objectives. They can serve as a source of regular income, a tool for capital preservation, or a way to adjust a portfolio's risk profile depending on the investor's stage of life. A young investor may hold a modest allocation to fixed income to moderate volatility, while someone nearing retirement may increase their bond holdings to prioritise stability and income generation. The allocation need not be static—it can evolve with the investor's needs, offering both structure and adaptability.

The bond market itself is vast and varied, encompassing a diverse array of issuers, maturities, credit qualities, and interest rate structures. Government bonds, such as UK Gilts or US Treasuries, are generally considered the safest, backed by the taxing power of sovereign governments. These securities tend to offer lower yields, reflecting their minimal default risk, but they provide unmatched security and liquidity. Corporate bonds, issued by companies to finance operations or expansion, typically offer higher yields to compensate for greater credit risk. Within this category, there is a spectrum ranging from investment-grade bonds—issued by financially robust companies—to high-yield, or "junk," bonds, which come with a greater risk of default but also the potential for higher returns.

Municipal bonds, common in the United States, are issued by local governments and can offer tax advantages to residents, though they are less prevalent in the UK and Europe. Inflation-linked bonds—such as Treasury Inflation-Protected Securities (TIPS) in the US or Index-Linked Gilts in the UK—adjust their principal and interest payments in line with inflation, making them useful in preserving real purchasing power.

Another important dimension is duration—the length of time until a bond matures. Duration affects not only the time horizon of the investment but also its sensitivity to interest rate changes. Generally, the longer the duration, the more a bond's price will fluctuate with changes in interest rates. For instance, if interest rates rise, the value of existing bonds tends to fall because their fixed payments become less attractive compared to newly issued bonds with higher yields. This inverse relationship between interest rates and bond prices is a fundamental feature of fixed income investing and one that becomes especially relevant in changing monetary policy environments.

Over the past decade, global interest rates have hovered at historically low levels, prompting some investors to question the role of bonds in their portfolios. With yields compressed, the income generated from bonds has diminished, leading to a reassessment of their utility. However, it is important to understand that fixed income's value does not rest solely on yield. Even in a low-rate environment, bonds continue to serve their stabilising function, and they can still act as a counterbalance to equity risk. Moreover, within the broad fixed income universe, there remain opportunities for strategic allocation—such as diversifying across credit tiers, geographies, or using bond ladders to manage reinvestment risk.

Another consideration is the growing accessibility of bond investments through mutual funds and exchange-traded funds (ETFs). For individual investors, buying a single bond directly often requires a substantial capital outlay and careful credit analysis. Bond funds, on the other hand, allow for diversified exposure with lower entry points and professional management. These funds can target specific sectors—such as emerging market debt or short-duration corporate bonds—or provide broad-market exposure. While bond funds come with their own set of risks, particularly around liquidity and interest rate sensitivity, they remain an effective vehicle for incorporating fixed income into a personal investment strategy.

It is also worth exploring the behavioural benefits of fixed income investing. The relative predictability of bond returns can provide psychological comfort during turbulent times, helping investors remain committed to their broader strategy. This emotional steadiness is often underestimated but plays a critical role in long-term investment success. A portfolio that combines growth assets with stabilising elements is more likely to weather market cycles and keep the investor invested, which is ultimately what drives compounded returns over time.

For those with specific income needs—retirees, for example—bonds can be structured into income ladders or bond ladders, where a series of bonds with staggered maturities provide regular cash flow while limiting exposure to interest rate risk. This tailored approach allows investors to match future liabilities with maturing assets, creating a more predictable and manageable retirement income stream.

Despite their virtues, bonds are not without risk. Credit risk, interest rate risk, reinvestment risk, and inflation risk must all be accounted for. A diversified and well-constructed fixed income strategy mitigates these concerns, but they cannot be ignored. Investors must be wary of chasing yield—particularly in lower-rated or exotic bonds—without a clear understanding of the underlying risks. As with all investments, discipline and due diligence are paramount.

The function of fixed income is not to dazzle with dramatic gains. It is to provide ballast, liquidity, and dependability. In a world that frequently rewards boldness and risk-taking, bonds remind us of the importance of caution, prudence, and the long view. They serve as the steady hand on the tiller—allowing investors to pursue higher returns elsewhere in the portfolio, knowing that a stable core is quietly doing its work.

In designing a balanced portfolio, bonds are not an optional afterthought—they are a strategic necessity. Their role in managing risk, preserving capital, and delivering income becomes more valuable as life circumstances shift and financial priorities evolve. Whether as a defensive layer, an income source, or a tool for strategic positioning, fixed income remains an essential component in the modern investor's toolkit.

To understand bonds is to understand the art of measured investing—where returns are earned not through speculation, but through structure, consistency, and alignment with purpose. For those willing to look beyond the noise of yield-chasing and short-term movements, bonds offer something far more enduring: the quiet confidence that your financial foundation is built on stable, thoughtfully chosen ground.

Mutual Funds vs. ETFs

As the landscape of personal investing has evolved, so too have the tools available to individual investors. Once the domain of stockbrokers and institutional players, diversified investment vehicles are now accessible to nearly anyone with a brokerage account and an internet connection. Among the most widely used of these tools are mutual funds and exchange-traded funds (ETFs). Both offer efficient ways to gain exposure to a diversified portfolio of securities, whether equities, bonds, or alternative assets. Yet despite their similarities, they differ in structure, cost, flexibility, and investment philosophy—most notably in their respective alignment with active versus passive strategies.

At a fundamental level, mutual funds and ETFs are pooled investment vehicles. Investors contribute money to a collective fund, which is then used to purchase a basket of assets managed by a fund manager or automated system. This pooling mechanism provides instant diversification, even with a relatively modest investment. Rather than selecting individual stocks or bonds, the investor gains exposure to dozens or even hundreds of holdings through a single purchase. This makes both mutual funds and ETFs attractive to those seeking convenience, risk mitigation, and broad market participation.

The key divergence between these two vehicles begins with how they are structured and traded. Mutual funds are traditionally offered by investment firms and are priced just once per day—after the market closes—at their net asset value (NAV). When an investor places a buy or sell order, it is executed at this end-of-day price, regardless of when the order was placed. ETFs, on the other hand, trade on stock exchanges throughout the trading day, just like individual shares. Their prices fluctuate in real time based on supply and demand, even though the value of their underlying assets changes more gradually. This intraday trading feature adds a layer of flexibility to ETFs that mutual funds inherently lack.

This difference in trading mechanism has practical implications. ETFs allow for greater tactical control. Investors can use limit orders, stop-losses, or even short-sell ETF shares—tools that can be useful in volatile markets. For example, during sharp intraday movements, ETF investors can respond instantly, while mutual fund investors must wait until the market closes to know the price at which their transaction was executed. For those who value precision and flexibility, especially in active trading or risk management, ETFs may offer a distinct advantage.

However, mutual funds are often better suited to systematic investing strategies. Because they are priced once per day, they encourage a long-term perspective and discourage reactionary behaviour. Many retirement plans and workplace savings schemes use mutual funds for this reason. The structure reduces temptation to time the market, which, for most investors, results in better long-term outcomes. Additionally, mutual funds often offer automatic investment and withdrawal plans, simplifying contributions to pensions, education savings, or income generation in retirement.

The question of whether to invest in mutual funds or ETFs is frequently tied to the broader debate between active and passive investing. Mutual funds, particularly those that are actively managed, employ professional fund managers who make decisions about which securities to buy and sell in an attempt to outperform a benchmark index. These managers rely on research, market analysis, and predictive modelling to identify undervalued securities or exploit market inefficiencies. The appeal of active management lies in its potential for outperformance—especially during periods of market dislocation or within less efficient sectors.

However, this potential comes at a cost. Active mutual funds typically charge higher management fees—known as the expense ratio—because of the costs associated with research, trading, and portfolio oversight. Furthermore, data over the past few decades has consistently shown that the majority of active fund managers underperform their benchmarks over extended periods. This underperformance is often exacerbated by fees, taxes, and turnover costs. As a result, many investors have grown sceptical of the value delivered by active management.

ETFs are typically associated with passive investing. They are often designed to track a specific market index—such as the FTSE 100, S&P 500, or MSCI World—rather than trying to outperform it. Because they follow a rules-based methodology, passive ETFs have significantly lower fees than actively managed mutual funds. This cost advantage, when compounded over time, can make a substantial difference in returns. For example, an index ETF with an annual fee of 0.10 percent will retain more of the investor's capital than a mutual fund charging 1.50 percent, particularly over a twenty- or thirty-year horizon.

The rise of passive investing through ETFs reflects a broader philosophical shift. It acknowledges the difficulty of consistently beating the market, even for professionals, and instead seeks to capture market returns efficiently and with minimal friction. This does not imply that ETFs are always superior to mutual funds, but it underscores the importance of clarity around investment goals and expectations. If one believes in the value of professional insight, is investing in less efficient markets (such as small-cap equities or emerging markets), or is willing to accept higher costs in exchange for potential outperformance, actively managed mutual funds may still hold appeal.

However, the landscape is changing. In recent years, actively managed ETFs have begun to emerge, blending the structural advantages of ETFs—liquidity, transparency, and tax efficiency—with the discretionary oversight of active managers. This hybrid model is gaining traction, particularly in specialised areas like thematic investing, where investors want exposure to niche sectors—such as clean energy, cybersecurity, or biotechnology—guided by expert insight. The rise of such products has further blurred the line between traditional mutual funds and ETFs, expanding choice while complicating the decision-making process.

Tax efficiency is another area where ETFs often have the upper hand. Because of the way ETFs are structured—using an "in-kind" creation and redemption mechanism—they are generally able to avoid triggering capital gains distributions when assets within the fund are bought or sold. This stands in contrast to mutual funds, which must distribute realised gains to shareholders at year-end, even if those investors didn't sell their fund units. For investors in taxable accounts, this difference can meaningfully impact after-tax returns, particularly for those with large holdings or in higher tax brackets.

Still, mutual funds maintain certain advantages. They often offer access to institutional share classes with lower fees for large investors, or they may include features such as target-date functionality, which automatically adjusts asset allocation over time. For investors contributing to long-term savings plans with set timelines—such as pensions or university funds—these features can provide both simplicity and strategic discipline.

Another important consideration is minimum investment thresholds. Many mutual funds require a relatively high initial investment—£1,000 or more—whereas ETFs can be purchased in smaller increments, limited only by the price of a single share or fraction thereof. This accessibility makes ETFs particularly attractive for younger investors or those starting with limited capital.

Ultimately, the decision between mutual funds and ETFs is not a binary one. Each has merits, and both can play a complementary role within a broader investment strategy. For example, one might use passive ETFs to form the core of a portfolio—tracking broad market indices at low cost—while allocating a portion to actively managed mutual funds that target specific opportunities or express particular convictions. This "core-satellite" approach allows for efficiency and diversification, while leaving room for strategic tilts or specialised insight.

Investor temperament also plays a role. Some may prefer the stability and systematic nature of mutual funds, avoiding the distraction of intraday trading and media noise. Others may value the control, flexibility, and cost advantages offered by ETFs, especially those who enjoy being more hands-on with their portfolio construction. What matters most is not the label, but how well the chosen vehicle aligns with one's financial objectives, risk tolerance, and behavioural inclinations.

As with any investment decision, due diligence is essential. Investors should evaluate not only fees and performance history but also the fund's objective, holdings, turnover rate, and the reputation of the management team. A well-constructed ETF or mutual fund should be transparent, cost-effective, and coherent in strategy. It should serve as a building block in a portfolio designed not for short-term speculation but for long-term success.

In the increasingly sophisticated world of personal finance, the proliferation of investment vehicles is a welcome development—but it also demands a higher level of discernment. Understanding the differences between mutual funds and ETFs, and recognising how each fits into a personal investment plan, empowers investors to build portfolios that are not only diversified, but intentional. Whether one leans towards active engagement or passive efficiency, the key lies in aligning tools with purpose—and in doing so, turning investment into a disciplined, effective, and ultimately rewarding pursuit.

Real Estate as a Long-Term Investment

Few asset classes carry the psychological weight, emotional significance, and generational impact of real estate. Property is more than a financial vehicle—it is shelter, status, and strategy woven into one. For centuries, owning land or property has symbolised stability and security, a tangible marker of prosperity. But beyond its social meaning, real estate stands as one of the most reliable methods of long-term wealth accumulation. It offers a distinctive combination of income, capital appreciation, and leverage, making it an essential component of many intergenerational wealth-building strategies.

The appeal of property investment lies in its dual nature. Unlike equities or bonds, which are financial abstractions tied to market sentiment, property is a physical asset. It can be seen, touched, improved, and leveraged in ways other investments cannot. This tangibility provides a sense of control, especially for those who value the ability to directly influence the performance of their investments. Renovating, re-leasing, or redeveloping a property can materially increase its value—something that cannot be said for most shares in a portfolio.

Yet real estate's true power as a long-term investment is revealed over decades, not years. Its ability to generate steady cash flow through rental income while appreciating in value through capital growth creates a compounding effect that builds slowly, then suddenly. A modest buy-to-let property acquired in one's early thirties and held into retirement can grow significantly in value, pay off its mortgage through tenant income, and eventually become a debt-free asset providing steady returns. Multiply this effect across multiple properties and generations, and one begins to understand how real estate serves not merely as an asset class, but as a vehicle for legacy.

Generational wealth-building through property often begins with leverage. Mortgages allow investors to control assets far greater in value than the capital initially committed. For example, with a 20 percent deposit on a £300,000 property, an investor gains exposure to the full value of the asset while only tying up £60,000 of their own capital. If the property appreciates by just 3 percent annually, the return on the investor's equity is substantially magnified. While leverage introduces risk—particularly in environments with rising interest rates or declining prices—it is also one of the defining features that distinguishes property investment from other forms of wealth accumulation.

The rental income generated from property adds another layer of benefit. Properly managed, a rental property can provide a steady stream of passive income that increases over time with inflation and market demand. This income can be reinvested, used to fund other investments, or serve as a retirement income stream. For families, this income-producing aspect of property can help support future generations—offsetting university costs, assisting with home purchases, or simply acting as a financial cushion. Unlike a lump sum inheritance, which can be quickly spent or mismanaged, an income-producing asset encourages stewardship and continuity.

Moreover, property benefits from scarcity. Land, especially in high-demand urban centres, is finite. As populations grow and cities become denser, well-located properties tend to become more valuable. Governments rarely manufacture new land, and zoning restrictions often constrain supply. This scarcity underpins the appreciation seen in desirable property markets. While bubbles and corrections do occur, over the long term, real estate in prime areas has shown a remarkable ability to preserve and increase wealth.

Consider the example of a family that purchased a Victorian terrace house in north London in the 1980s for £80,000. Over the next four decades, that property could appreciate to over £1 million, depending on location and improvements. In the meantime, it might generate tens of thousands in rental income, or house family members through different life stages. That single decision, made decades ago, can become a cornerstone of financial security not just for the buyer, but for their children and grandchildren.

However, the power of real estate is not purely passive. It rewards initiative and long-term thinking. Value can be added through renovations, better tenant management, or strategic refinancing. Tax-efficient ownership structures—such as holding property within a limited company or family trust—can preserve more of the gains for future generations. There are opportunities to scale, to optimise, and to professionalise. Real estate is not a "set and forget" asset; it requires engagement, but that engagement can generate outsize rewards.

That said, property investing is not without risk or complexity. Markets fluctuate. Properties can sit vacant. Tenants can default. Maintenance costs can escalate. Regulatory changes—such as restrictions on landlord tax relief or new compliance standards—can alter the economics significantly. Overleveraging can turn a promising portfolio into a financial burden. For these reasons, property must be approached with the same rigour and prudence as any other investment. Emotional attachment to property can cloud judgment, and assuming that all real estate investments will perform uniformly is a mistake.

Real estate also poses unique challenges related to liquidity. Unlike stocks or bonds, which can be sold quickly in liquid markets, property transactions take time and incur significant costs. Selling a house may involve weeks or months of marketing, legal review, inspections, and negotiation. These barriers to exit can complicate cash flow planning or force investors to sell at unfavourable times. While this illiquidity protects property from the rapid fluctuations of the financial markets, it also requires careful portfolio design to ensure that capital needs can be met without sacrificing long-term assets.

Despite these limitations, the role of real estate in building generational wealth remains robust. It provides not only economic returns but also cultural continuity. A family home becomes a repository of memory and identity. A portfolio of rental properties becomes a shared responsibility and a collective asset. Unlike intangible investments that may be abstract to younger generations, property is immediate and tangible. It can be walked through, lived in, and passed on.

In an era marked by financial instability, inflation, and the erosion of trust in traditional pensions, property offers a degree of autonomy. It allows families to take control of their financial future, to craft a legacy that is resilient and rooted in something real. When integrated thoughtfully into an investment strategy—balanced with liquid assets, diversified across locations and property types, and managed with attention to both risk and reward—real estate becomes far more than an income stream or an appreciating asset. It becomes a cornerstone of intergenerational security.

Many of the world's wealthiest families have long understood this. Their fortunes are rarely built on property alone, but they are often sustained by it. It offers a form of permanence amidst the volatility of markets and the impermanence of trends. It anchors a portfolio, offers leverage without excessive risk when managed prudently, and creates a bridge between generations.

For the individual investor, the decision to include property in a long-term plan should be informed by purpose, not just potential return. What role should the property play? Is it intended to generate income, provide a home, serve as a store of value, or support future generations? Each of these objectives demands different strategies, financing, and timelines. Aligning the structure of the investment with the family's broader goals ensures that the property remains an asset—not a burden—as circumstances change.

Ultimately, real estate's most enduring appeal lies in its dual character: physical yet financial, personal yet strategic. It is an investment in place, permanence, and people. When acquired with discernment, financed responsibly, and managed with care, it becomes not just a home or an income source, but a foundation—one upon which families can build, grow, and thrive across decades.

Alternative Investments (Gold, Crypto, Private Equity)

For generations, mainstream investing has revolved around a familiar axis: equities, bonds, and cash. These traditional asset classes form the foundation of most portfolios, offering a balance between growth, income, and liquidity. However, as markets become more complex and investors seek broader diversification and exposure to asymmetric returns, alternative investments are playing an increasingly prominent role in long-term wealth strategies. Gold, cryptocurrencies, and private equity represent three distinctly different non-traditional assets—each with its own opportunities, risks, and philosophies. While none are inherently superior or inferior to conventional investments, each offers characteristics that can enhance a portfolio when used judiciously.

Gold is arguably the most enduring of all alternative investments. Revered for millennia as a store of value, it has retained purchasing power across civilisations and crises. Unlike currencies or shares, gold is not tied to the fortunes of any particular government or company. It is finite, tangible, and universally accepted. Investors often turn to gold in times of uncertainty—whether geopolitical, economic, or financial—viewing it as a safe haven that can preserve capital when other assets falter.

The strategic case for gold lies in its role as a hedge. It tends to move independently of equities and bonds, and it often performs well during periods of inflation or currency devaluation. During the global financial crisis of 2008, for instance, gold prices surged as central banks slashed interest rates and investors lost faith in the stability of financial institutions. Similarly, the quantitative easing era of the 2010s, and more recently the inflationary pressures of the 2020s, have seen gold regain prominence as a protective asset.

Yet gold is not without limitations. It does not generate income, its price can be volatile, and its long-term real return—while positive—is modest compared to equities. Additionally, gold's value is driven largely by sentiment and macroeconomic factors rather than fundamentals. There are no earnings, dividends, or cash flows to analyse. For this reason, gold should not be viewed as a growth asset but rather as a form of portfolio insurance. Allocating a modest percentage of total wealth to gold can add resilience, particularly for those concerned about systemic risks or long-term inflation.

Cryptocurrencies, by contrast, represent a far more recent—and controversial—alternative investment. Bitcoin, launched in 2009, introduced a novel concept: a decentralised digital currency that operates independently of central banks, intermediaries, and national borders. Built on blockchain technology, cryptocurrencies promise transparency, security, and programmability. Over the past decade, this innovation has spurred an explosion of digital assets, including Ethereum, Solana, and thousands of others. Proponents view crypto not merely as a new asset class, but as the foundation for a new financial system.

From a portfolio perspective, cryptocurrencies offer unique attributes. They are uncorrelated with traditional assets, highly liquid (in major coins), and have demonstrated extraordinary growth.

Investors drawn to crypto often cite its potential to outperform due to network effects, technological adoption, and the macroeconomic appeal of decentralised money. Indeed, early adopters of Bitcoin have realised staggering returns—turning modest investments into substantial wealth.

However, these rewards have come with extreme volatility and existential uncertainty. The crypto market is notorious for price swings, regulatory scrutiny, technological vulnerabilities, and speculative fervour. Events such as exchange hacks, algorithmic stablecoin collapses, or crackdowns by governments can send shockwaves through digital asset markets. The collapse of platforms like FTX in 2022 or the dramatic valuation swings of major coins have served as reminders that this is still an emerging, experimental space.

Investing in crypto requires a clear understanding of risk appetite, time horizon, and purpose. For those with a long-term outlook and tolerance for significant drawdowns, a small allocation to digital assets may serve as a high-risk, high-reward satellite within a diversified portfolio. However, crypto should never be mistaken for a reliable store of value or a replacement for more established asset classes. Nor should it be pursued purely on the basis of hype or momentum. Education, security, and strategic discipline are essential for any investor exploring this space.

In contrast to both gold and crypto, private equity represents an alternative asset class that is less visible but deeply embedded in institutional wealth-building. Private equity refers to investments in companies that are not publicly traded. This can involve early-stage venture capital, growth equity in expanding firms, or buyouts of mature businesses. Investors in private equity typically commit capital to a fund managed by a professional team, which then deploys that capital across multiple private businesses with the aim of driving operational improvement, strategic growth, and eventual exit—either through sale or public offering.

The appeal of private equity lies in its potential for superior returns. Because private companies are not subject to the short-term pressures of public markets, they can take a longer-term approach to innovation, restructuring, and market penetration. Furthermore, private equity managers often take an active role in governance, aligning incentives and unlocking value that passive investors in public stocks may never access. Historical performance data, particularly from top-quartile funds, has shown that private equity can outperform public markets—though such results are by no means guaranteed.

That said, private equity is not for everyone. These investments are illiquid, with capital often locked up for seven to ten years. Minimum investment thresholds are high, fees can be substantial, and access is typically limited to institutional or accredited investors. Transparency is lower than in public markets, and performance varies widely across funds. Moreover, because private equity relies on a concentrated number of investments and exit opportunities, outcomes can be highly idiosyncratic. Investors must have patience, confidence in the fund's management team, and a long-term commitment to capital deployment.

Despite these hurdles, private equity has become a cornerstone of many sophisticated portfolios—particularly among family offices, endowments, and pension funds. Its inclusion reflects a belief not only in diversification, but in the value of long-term engagement with private enterprise. For individual investors seeking exposure, options have expanded in recent years through publicly listed private equity vehicles, secondary markets, or lower-minimum feeder funds, though these come with their own nuances and risks.

Weighing the pros and cons of alternative investments ultimately comes down to strategic alignment. These assets should serve specific purposes within a broader framework—not dominate a portfolio out of novelty or fear of missing out. Gold can hedge against inflation and crisis. Cryptocurrencies offer speculative upside and exposure to digital innovation. Private equity delivers access to the unlisted economy and the potential for high alpha. But each comes with trade-offs: reduced liquidity, increased volatility, higher fees, or uncertain regulation.

It is therefore critical for investors to be clear on their objectives. Are you seeking diversification? Protection against systemic risk?

Asymmetric return potential? A hedge against currency devaluation? Each motivation demands a different mix of exposure and a different tolerance for complexity. Incorporating alternatives successfully requires not just knowledge, but humility—an understanding that these assets behave differently, require more diligence, and demand patience.

From a behavioural standpoint, alternative investments also pose challenges. Their novelty, opacity, and media-driven narratives can provoke emotional decision-making. Gold can tempt over-allocation during economic panic. Crypto can inspire reckless risk-taking during bull runs. Private equity can breed overconfidence in illiquid commitments. Sound investment behaviour—grounded in discipline, planning, and long-term thinking—remains the foundation upon which all successful portfolios are built.

In constructing a robust portfolio, the inclusion of alternative assets should be deliberate, measured, and continuously reviewed. A thoughtful allocation—often no more than 5 to 15 percent of total investable assets—can provide valuable diversification and complement traditional holdings. But these positions must be earned through understanding, not purchased through impulse.

In today's evolving financial landscape, alternative investments are no longer exotic outliers—they are part of the mainstream conversation. They reflect changing economic conditions, technological disruption, and the search for new sources of value. When understood and integrated appropriately, they can add meaningful depth to a portfolio. When misunderstood or misapplied, they can undermine even the best-laid plans. The task for the modern investor is not to avoid these assets, but to approach them with curiosity, caution, and clarity—recognising that diversification is not simply about owning more things, but about owning the right things for the right reasons.

Chapter 5
Risk Management - Protecting Your Wealth

Every investor, whether novice or seasoned, must come to terms with a fundamental truth: risk and reward are inextricably linked. Financial markets, for all their promise of wealth accumulation, remain riddled with uncertainty. Economic upheavals, corporate blunders, shifts in interest rates, political upheavals, even the collective mood of investors—all have the power to unsettle the most carefully devised plans. Managing these risks is far more than a technical exercise; it is the bedrock of prudent investing. Without it, ambition drifts into speculation. With it, growth finds a solid, measured footing.

Risk management isn't about banishing risk altogether—that would be a fool's errand, as impossible as it is undesirable. Instead, it demands recognising potential threats to one's capital, gauging their possible consequences, and establishing safeguards that bolster resilience amid inevitable uncertainties. Viewed in this light, managing risk is far from a defensive stance—it is an active, deliberate stewardship of resources, requiring both wisdom and foresight.

To navigate this terrain, one must first grasp the various types of financial risk investors encounter. Market risk, often labelled systematic risk, affects virtually all investments, driven by sweeping economic forces like recessions, inflation, interest rate shifts, or geopolitical strife. This risk cannot be eradicated through diversification alone but can be tempered by prudent asset allocation and patience. Conversely, specific—or unsystematic—risk pertains to individual companies or sectors. A sudden leadership shake-up, a failed product launch, or regulatory penalties can quickly batter a single stock. Fortunately, this type of risk can be substantially lowered through diversification, one of the oldest and most trusted principles of risk management.

Credit risk comes into play mostly with bonds and lending: the peril that a borrower may default. For instance, UK government bonds are typically low-risk, while high-yield corporate bonds come with greater credit risk, balanced by the prospect of higher returns. Liquidity risk differs slightly—it's the threat that an asset cannot be sold swiftly enough to stave off losses, a concern especially relevant in property or private equity where funds can be tied up for extended periods.

Then there's inflation risk—the stealthy erosion of purchasing power over time. Parking too much cash or clinging to low-yield fixed income during inflationary times may feel safe, yet this strategy quietly chips away at real value. Currency risk also matters for those with overseas investments, as exchange rate swings can influence the value of foreign-denominated assets. Acknowledging and incorporating these risks into a coherent, long-term plan is essential.

Among all strategies, diversification stands out as one of the most potent and accessible shields against risk. By distributing investments across various asset classes, industries, and regions, an investor softens the blow of any single failure. Portfolios that blend equities, bonds, property, and alternative assets generally fare better against shocks than those heavily concentrated in one sector or geography. Within equities, diversification might span sectors—technology, healthcare, financials—and regions, from developed to emerging markets. Bonds, too, can be diversified by mixing short and long maturities and varying credit qualities. The goal isn't to eliminate volatility but to ensure that losses in one pocket are cushioned by gains or steadiness elsewhere.

History offers lessons in this regard. Take the 2008 financial crisis, for example. Equities plunged worldwide, yet portfolios fortified with long-dated government bonds, gold, or cash equivalents fared noticeably better. Likewise, during the market turmoil at the start of the COVID-19 pandemic in early 2020, those with diversified holdings bounced back faster than investors clinging to narrow, high-risk positions. While diversification doesn't promise immunity from losses, it mitigates severity and duration, boosting the odds of weathering storms and eventually reaping rewards.

Navigating market volatility is another pillar of effective risk management. Price swings, though inevitable, can unleash powerful emotions: fear, anxiety, impatience. All too often, these feelings provoke damaging reactions—panic selling at market lows, chasing the latest hot asset, abandoning well-thought-out strategies in favour of fleeting trends. Ironically, such emotional responses can inflict greater harm than the market's ups and downs.

Managing volatility calls for setting realistic expectations. Markets don't travel in straight lines; even during robust bull runs, corrections of 10% or more are common, while bear markets—declines of 20% or beyond—arrive from time to time. Yet history shows markets' remarkable capacity to recover and advance over the long haul. The real winners are those who endure volatility, who resist panic, maintain composure during downturns, and continue investing steadily. It's this discipline that often separates successful investors from the rest.

Practical tools like rebalancing and dollar-cost averaging aid in weathering volatility. Rebalancing involves periodically adjusting a portfolio back to its target asset mix—selling parts of those that have risen and buying into those that have fallen—thus removing emotion from decisions and reinforcing long-term aims. Dollar-cost averaging, meanwhile, entails investing fixed sums regularly, smoothing the purchase price over time and reducing the risk of unfortunate timing.

Beyond behavioural tactics, structural methods also play a vital role. Insurance, frequently overlooked in investment discussions, is indispensable in comprehensive financial planning. Life insurance, income protection, and critical illness cover offer buffers against unforeseen events that could derail wealth-building efforts. For high-net-worth individuals or entrepreneurs, specialised policies may guard against liabilities, asset loss, or succession complications.

Hedging strategies, usually reserved for sophisticated investors, involve using financial derivatives like options, futures, or inverse ETFs to offset potential losses. For example, a portfolio manager expecting short-term turbulence might buy put options to shield part of their equity holdings. While hedging can be effective, it brings complexity, costs, and risk of missteps, thus demanding careful consideration and expertise.

Lastly, an often-neglected aspect of risk management is knowing when to exit an investment. Too many fixate on when to buy, but selling deserves equal foresight. Exit strategies should be integral to the investment plan—what conditions trigger a sale? A shift in fundamentals, liquidity needs, or evolving goals? Selling must be deliberate, not emotional. For instance, an investor who achieves their target might gradually reduce exposure to equities, moving into bonds or income-generating assets.

Tax consequences, transaction expenses, and overall financial impact are crucial when planning exits. Sometimes partial sales or strategic reallocations trump wholesale divestments. Moreover, investors must beware of anchoring—clinging stubbornly to a target price or refusing to cut losses in hopes of a rebound. Such habits tie up capital in underperforming assets, hindering progress toward more productive aims.

In truth, risk management is not a symptom of fear but a mark of resilience, adaptability, and thoughtful foresight. It turns investing from a gamble into a rational, evidence-based endeavour. Above all, it preserves not just capital but the investor's confidence—the confidence to remain engaged, make informed decisions, and pursue long-term ambitions with clarity.

As we delve deeper into this chapter, we will explore each dimension of risk management—from understanding and categorising risks, through crafting diversified portfolios, managing emotional responses, applying protective measures, to executing well-planned exits. The goal is not merely to survive market turbulence but to emerge stronger, wiser, and more prepared. After all, true wealth is measured not only by what is gained in prosperous times but by what is safeguarded and sustained through all seasons.

Understanding Investment Risks

Risk is an unavoidable companion to any form of investing. The moment an individual decides to place capital into a financial vehicle—whether stocks, bonds, property, or alternative assets—they are exposed to uncertainty. What they receive in return, however, is the potential for reward. Without risk, there would be no return. Understanding the nature of investment risks—how they function, where they emerge, and how they can be controlled—is fundamental to making sound financial decisions and achieving long-term stability. Risk management is not a reactive task; it begins with knowledge, structure, and foresight.

Investment risk is not a monolithic concept. It comes in many forms, each with different implications depending on the context, the investor's goals, and the chosen asset class. At its broadest level, risk refers to the possibility that an investment's actual returns will deviate from expected outcomes. These deviations can be mild or severe, temporary or permanent, but they are always instructive. Rather than seeing risk as something to fear or avoid, investors should view it as a factor to be identified, measured, and managed within a strategic framework.

Market risk, also known as systematic risk, is perhaps the most familiar. This refers to the risk of loss due to movements in the overall financial markets—such as downturns in stock indices, rising interest rates, inflationary shocks, or geopolitical events. No amount of diversification can eliminate market risk because it affects nearly all assets simultaneously to varying degrees. During the global financial crisis of 2008, for example, stock markets around the world fell sharply, regardless of sector or geography. Similarly, the COVID-19 pandemic triggered a swift and widespread sell-off across nearly every asset class in early 2020, illustrating the systemic nature of such events.

While market risk cannot be eradicated, it can be mitigated through thoughtful asset allocation and long-term positioning. A portfolio that is heavily weighted towards equities may suffer during a downturn, but a balanced portfolio with allocations to bonds, cash, real assets, and perhaps some alternatives will typically experience less volatility and recover more predictably. Time horizon plays a crucial role here. Market risk is often most damaging to those with short-term needs, whereas long-term investors have the advantage of time to weather volatility and benefit from eventual recovery.

Closely related, but more controllable, is specific risk—or unsystematic risk. This refers to risks that affect individual companies, sectors, or geographic regions. Examples include poor corporate governance, product recalls, management scandals, or regulatory changes affecting a particular industry. Specific risk is highly relevant in equity investing, where the fate of a single stock can diverge sharply from the broader market. In 2001, investors in Enron learned this lesson harshly when the company collapsed due to accounting fraud, causing massive losses even as the broader market remained intact.

The primary tool for managing specific risk is diversification. By spreading investments across a broad mix of securities, industries, and countries, the impact of any single adverse event is diluted. A well-diversified equity portfolio might include hundreds of companies, making it unlikely that the failure of one will cause disproportionate damage. Similarly, a fixed income portfolio might span different credit ratings, maturities, and issuers to avoid overexposure to a single borrower. While diversification does not protect against market-wide declines, it significantly reduces the likelihood of catastrophic loss due to concentrated exposure.

Credit risk, particularly relevant in fixed income investing, refers to the risk that a bond issuer will default on its payment obligations—either failing to pay interest or return the principal. Government bonds from countries with stable fiscal reputations tend to carry very low credit risk, which is reflected in their lower yields. Corporate bonds, especially those issued by companies with weaker balance sheets, offer higher yields to compensate for increased default risk. Investors must assess the trade-off between yield and reliability, ideally by evaluating credit ratings, debt ratios, and industry conditions.

Liquidity risk is often underappreciated, particularly by retail investors. This is the risk that an asset cannot be sold quickly or at its fair value without incurring a significant loss. Real estate, for instance, is highly illiquid—properties may take months to sell, and pricing can be influenced by local demand or economic cycles. Thinly traded shares, private equity stakes, or collectibles also carry liquidity risk. During periods of market stress, even assets typically considered liquid—such as corporate bonds or small-cap stocks—can become difficult to sell without sharp price concessions.

To manage liquidity risk, investors should ensure that a portion of their portfolio is held in easily tradable assets such as cash, money market funds, or liquid ETFs. Emergency reserves, short-term needs, and anticipated expenditures should never be invested in illiquid instruments. Moreover, the overall asset mix should be structured so that liquidity is matched to horizon—short-term money in short-term vehicles, long-term capital in long-term assets.

Inflation risk is the threat that rising prices will erode the real value of investment returns. It is particularly dangerous for conservative portfolios heavily weighted toward cash or fixed income, where nominal yields may not keep pace with the cost of living. Over time, even modest inflation can significantly diminish purchasing power. A savings account yielding 2 percent in an environment where inflation is running at 4 percent results in a real loss of value, despite the appearance of gain.

Mitigating inflation risk requires investing in assets that have historically outpaced inflation. Equities, property, inflation-linked bonds, and certain commodities such as gold tend to perform better during inflationary periods. Additionally, maintaining a dynamic, regularly reviewed asset allocation can help reposition the portfolio in response to shifting macroeconomic conditions.

Currency risk arises when investors hold assets denominated in foreign currencies. If the value of the domestic currency strengthens relative to the foreign currency, the value of the foreign investment declines when converted back. For example, a British investor holding US-based assets will see the value of those assets fall in pound terms if the dollar weakens significantly. Currency risk can affect equities, bonds, property, and even cash holdings abroad.

Some investors choose to hedge currency exposure using financial instruments such as forwards or options, but these strategies can be costly and complex. A more accessible approach is to balance international exposure across multiple regions and currencies, or to favour assets that generate returns from local economies but report in the investor's home currency.

Another nuanced but critical risk is behavioural risk—stemming not from external events but from the investor's own decision-making. Emotional responses to market movements, such as fear during downturns or greed during rallies, can prompt poor choices: selling low, buying high, overtrading, or abandoning a carefully constructed plan. Behavioural biases such as confirmation bias, loss aversion, and herd mentality are well documented in behavioural finance and have tangible financial consequences.

The most effective mitigation for behavioural risk is education, planning, and discipline. A clear investment policy statement, a well-defined asset allocation, and periodic reviews—preferably with a trusted adviser—can provide a framework that reduces the likelihood of reactive decisions. Automated investing tools, such as standing orders, portfolio rebalancing, and target-date funds, can further reduce emotional interference.

Even sophisticated investors must navigate political and regulatory risk. Changes in tax law, financial regulation, trade policy, or political stability can impact asset valuations. This is especially pertinent for international investing, where local governance, legal systems, and economic policy differ substantially from domestic norms. A favourable environment can shift abruptly, as seen in markets that experience capital controls, expropriation, or sudden regulatory overhauls.

To manage these risks, investors must conduct proper due diligence, favour jurisdictions with strong institutions, and avoid overexposure to high-risk environments. Political risk insurance or structuring investments through diversified global funds can also reduce the potential for loss from localised shocks.

Understanding investment risks requires both a macro and micro lens. It is not enough to recognise that markets fluctuate or that companies can falter. One must also appreciate how these risks interact within a portfolio, how they align with personal financial objectives, and how they evolve over time. Risk is not static—it changes with market conditions, life events, and economic policy. An investor's risk profile at thirty will likely differ from their risk profile at sixty. The tools for mitigation must therefore be flexible and reviewed regularly.

To invest wisely is not to avoid risk, but to respect it. It is to measure risk against expected reward, to make informed trade-offs, and to remain calm in the face of uncertainty. When understood and integrated properly, risk becomes not a threat, but a guide. It helps define what matters most, clarifies priorities, and shapes a portfolio designed not only to grow, but to endure. Through knowledge, preparation, and discipline, investors can transform risk from a source of fear into a source of strength—fortifying wealth across cycles, conditions, and generations.

The Role of Diversification

Among all the principles of sound investing, few are as enduring—or as often misunderstood—as diversification. At its essence, diversification is the practice of spreading investments across different assets to reduce exposure to any single source of risk. It does not guarantee profits, nor does it eliminate losses entirely, but it does serve as one of the most reliable tools for managing uncertainty. In an unpredictable world, diversification is a form of intellectual humility—an acknowledgement that no one can consistently predict which asset, sector, or market will outperform, and therefore prudence lies in balance.

To appreciate the value of diversification, it is first necessary to understand the anatomy of investment risk. Financial markets are complex ecosystems, driven by countless variables—economic indicators, company performance, geopolitical shifts, technological innovation, and investor sentiment, to name only a few. These variables do not move in synchrony, which means that assets often respond differently to the same events. While a recession may send equity prices downward, government bonds might rise. Commodity prices may surge during inflationary periods even as real estate slows. Diversification leverages these different response patterns to smooth out a portfolio's returns over time.

The historical data is instructive. Over the decades, financial markets have witnessed sharp booms and severe busts. The dot-com crash of the early 2000s, the 2008 financial crisis, the COVID-19 shock in 2020—all underscore how rapidly sentiment and valuations can shift. Investors heavily concentrated in a single sector, such as technology in the late 1990s or property-related equities in the mid-2000s, suffered outsized losses when those bubbles burst. Those with diversified holdings fared better—not because they avoided losses altogether, but because their exposure was cushioned by more stable or countercyclical assets.

A well-diversified portfolio incorporates a mix of asset classes—equities, fixed income, real estate, cash, and potentially alternatives like commodities or private equity. Within each category, further layers of diversification can be applied. In equities, for instance, one can diversify across regions (domestic and international), capitalisations (large-cap, mid-cap, small-cap), and sectors (such as healthcare, technology, industrials). Fixed income portfolios can include a spread of government and corporate bonds with varied maturities and credit ratings. Real estate holdings may include both residential and commercial property in different geographic markets.

The rationale behind this complexity is not to complicate the investor's life, but to manage correlation. Correlation measures how assets move in relation to one another. Two assets that are perfectly correlated offer little diversification benefit, as they tend to rise and fall together. Assets with low or negative correlation can offset each other's volatility. For example, during a stock market downturn, high-quality bonds often gain in value as investors seek safer havens. Holding both provides a balancing effect, reducing the overall volatility of the portfolio.

Diversification also plays a critical role in behaviour management. One of the greatest threats to investor returns is not market volatility, but emotional reaction to it. Investors tend to panic during downturns, abandoning sound strategies in favour of short-term safety, often at precisely the wrong time. A diversified portfolio that performs more consistently—even if it doesn't deliver the absolute highest returns—can help prevent these emotional swings. By reducing the amplitude of losses during market declines, diversification makes it psychologically easier to stay the course and remain invested.

Real-world investors regularly benefit from this approach. Consider a retiree drawing income from their portfolio. If they were invested solely in equities, a sharp market correction could force them to sell assets at depressed prices to fund their living expenses, accelerating depletion of their capital. A diversified portfolio, including bonds and cash equivalents, would provide alternative sources of income and reduce the need to liquidate risk assets at inopportune moments. Diversification, in this sense, is not just a risk-reduction tool—it is a preservation strategy.

Yet it is important to recognise that diversification is not about spreading investments blindly or indiscriminately. True diversification is strategic. It requires careful assessment of how different assets interact and respond to macroeconomic conditions. Investing in ten different technology stocks may feel diversified because of the number of holdings, but if they are all driven by similar business models, regulatory risks, and valuation metrics, they may behave as one in a downturn. Conversely, a portfolio holding fewer but fundamentally distinct asset classes may be far more robust. Effective diversification demands a nuanced understanding of where risks converge and where they diverge.

One area where investors often under-diversify is geographic exposure. Home bias—the tendency to invest disproportionately in one's domestic market—is common, even among sophisticated investors. While familiarity offers comfort, it also limits opportunity and increases concentration risk. The UK equity market, for instance, represents only a small fraction of global market capitalisation. Failing to include US, European, Asian, and emerging market equities leaves investors vulnerable to domestic shocks and deprives them of the growth potential found in other regions.

Currency diversification, while introducing its own set of considerations, can further hedge against local economic downturns.

Another misunderstood aspect of diversification is time. Investors often focus on asset diversification without considering the diversification of timing. Systematic investing—regularly investing fixed amounts over time regardless of market conditions—introduces what is known as temporal diversification. This approach, often referred to as pound-cost averaging, reduces the risk of investing a large sum at a market peak. It also instils discipline by encouraging consistent contributions and reducing the temptation to time the market, which even seasoned professionals struggle to do effectively.

Alternative assets also provide an increasingly important avenue for diversification. These include commodities, hedge funds, infrastructure, and private capital. Gold, for example, may act as a hedge against inflation or currency devaluation. Infrastructure assets, such as toll roads or utilities, can offer stable cash flows and low correlation with traditional securities. While alternatives often come with higher complexity, lower liquidity, and different fee structures, they can be valuable tools for reducing portfolio risk and improving risk-adjusted returns when used appropriately.

Of course, diversification has its limits. In periods of extreme market stress—such as during the 2008 crisis—correlations between assets can spike, reducing the effectiveness of diversification in the short term. However, such periods are rare, and over longer time horizons, diversification remains one of the few reliable ways to manage volatility and enhance consistency. The goal is not to eliminate all risk, but to ensure that no single risk dominates or jeopardises the portfolio's ability to meet its objectives.

Importantly, diversification should not be static. Portfolios must evolve in line with changing financial goals, life stages, and economic conditions. A young professional might embrace a high-equity portfolio for long-term growth, gradually incorporating more bonds and income-producing assets as retirement nears. A family office might increase exposure to real assets or private markets as a hedge against inflation or public market saturation. Periodic rebalancing is essential to ensure that the portfolio remains aligned with the investor's intent and does not drift unintentionally due to market movements.

Ultimately, diversification is not just a technical solution—it is a mindset. It reflects an understanding that investing is an exercise in uncertainty, and that resilience, not prediction, is the key to enduring success. By embracing variety, balance, and strategic distribution, investors reduce their dependence on any single outcome and improve their chances of achieving long-term financial stability. It is a quietly powerful discipline, one that does not draw headlines or promise excitement, but that builds wealth sustainably, sensibly, and with respect for the unpredictable nature of markets.

Market Volatility and How to Handle It

Volatility is an intrinsic characteristic of financial markets. Prices go up, they go down, and at times they swing between extremes with unnerving speed. While these fluctuations are a natural consequence of the market's function—where prices reflect a constant negotiation between buyers and sellers—they can also be deeply unsettling for investors. The sight of one's portfolio losing value, sometimes dramatically, can trigger anxiety and lead to decisions that are emotionally satisfying in the short term but financially damaging over the long term. Handling market volatility, then, is not simply about financial theory—it is about psychological resilience, strategic discipline, and an understanding of the mechanisms at play.

To begin with, it is important to demystify what volatility actually represents. In technical terms, it refers to the degree of variation in the price of an asset over time. A highly volatile asset is one whose price moves sharply in either direction within short periods. Volatility is often perceived as a form of risk, and in a behavioural sense, that perception is justified—most people are loss averse and react more strongly to losses than to gains. But volatility is not inherently bad. In fact, without it, there would be no opportunity for growth. Prices that never move offer no reward. It is only through fluctuation that value is discovered, inefficiencies are corrected, and long-term returns are earned.

What unsettles investors is not volatility itself, but their reaction to it. History shows that markets experience downturns regularly. Corrections, defined as declines of 10 per cent or more, occur on average once every couple of years. Bear markets, which entail falls of 20 per cent or more, happen less frequently but are inevitable. Yet, over time, markets have always recovered, often reaching new highs within a few years. The long-term trajectory of well-diversified equity portfolios has been upward, despite periods of severe turbulence.

Take the global financial crisis of 2008. During that period, global stock markets lost nearly half their value in a matter of months. Many investors, gripped by fear, sold their holdings and retreated to cash. Those who remained invested, or better yet, who continued contributing through systematic investment plans, saw their portfolios recover and grow significantly in the decade that followed. Similarly, during the COVID-19 shock in March 2020, equity markets fell by more than 30 per cent in a matter of weeks. The panic was widespread. Yet within six months, most major indices had rebounded, and by the end of 2020, many had posted positive returns for the year.

These examples are not offered to trivialise market declines, but to reinforce a crucial point: volatility is temporary; the consequences of impulsive behaviour are not. Selling in response to fear often results in realising losses that might otherwise have been recovered. Missing just a few of the best-performing days in the market can drastically reduce long-term returns. Timing the market—attempting to exit before declines and re-enter before rallies—is notoriously difficult, even for seasoned professionals. More often than not, it leads to suboptimal outcomes.

The emotional challenge of volatility can be managed with preparation and context. A well-structured investment plan, grounded in realistic expectations and aligned with one's financial goals, serves as a psychological anchor during turbulent times. When investors understand why they are invested in a particular way, and what they are working toward, they are less likely to be swayed by short-term noise. This requires clarity not just on return targets, but also on risk tolerance, time horizon, and liquidity needs.

Time is one of the most powerful antidotes to volatility. While daily or monthly price movements may seem chaotic, long-term trends tend to be more predictable. Over ten-year periods, equity markets have historically delivered positive returns in the vast majority of cases, despite experiencing numerous downturns along the way. This means that volatility, though distressing, is survivable—so long as one's investment horizon is sufficiently long and their portfolio is appropriately diversified.

Diversification, of course, plays a central role in tempering the effects of volatility. By spreading investments across asset classes, sectors, and geographies, investors reduce their exposure to any single source of instability. Bonds may provide stability during equity sell-offs. Cash holdings can provide liquidity without requiring the sale of depressed assets. Real assets, such as property or commodities, may behave differently under inflationary or crisis conditions. A diversified portfolio doesn't eliminate volatility, but it makes it more manageable.

For those actively contributing to their investments, market volatility can actually be beneficial. When prices fall, new contributions buy more units, effectively reducing the average cost of the investment. This process, known as pound-cost averaging, turns market dips into opportunities. It requires a shift in mindset—from seeing volatility as a threat to viewing it as a feature of the system, one that offers long-term investors a way to build wealth more efficiently.

Behavioural discipline is also essential. Investors are often influenced by cognitive biases that distort their perception of risk and reward. Recency bias leads people to overweight recent losses and extrapolate them indefinitely. Confirmation bias causes them to seek out information that supports their fears while ignoring contrary evidence. Herd behaviour results in mass sell-offs, not because the fundamentals have changed, but because others are doing the same. Awareness of these tendencies is the first step toward neutralising their effect.

Practical strategies can support emotional resilience during downturns. Turning off financial news, which thrives on fear and sensationalism, can help reduce anxiety. Reviewing long-term performance charts rather than daily price movements provides perspective. Focusing on cash flow and income—such as dividends, bond interest, or rental yields—can reinforce the idea that not all value is reflected in short-term price changes. Regularly revisiting and reaffirming one's investment plan with a trusted adviser can also provide reassurance and accountability.

Importantly, volatility also provides an opportunity for reflection. When markets fall, investors have a chance to test their true risk tolerance. Did the recent downturn feel uncomfortable, or did it feel unbearable? Were you tempted to sell, or did you see it as a chance to buy? These reactions can inform future asset allocation decisions, helping refine a strategy that matches not just theoretical risk appetite, but lived experience.

Volatility also invites a reassessment of liquidity needs. An investor who finds themselves having to sell risk assets during a downturn to fund expenses may need to adjust their cash reserves or include more stable instruments in their portfolio. Ensuring that emergency funds and short-term liabilities are covered by low-volatility holdings reduces the likelihood of needing to sell at a loss.

There is also a broader philosophical dimension to navigating market volatility. Investing is ultimately about patience, resilience, and deferred gratification. It is an exercise in long-term thinking in a culture increasingly driven by short-term results. Remaining calm in the face of market swings is not a natural behaviour—it is a learned discipline. It requires investors to trust in the process, to look beyond the immediate, and to stay focused on the horizon even when the path seems uncertain.

This discipline is what separates successful investors from the merely lucky. It is what enables some to build wealth steadily, sustainably, and with confidence, while others falter under pressure. Volatility, viewed through this lens, becomes less of a threat and more of a test—a recurring opportunity to reaffirm commitment, assess alignment, and stay anchored to one's goals.

No one enjoys watching the value of their investments decline. But understanding that such movements are normal, temporary, and often necessary for long-term returns helps put them into perspective. Markets breathe. They contract and expand. Accepting this rhythm is key to building a lasting, resilient financial future.

As with all aspects of investing, success during volatile periods comes not from reacting to events, but from preparing for them in advance. A diversified portfolio, a clear plan, and a calm mindset—these are the tools that allow investors not only to survive volatility, but to emerge from it stronger, wiser, and more grounded. Markets will always move. The only question is whether the investor is prepared to move with them, with steadiness and resolve, or to be moved by them in ways they did not intend.

Insurance and Hedging Strategies

In the architecture of long-term wealth building, insurance and hedging are often relegated to the margins—seen as defensive tactics rather than core strategic components. Yet for those who aim not only to accumulate wealth but to preserve it across changing circumstances, these financial safety nets are indispensable. Just as diversification spreads exposure across asset classes, insurance and hedging serve to mitigate specific, potentially catastrophic risks that could otherwise unravel years of careful planning.

At the most fundamental level, insurance addresses risks that cannot be diversified away or recovered from through traditional investment management. While a diversified portfolio can protect against market volatility or sector-specific downturns, it offers no shield against personal misfortunes such as illness, disability, premature death, or liability claims. These events, while statistically infrequent, can have disproportionate consequences. They are what the financial planning community often calls "low-probability, high-impact" events—and they are precisely where insurance plays a vital role.

Consider life insurance. For families with dependents, it is not simply a policy but a contingency plan. The premature loss of a primary income earner can devastate a household's financial stability, compromise children's education plans, or force the sale of assets at an unfavourable time. A properly structured life insurance policy ensures that, in such an event, liquidity is available to maintain quality of life and long-term goals. This liquidity is especially valuable when wealth is tied up in illiquid assets, such as property or business equity.

Similarly, income protection insurance offers a layer of defence against the risk of losing one's earning capacity due to illness or injury. The ability to earn an income is, for most people, their most valuable asset—yet it is rarely protected with the same care as investments or property. Income protection policies typically replace a significant portion of lost earnings, providing financial continuity during periods when working is impossible. For professionals, entrepreneurs, and sole traders, this form of cover can be the difference between temporary hardship and permanent financial derailment.

Critical illness cover serves a related purpose, paying a lump sum upon diagnosis of specific serious conditions. While advances in medicine have increased survival rates for diseases like cancer and heart attacks, the associated costs—treatment, rehabilitation, lost income—can still be profound. A well-structured critical illness policy does not just support recovery; it preserves financial independence at a time when physical health is compromised.

Beyond personal protection, insurance also plays a pivotal role in preserving capital for high-net-worth individuals and business owners. Estate planning often relies on life insurance to provide liquidity for inheritance tax liabilities, allowing assets to pass to heirs intact rather than being sold under duress. In family businesses, insurance can fund buy-sell agreements, ensuring that ownership transitions are handled smoothly in the event of a partner's death. Directors' and officers' liability insurance protects business leaders from legal claims related to their management decisions—a growing concern in today's litigious environment.

But while insurance tends to be more familiar to most individuals, hedging remains less understood—often perceived as a tool for institutions or speculative traders rather than everyday investors. In reality, hedging is a strategic technique that, when applied thoughtfully, can shield portfolios from specific risks without sacrificing overall return potential.

Hedging involves taking an offsetting position in a related asset to reduce the impact of adverse price movements. The classic example is the use of put options to hedge equity exposure. A put option gives the holder the right, but not the obligation, to sell a security at a predetermined price within a set timeframe. If the market declines, the put increases in value, partially offsetting the losses in the underlying portfolio. This approach can be likened to paying a premium for downside insurance—it doesn't eliminate the loss entirely, but it cushions the blow.

For investors holding concentrated positions in a single stock—perhaps due to employer equity compensation—hedging becomes particularly relevant. Through options or structured notes, they can reduce their exposure to sharp declines while retaining upside potential. Likewise, currency hedging allows investors with international holdings to protect against unfavourable exchange rate movements. A British investor with substantial US-dollar-denominated assets may use forward contracts to lock in conversion rates, thereby preserving the domestic value of those holdings despite currency volatility.

Hedging also extends to commodities and interest rates. Businesses whose operations are sensitive to input costs—airlines facing fluctuating fuel prices, for example—often hedge those costs using futures contracts. Investors in fixed income may use interest rate swaps or futures to protect against rising rates that would erode bond values. These tools are not merely speculative instruments; they are mechanisms for stabilising cash flows, preserving purchasing power, and aligning asset performance with liability obligations.

Yet, hedging is not without trade-offs. It introduces complexity, requires ongoing monitoring, and comes at a cost—often in the form of premiums or foregone gains. For this reason, hedging should be purpose-driven, not habitual. It should serve to protect specific exposures or strategic vulnerabilities, not to eliminate risk altogether. After all, risk is the source of investment return. The aim is not to insulate oneself completely, but to ensure that risks taken are intentional and proportionate to one's objectives.

Moreover, it is critical to distinguish between genuine hedging and speculative behaviour disguised as risk management. A portfolio that becomes overly reliant on complex derivatives or leverages one side of a trade too heavily can quickly veer into dangerous territory. Hedging should enhance portfolio stability, not introduce new layers of fragility. This underscores the importance of education and, where appropriate, professional advice. Investors should fully understand the instruments they use and the scenarios in which they function—or fail.

From a psychological perspective, both insurance and hedging also offer emotional utility. Knowing that one is protected against catastrophic loss can reduce anxiety and support more rational decision-making. During market turbulence, for example, the presence of protective positions can make it easier to remain invested, avoid panic selling, and focus on long-term goals. In life, knowing that family, income, or business interests are safeguarded allows individuals to plan with confidence and sleep with greater peace of mind.

Practical implementation of these strategies begins with identifying exposure. What are the key vulnerabilities in your financial life or investment portfolio? Which events would cause irreparable damage or force a change in lifestyle or long-term goals? Once these are mapped out, appropriate tools—insurance policies, options, contracts—can be selected to address each. The cost-benefit analysis should always be part of the conversation: what premium or hedge cost is worth paying for peace of mind and stability?

It is also essential to regularly review coverage and positions. Insurance needs evolve over time. A young family with children has different protection requirements than a retired couple. Similarly, as investment portfolios grow in size or complexity, new hedging opportunities or risks may arise. An annual review, ideally in conjunction with broader financial planning, ensures that safety nets remain relevant and effective.

In building lasting wealth, the focus often falls on growth strategies: selecting the right funds, timing the market, maximising returns. But sustainable wealth is not just about what you earn—it is about what you protect. Insurance and hedging may not generate eye-catching returns, but they preserve the foundation upon which those returns rest. They are not defensive in the pejorative sense, but foundational in the most meaningful one.

Wealth, after all, is not merely about accumulation. It is about continuity, security, and resilience. It is about ensuring that plans made today can withstand the unpredictability of tomorrow. Insurance and hedging, when applied with clarity and intention, serve precisely that purpose. They do not remove risk, but they place a buffer between risk and ruin. They offer investors the freedom to pursue opportunity—knowing that if the unexpected occurs, they are not starting again from zero.

In an age where uncertainty is both pervasive and rapidly transmitted, these tools are more valuable than ever. The prudent investor understands that growth and protection are not opposing forces, but complementary strategies—each essential, each reinforcing the other. With the right safety nets in place, investing becomes not a leap of faith, but a calculated step forward.

Exit Strategies and When to Sell

While the focus in investing is often on what to buy and when to enter the market, the more difficult and often overlooked question is when to sell. Exiting an investment—whether partially or fully—is a decision that carries as much weight as the initial purchase, yet it is frequently governed by emotion, impulse, or arbitrary rules rather than deliberate strategy. Knowing when and how to sell is not simply about taking profit or avoiding loss; it is about aligning actions with goals, managing tax consequences, adjusting to changes in circumstances, and maintaining discipline in an ever-shifting market.

Selling is difficult for several reasons. First, it requires the investor to let go of an asset that may have performed well, or that carries sentimental or psychological weight. Second, it often involves admitting error—either in the original investment thesis or in the timing. Third, and perhaps most importantly, selling demands forward-looking judgement. Unlike buying, where the only unknown is future performance, selling requires a view not only on the current asset but on the alternatives available. If you exit a position, where will the proceeds go? If the answer is uncertain, the decision to sell can be paralysing.

A well-conceived exit strategy begins with purpose. Every investment should have a rationale at the time of entry: what role does it play in the portfolio, what is the expected time horizon, and what would prompt a re-evaluation? Unfortunately, many investors enter positions without this clarity, making the sell decision reactive rather than proactive. By contrast, those who define their objectives up front—whether it is a target valuation, a required rate of return, or a life event like retirement or a home purchase—have a clear framework for exit. Selling becomes a function of plan execution, not panic or profit-chasing.

There are several circumstances where selling is not only appropriate but necessary. One of the most common is a material change in the fundamentals of an investment. If a company's competitive position deteriorates, its management loses credibility, or its financial health declines, the original investment thesis may no longer hold. Clinging to such a position in the hope of recovery is rarely rewarded. Investors must be willing to reassess dispassionately. Just as a good doctor changes a treatment when the diagnosis evolves, a good investor must adjust when the facts do.

Another legitimate reason to sell is rebalancing. Over time, the relative weights of assets in a portfolio will shift due to differential performance. Left unchecked, this drift can alter the portfolio's risk profile and lead to overexposure in outperforming sectors or geographies. Rebalancing restores the intended allocation by selling portions of the winners and redeploying capital into lagging areas. Though counterintuitive—selling what has done well to buy what has underperformed—it is a disciplined method for maintaining risk control and capitalising on mean reversion.

A life stage change or financial need may also necessitate an exit. An investor nearing retirement might shift from growth-oriented equities to income-producing assets or cash equivalents. A family preparing to fund university fees may sell investments to meet upcoming expenses. These sales are not signs of failure or misjudgement; they are part of translating financial assets into real-world utility. Planning for such events in advance, and structuring investments with appropriate liquidity and timing, ensures that necessary exits can be made on favourable terms rather than forced by urgency.

Tax planning is another crucial, yet often neglected, factor in selling decisions. Realising gains can trigger capital gains tax, particularly if the asset has appreciated significantly. In some cases, it may be beneficial to spread sales over multiple tax years, offset gains with losses elsewhere in the portfolio, or utilise tax-advantaged accounts. Selling purely for performance reasons, without considering tax consequences, can erode returns substantially. Conversely, strategic tax-loss harvesting—selling positions at a loss to offset gains—can enhance after-tax performance without materially altering the portfolio's long-term strategy.

Then there is the challenge of behavioural bias. Investors are prone to a range of psychological traps that distort selling decisions. Anchoring to a past high can prevent the sale of a declining asset, even when recovery is unlikely. Loss aversion leads individuals to hold onto losing positions longer than they should, unwilling to crystallise a loss that is already real. The endowment effect creates an illusion of increased value simply because one owns the asset. These biases, while deeply human, are financial liabilities. A structured exit framework, preferably developed in advance, helps sidestep these cognitive distortions.

Consider the experience of investors during the dot-com boom of the late 1990s. Many held internet stocks that soared in value, often without supporting business models or profitability. When the bubble burst in 2000, those who failed to establish an exit strategy saw their paper gains evaporate. Similarly, in the housing market crash of 2008, investors who had overextended into property without contingency plans were forced into distress sales. These episodes highlight that selling is not only about capturing gains—it is also about limiting losses, reallocating risk, and preserving capital for future opportunities.

Timing exits is inherently difficult, and even professionals struggle to get it right consistently. The market rarely sends a clear signal that it has peaked or bottomed. Attempting to sell at the top is a seductive fantasy, but often leads to missed gains or premature exits. A more realistic approach is to define exit zones rather than single points—ranges within which selling makes sense based on valuation, target return, or life events. This method acknowledges uncertainty while allowing for flexibility and pragmatism.

For income-focused investors, exit decisions can take a different form. Rather than selling principal, they may focus on the sustainability and reliability of income streams. If a dividend is cut or a bond issuer shows signs of distress, the asset may no longer serve its intended purpose, prompting a reallocation. Conversely, if income needs increase—due to inflation or rising costs—some capital may need to be liquidated in a structured way. Planning withdrawals around asset performance, tax brackets, and cash flow projections becomes essential.

Exit strategy also matters for illiquid investments such as private equity, real estate, or collectibles. These assets cannot be sold quickly or easily, so the decision to exit must be made well in advance and often through staged processes. For instance, a property sale may take months and involve market conditions, buyer negotiations, and legal formalities. Having an exit timeline and contingency options is critical to avoiding fire sales or missed targets.

Institutional investors, such as pension funds or endowments, often use policy statements to define their exit parameters. These documents articulate the goals of each investment, acceptable risk thresholds, and conditions under which an asset will be reviewed or removed. Retail investors can benefit from adopting similar disciplines. A personal investment policy statement can codify intentions, reduce emotional interference, and provide a basis for evaluating decisions after the fact.

Technology can support this process. Automated alerts, stop-loss orders, and target-based notifications can help track when a position reaches predefined criteria. However, automation should complement, not replace, critical thinking. Market anomalies, company news, or economic shifts may justify overriding preset rules. The key is not rigidity, but responsiveness within a framework.

At the heart of all effective exit strategies is clarity of purpose. Investors who know what they own, why they own it, and what conditions would prompt them to change that position are far better equipped to act decisively and rationally. Selling should be as intentional as buying—not driven by fear, fashion, or fatigue, but by alignment with goals, risk tolerance, and a coherent investment philosophy.

Ultimately, an exit strategy is not about quitting; it is about evolving. It is about recognising that investing is not static, that portfolios must adapt, and that flexibility is a strength, not a compromise. By thinking in terms of both entry and exit, investors take a holistic view of their capital—one that values preservation as much as accumulation, prudence as much as ambition, and intentionality above impulse. In this light, selling becomes not a retreat from opportunity, but a step toward sustained, purposeful financial stewardship.

Chapter 6
Market Cycles - How to Navigate Ups and Downs

Financial markets rarely trace a neat, predictable path. Instead, they ebb and flow—sometimes rising steadily, other times faltering, pausing, or surging with little warning. It's tempting to see this as mere randomness, but in truth, these movements are the visible footprints of deeper economic and psychological currents intertwining over time. For anyone committed to investing over the long haul, understanding how markets transition through their natural phases—growth, contraction, and recovery—is more than an intellectual exercise. It's a vital compass, not so much for timing the market, which is notoriously tricky, but for making informed choices and maintaining emotional steadiness. Navigating these cycles with a mix of awareness and discipline often separates steady wealth accumulation from costly mistakes born of panic or excessive optimism.

Economic and market cycles are as inevitable as the seasons. While each cycle bears its own unique traits shaped by particular causes and circumstances, a familiar pattern persists. Typically, an economy expands as productivity rises, employment picks up, and consumer confidence feeds spending. Yet growth rarely stays perfectly in sync with fundamentals. Eventually, asset prices become stretched, borrowing escalates, and imbalances creep in. A correction then follows—sometimes a minor setback, other times a full-blown recession or financial crisis. After the dust settles, markets regain their footing, confidence rebuilds, and growth resumes. These cycles don't operate on a strict timetable, nor do they unfold like clockwork, but their presence is an enduring feature of market economies.

The investing landscape is punctuated by bull and bear markets—extended stretches of rising and falling prices. Each phase tests investors in distinct ways. Bull markets, while often rewarding, can foster complacency, hubris, and speculative excess. It's all too easy to assume that recent gains will continue unabated, to take on risk without proper scrutiny, or to chase after the hottest trends. Bear markets, by contrast, test one's nerve. Fear and uncertainty dominate the narrative; losses feel irrevocable. Strategies are questioned, positions are sold in haste, and long-held convictions are abandoned. Both phases challenge rationality, yet it is often during the bear markets that the deepest damage occurs—not from the markets themselves, but from the reactions they provoke.

Behavioural finance has cast light on these emotional undercurrents. Humans are wired to seek patterns and favour short-term safety over probabilistic reasoning or delayed rewards. This predisposition leaves investors vulnerable to cognitive biases. When markets fall, loss aversion amplifies pain—what might be a normal correction can feel catastrophic. Herd mentality nudges people to follow the crowd—buying during frenzies or selling amid panic—not because of sound analysis, but simply because others do so.

One of the gravest missteps investors make in volatile times is trying to time the market. The logic is seductive: sell before prices plunge, buy at the bottom, dodge losses, and reap gains. Yet, market timing eludes even the most skilled professionals. Two simple yet profound reasons explain why. First, markets are forward-looking creatures. Prices incorporate not just current conditions but expectations about the future. By the time economic data confirms a downturn, markets may already have absorbed that news. Conversely, by the time a recovery becomes apparent, much of the upside may be behind us. Second, successful timing requires two perfectly timed moves: an exit and a re-entry. Missing just a handful of the best days can drastically reduce long-term returns.

Consider the investor who exited equities during the frantic sell-off in early 2020, triggered by the COVID-19 panic. If they waited for certainty before stepping back in, they almost certainly missed the swift and powerful rebound that followed. The market recovered far quicker than the economy, rewarding those who remained invested. This is hardly an isolated case. After the 2008 financial crisis, those who stayed put enjoyed a historic bull market over the following decade, while those who fled and waited missed out on substantial gains.

Remaining invested through crashes calls for a shift in mindset. It means stepping away from obsessing over daily portfolio values and focusing instead on the long term. Admittedly, this is far easier said than done. Watching one's investments shrink, especially amid negative headlines, social unease, or personal financial pressure, can provoke a desperate urge to act. But history teaches that disciplined investors—those who stay the course, rebalance thoughtfully, and continue contributing during downturns—are consistently rewarded. Market declines, however painful, often present some of the finest buying opportunities, allowing one to acquire quality assets at reduced prices and boost future returns.

That said, staying invested doesn't imply remaining rigid or passive. It means adapting within a coherent strategy. During downturns, investors might increase exposure to undervalued sectors, deploy cash reserves judiciously, or rebalance towards risk assets while maintaining adequate diversification. The objective is not to predict the exact bottom but to ensure participation in the recovery when it comes. Avoiding the extremes of going "all in" or "all out" preserves flexibility and underpins steady portfolio growth over time.

A vital aid in maintaining this discipline is the investment policy statement—a document that sets out objectives, risk tolerance, time horizon, and strategic allocations. Crafted in calmer moments, it serves as a touchstone during stressful times, reminding investors that investing is a process, not a knee-jerk reaction. Temporary setbacks are part and parcel of a longer journey toward wealth accumulation.

Concrete examples illustrate these truths. Take two investors caught in the dot-com crash of the early 2000s. One, disillusioned by tumbling tech stocks, liquidated their equity holdings and parked cash on the sidelines. The other, though shaken, held a diversified portfolio, rebalanced when necessary, and resisted panic. A decade later, their results diverged sharply. The first missed the early stages of recovery and re-entered late, capturing lower returns. The second not only recouped losses but enjoyed significant gains as markets recovered and diversified portfolios regained momentum.

These outcomes aren't products of luck or clairvoyance. They stem from preparation, discipline, and perspective. Market cycles aren't anomalies; they're fundamental to how economies function and how prices react to new information. Recognising this allows investors to welcome volatility rather than dread it. Viewed rightly, fluctuations are not threats but features of the system—opportunities in disguise.

Ultimately, the greatest lesson of market cycles is that perseverance—riding out the peaks and troughs—is often the most effective approach. This does not mean ignoring risk or resisting adaptation. Rather, it entails committing to a thoughtful, evidence-based plan rooted in realistic expectations and designed to withstand turbulence. Investors who do so are hardly passive; they are purposeful. They appreciate that compounding is as much about consistency as about returns. Time spent in the market, rather than timing the market, remains the true driver of wealth.

As we delve deeper into the anatomy of market cycles, the focus will shift to practical insights and historical lessons—tools to help investors steer with greater confidence and clarity. Bull markets, bear markets, corrections, recoveries—all possess distinct traits, challenges, and chances. Yet all are threads in a larger narrative where patience, preparation, and perspective transform volatility from a foe into a formidable ally. For those who learn to ride the waves, rather than fear them, market cycles become less an obstacle and more a skill to master.

Understanding Economic Cycles

To navigate financial markets with confidence and composure, one must develop an appreciation for the natural ebb and flow of economic cycles. These broad, recurring patterns in economic activity shape investor behaviour, business decisions, government policy, and, crucially, portfolio performance. At their core, economic cycles reflect shifts in production, employment, consumption, and investment over time—fluctuations that, while sometimes abrupt or severe, follow recognisable rhythms. Understanding these cycles, particularly the impact of bull and bear markets, equips investors to respond not with panic or euphoria, but with perspective and prudence.

An economic cycle typically comprises four phases: expansion, peak, contraction, and trough. During expansion, economic indicators such as GDP growth, employment, corporate earnings, and consumer spending rise. Optimism is high, markets perform strongly, and investors gain confidence. As the cycle matures, this growth begins to slow, often due to inflationary pressures, monetary tightening, or supply constraints. The peak marks a turning point, followed by contraction—a period of reduced economic activity, rising unemployment, falling asset prices, and dampened sentiment. Eventually, stabilisation occurs, often through policy support or natural rebalancing, leading into recovery and a new phase of expansion.

Financial markets do not merely follow these cycles—they anticipate them. Equity prices, in particular, are forward-looking, reflecting investor expectations about future earnings, interest rates, and economic health. This anticipatory nature means markets often rise before economic recoveries are clearly underway, and fall before economic slowdowns are officially recognised. As such, market cycles tend to lead economic cycles, not lag them. Investors who understand this relationship are better positioned to interpret market movements without being misled by current headlines.

The most visible expressions of market cycles are bull and bear markets. A bull market is characterised by sustained upward movement in asset prices, typically fuelled by strong economic performance, rising corporate profits, and investor optimism. These periods often last for years and generate significant wealth for those who remain invested. However, they are not without danger. Extended bull markets can create bubbles, driven by speculative excess and unrealistic expectations. The dot-com boom of the late 1990s is a classic example, where valuations detached from fundamentals and investors piled into technology stocks with little regard for earnings or sustainability.

Conversely, a bear market is defined by a decline of 20 per cent or more from recent highs, accompanied by widespread pessimism and risk aversion. These downturns are emotionally taxing and financially damaging, especially for those caught off guard or overexposed to volatile assets. Yet bear markets also serve an essential function: they correct excess, reprice risk, and reset expectations. They are not anomalies but necessary phases that cleanse the system of inefficiency and excess leverage.

One of the key lessons from history is that bear markets are temporary, while the long-term trajectory of markets is upward. The global financial crisis of 2008, one of the most severe downturns in modern times, saw global equity markets decline by more than 50 per cent. Investors who capitulated during the lows locked in massive losses. Those who stayed the course, or added to their holdings when valuations were depressed, saw their portfolios recover and, over time, reach new highs. Similarly, the COVID-19 pandemic triggered a rapid bear market in early 2020, with markets falling sharply as lockdowns froze economic activity. Yet the subsequent recovery was one of the fastest in history, propelled by fiscal stimulus, monetary easing, and technological resilience.

Understanding economic cycles is not about predicting precise timing—no model or expert has consistently forecasted the beginning or end of cycles with accuracy. Rather, it is about recognising where we might be within a cycle and adjusting expectations accordingly. During the late stages of expansion, for instance, investors might reduce exposure to overheated sectors, rebalance towards defensive assets, or increase cash reserves. In early recovery phases, where valuations are attractive and sentiment is subdued, increasing exposure to equities or cyclical sectors may prove beneficial.

It is also important to differentiate between short-term market corrections and full-scale cyclical downturns. A correction—a decline of 10 to 20 per cent—is common and can occur within ongoing bull markets. These pullbacks are often triggered by external shocks, policy announcements, or changes in sentiment, and may not reflect deteriorating economic fundamentals. While unnerving, corrections can provide valuable entry points for long-term investors. Panic selling during these episodes often proves costly.

Economic cycles also vary in length and intensity, influenced by structural factors such as demographic trends, technological innovation, global trade dynamics, and central bank policy. The post-

2009 expansion, for instance, was one of the longest on record, lasting over a decade before being interrupted by the pandemic. Its longevity was supported by low inflation, moderate growth, and accommodative monetary policy. Earlier cycles, such as those in the 1970s and 1980s, were more volatile due to oil shocks, inflationary surges, and less sophisticated policy tools.

Globalisation has also altered the nature of economic cycles. The interconnectedness of markets means that crises can spread quickly across borders, but also that recovery in one region can support others. The 1997 Asian financial crisis, the 2011 Eurozone debt crisis, and the synchronised stimulus following COVID-19 all demonstrate how local disturbances can become global phenomena. Investors must therefore adopt a global perspective, understanding how different regions may be at different points in their cycles and how cross-border capital flows influence markets.

For individual investors, the practical application of cycle awareness lies in strategy rather than speculation. Asset allocation, rebalancing, and risk management should be informed by cyclical context but not dominated by it. A portfolio designed for long-term objectives—such as retirement or generational wealth transfer—should remain anchored to a coherent plan, even as economic conditions change. Trying to exit and re-enter markets based on perceived cycle shifts is more likely to introduce timing errors than to enhance returns.

Professional investors, including fund managers and institutions, may use macroeconomic indicators—such as yield curves, leading economic indices, corporate earnings forecasts, and inflation data—to inform tactical decisions. However, even they emphasise discipline over prediction. Diversification across asset classes, regions, and sectors remains the most reliable defence against cycle-driven volatility.

Education and expectation management are also critical. Investors who understand that downturns are normal, that losses can be temporary, and that compounding requires time are more likely to stay invested and realise their goals. Communication from advisers during market stress, grounded in historical perspective and data, can prevent rash decisions and reinforce commitment to long-term strategies.

In summing up the role of economic cycles in investing, one must appreciate their dual nature: they are both disruptors and enablers. They challenge investors to remain resilient, yet they create the very conditions that allow disciplined strategies to outperform. Each cycle is different, but the underlying behaviours—fear, greed, doubt, and hope—are perennial. Learning to observe cycles with detachment, respond with informed judgement, and resist the urge to overreact is what separates enduring success from transient gain.

Understanding economic cycles, then, is not about prediction—it is about preparation. It is about equipping oneself with the tools, habits, and mindset needed to make sound decisions in the face of uncertainty. For those willing to cultivate this awareness, economic cycles become less of a threat and more of a framework—an essential lens through which to interpret market movements, protect capital, and invest with confidence through all conditions.

Behavioural Investing and Market Emotions

For all its equations, models, and data-driven sophistication, investing remains deeply human. It is not merely an exercise in analysis, but a test of temperament. Behavioural investing—an area that explores the psychological forces shaping financial decisions—has emerged as a critical field of study precisely because traditional finance alone cannot explain why investors so often act against their own interests. Time and again, individuals with access to accurate information and clear strategy deviate from both under the pressure of emotion. Understanding these impulses—and how to manage them—is essential for building and protecting long-term wealth.

At the heart of behavioural investing is the recognition that human beings are not entirely rational agents. While we may intend to make decisions based on logic and evidence, our actions are frequently coloured by fear, greed, overconfidence, and herd mentality. These behavioural biases are not signs of weakness, but reflections of cognitive shortcuts that evolved for survival in uncertain environments. The problem is that what once helped us avoid danger on the savannah now leads to poor decisions in capital markets.

One of the most common emotional pitfalls is panic selling. The moment markets begin to fall sharply, a deep, primal instinct is triggered: avoid further loss at all costs. This response is understandable. Watching hard-earned savings decline in value evokes a powerful sense of vulnerability. For many, it feels less like a paper loss and more like a personal failure. Yet history demonstrates that selling during downturns is rarely a wise move. Market corrections and bear markets, while painful, are temporary. The most damaging financial outcomes often result not from the decline itself, but from locking in losses and missing the subsequent recovery.

The 2008 global financial crisis provides a stark example. As markets plummeted and headlines grew increasingly dire, countless investors sold out of equities and moved into cash or bonds. Those who did so often missed the strong recovery that began in 2009 and continued for more than a decade. Similarly, in March 2020, global markets fell precipitously in response to the coronavirus pandemic. Panic was widespread, with many fearing an economic depression. Yet within months, major indices had not only rebounded but surpassed pre-crash levels. Investors who remained invested—or even rebalanced into equities—benefited enormously.

These episodes reveal a fundamental truth: market sentiment often swings to extremes, detaching from underlying fundamentals. Prices rise and fall faster than long-term values change. Emotional responses to these swings can be deeply misleading. A temporary drawdown feels permanent in the moment. A rally feels unstoppable. These perceptions drive behaviour, which in turn reinforces the cycle. Fear begets selling, selling drives prices down further, and the downward spiral accelerates—until it reverses.

Understanding this pattern does not immunise one from it, but it provides a framework for managing responses. The key lies in cultivating emotional self-awareness and structural discipline. Investors must recognise that their instincts, though compelling, are not always accurate guides. A drop in portfolio value does not necessarily mean something is wrong with the strategy. Market volatility, even when dramatic, is not a call to abandon long-term plans.

To counteract these impulses, many successful investors rely on systems rather than feelings. They commit to asset allocation targets, rebalance periodically, and automate contributions. These mechanisms remove emotion from the equation and ensure that decisions are made based on predetermined rules rather than transient moods. A structured approach creates guardrails, preventing short-term emotion from dictating long-term outcomes.

Another critical emotional trap is overconfidence. During bull markets, investors often mistake good fortune for skill. Rising markets flatter all portfolios, and it becomes tempting to believe that one has found the key to consistent outperformance. This illusion fuels risk-taking, concentration in favourite sectors, and disregard for diversification. When the tide turns, these overly confident positions can lead to steep losses.

The technology bubble of the late 1990s offers a powerful illustration. As tech stocks surged, investors poured money into internet companies, many of which had little or no revenue. Valuations reached levels untethered to earnings or cash flow. Pundits proclaimed a new economic paradigm. Yet when reality reasserted itself in 2000, the bubble burst, wiping out trillions in market capitalisation. The same dynamic repeated in various forms during the cryptocurrency mania of the late 2010s and the meme stock phenomenon of 2021, where social media-fuelled speculation detached price from value.

Greed, like fear, distorts judgement. It encourages short-termism, leverage, and unrealistic expectations. It can lead investors to abandon sound strategy in pursuit of higher returns, often at the worst possible time. Guarding against this requires humility—an understanding that markets are unpredictable, that no strategy works all the time, and that preserving capital is just as important as growing it.

Another powerful behavioural influence is herd mentality. Human beings are social creatures. We take cues from others, especially in uncertain situations. When markets are surging, it feels safe to buy. When others are selling, it feels dangerous to hold. This herd effect is amplified by the media, which thrives on drama. Sensational headlines, dire forecasts, and breathless commentary can heighten anxiety and create a sense of urgency. But following the crowd is rarely a winning strategy in investing. By the time a trend is widely recognised, it is often too late to benefit. Conversely, the best opportunities often arise when sentiment is bleak and confidence is low.

The antidote to herd behaviour is independent thinking. This does not mean contrarianism for its own sake, but rather a willingness to base decisions on analysis rather than emotion or consensus. It means asking: What are the fundamentals? What is priced in? What are the risks? This mindset is not easy to maintain, particularly when emotions are running high, but it is essential for sound decision-making.

Behavioural discipline is not only about avoiding mistakes—it is about sustaining constructive habits. Regular saving, consistent investing, rebalancing, and reviewing plans all contribute to better outcomes. These actions reinforce a sense of control, reduce the temptation to act impulsively, and align behaviour with long-term goals.

Education also plays a vital role. Investors who understand how markets work, how volatility is normal, and how compounding functions over time are less likely to panic when setbacks occur. They are more likely to stay the course, weather downturns, and reap the rewards of patient investing. Education transforms uncertainty from a threat into a challenge—one that can be managed with the right tools and mindset.

Professional guidance can further support behavioural discipline. Advisers serve not just as technical experts but as behavioural coaches, helping clients maintain perspective, avoid reactive decisions, and stay aligned with their objectives. In this capacity, the value of advice is not measured solely in returns, but in improved outcomes born of better decision-making.

Ultimately, successful investing is not about brilliance or bold predictions—it is about temperament. It is about managing oneself as much as managing assets. Behavioural investing teaches us that the greatest risks often lie not in the markets, but in how we respond to them. It encourages humility, discipline, and emotional intelligence—qualities that foster resilience across cycles, crises, and market regimes.

When markets become volatile, headlines scream catastrophe, and anxiety sets in, the investors who thrive are those who can step back, breathe, and act with intent rather than instinct. They recognise that emotions are data, not directives. They trust in process over impulse, in strategy over sentiment. In a world of constant noise and shifting narratives, this behavioural clarity becomes not only a competitive advantage, but a safeguard—one that protects wealth, preserves composure, and ultimately ensures that investment decisions remain anchored to what matters most.

Why Market Timing Fails

Among the most persistent temptations in investing is the belief that one can predict market movements with enough accuracy to buy low and sell high consistently. This idea, known as market timing, appeals deeply to our desire for control, precision, and protection from loss. The notion is simple and intuitively appealing: if an investor could exit just before markets fall and re-enter just before they recover, they would maximise returns and minimise risk. But as with many elegant ideas, the reality is more complex and far less forgiving. Time and again, evidence has shown that market timing not only fails more often than it succeeds—it often leads to poorer outcomes than doing nothing at all.

The failure of market timing is not merely theoretical. It is grounded in decades of data, investor behaviour studies, and historical case studies. Financial markets are complex, adaptive systems influenced by countless variables—economic data, corporate earnings, central bank policy, geopolitical events, sentiment, and human psychology. These variables do not operate in a vacuum, nor do they produce linear outcomes. Prices reflect not just facts but expectations. They move in anticipation of future developments, many of which are unknowable. By the time an economic trend is confirmed, markets have often already reacted. This temporal mismatch is one of the core reasons why timing efforts fall short.

To appreciate the difficulty of timing, one must consider what is required for success. It is not enough to correctly anticipate a market downturn. One must also know when to get back in. That second decision is often harder than the first. Fear, uncertainty, and psychological inertia tend to linger after a decline, making re-entry difficult. Waiting for clarity often results in missing the early stages of a recovery—the phase where returns are most dramatic. Investors who sit on the sidelines during this period often re-enter only after prices have risen significantly, thereby locking in earlier losses and forfeiting gains.

Consider the market crash of 2008–2009. Investors who exited equity positions during the height of the financial crisis might have felt vindicated as markets continued to decline. But few anticipated the strength or timing of the recovery that began in March 2009. Those who remained in cash or low-risk assets missed out on one of the longest and most powerful bull markets in history. By the time they returned to the market—often years later—prices had already surged, and the opportunity for meaningful catch-up had passed.

This pattern repeated during the COVID-19 crash in 2020. Global equity markets fell by over 30 percent in a matter of weeks, triggering panic and widespread selling. Yet the recovery was swift and counterintuitive. Despite ongoing economic uncertainty, markets began rising in April, well before vaccines, reopenings, or robust growth returned. Those who had moved to cash in March often remained frozen by uncertainty, watching the rebound from the sidelines. Missing just a few of the best days during that recovery significantly reduced long-term portfolio performance.

The cost of missing these key days is not trivial. Numerous studies have shown that the vast majority of market returns come from a relatively small number of days. Being absent for even a handful can decimate long-term gains. For example, data from global markets over multiple decades reveals that missing the ten best days in a given decade can reduce overall returns by more than half. The problem is that these days are not predictable. They often occur during periods of high volatility or when sentiment is negative. Attempting to avoid downside by timing the market often means being absent for the upside as well.

Furthermore, market timing introduces behavioural risk. Investors who try to time their exposure are often influenced by emotional and cognitive biases. Overconfidence can lead them to believe they can outsmart the market based on gut feeling or incomplete analysis. Recency bias causes them to assume that recent trends will continue indefinitely. Herd behaviour pushes them to act in sync with prevailing sentiment, buying when others are euphoric and selling when others are afraid. These psychological patterns are not only common—they are deeply ingrained, making market timing as much an emotional gamble as an analytical one.

It is important to recognise that even professional investors with access to superior data, analytical tools, and decades of experience rarely succeed at market timing. Numerous studies of actively managed funds reveal that very few managers consistently outperform their benchmarks, particularly after fees. Those who do are often unable to repeat their performance across cycles. If full-time experts struggle to time markets accurately, it is unreasonable to expect that individual investors with limited resources can do so consistently and effectively.

The appeal of market timing also stems from a misunderstanding of risk. Investors often equate being out of the market with safety. But sitting in cash or low-yielding instruments while inflation erodes purchasing power carries its own form of risk—opportunity cost. Avoiding market downturns may preserve capital in the short term, but missing the subsequent recovery reduces long-term compounding. Over decades, the impact is substantial. The real risk is not short-term volatility, but permanent loss due to suboptimal strategy and inconsistent exposure.

The alternative to market timing is time in the market—remaining invested through cycles with a well-constructed, diversified portfolio aligned to one's objectives and risk tolerance. This approach may seem less exciting, but it is far more reliable. By staying invested, investors capture both the downturns and the recoveries, allowing compounding to do its work. Volatility is accepted as a necessary condition of long-term growth, not an aberration to be avoided.

This does not mean investors should never make adjustments. Rebalancing, strategic shifts based on life changes, or adjusting for altered time horizons are all prudent practices. But these changes should be driven by financial planning and strategy, not by fear or speculation. Selling assets because they have declined, or because a recession is feared, is reactive. Rebalancing to restore target allocations after a market move, on the other hand, is proactive and structured.

There is also value in process-driven investing. Setting up automated contributions through dollar-cost averaging helps mitigate the impact of short-term price swings. It encourages discipline, removes the temptation to time entries, and ensures consistent participation in the market. Over time, this method has been shown to reduce average purchase costs and improve behavioural outcomes.

Real-world investors who adhere to process over prediction tend to perform better not because they outguess the market, but because they avoid its most dangerous traps. They resist the allure of perfect timing. They understand that staying invested, even through discomfort, is a rational response to uncertainty. They embrace the idea that markets are unpredictable, but long-term trends are reliable. This mindset is not passive—it is intentional, disciplined, and grounded in evidence.

At its heart, the failure of market timing is not a technical problem—it is a behavioural one. The desire to avoid loss, to control outcomes, to be right, is deeply human. But investing is not about being right all the time. It is about being resilient, thoughtful, and consistent. By letting go of the illusion that market turns can be anticipated with precision, investors free themselves to focus on what truly matters:

building a strategy that aligns with their goals, managing risk with care, and allowing time and compounding to do the heavy lifting.

Markets will rise and fall. News cycles will shift from optimism to despair and back again. Predictions will abound, and many will be wrong. But through it all, the disciplined investor who remains engaged—who recognises that the attempt to avoid every downturn usually results in missing the most important upswings—will be rewarded. Market timing may promise clarity and control, but time-tested evidence reveals its fragility. Patience, perspective, and process, on the other hand, offer something far more powerful: enduring success.

How to Stay Invested During Crashes

Market crashes are a rite of passage for any investor. At some point—often more than once—every portfolio faces a severe downturn that tests not only the strength of its holdings but the resolve of its owner. These events, marked by sudden and steep declines in asset prices, bring fear, uncertainty, and often chaos. They are accompanied by alarming headlines, dire forecasts, and an overwhelming sense that the rules of the past may no longer apply. Yet history suggests that those who endure these moments, rather than flee from them, are the ones most likely to achieve long-term success.

Staying invested during market crashes is not a matter of blind optimism. It is a discipline rooted in perspective—an understanding that while markets may falter in the short term, they have always rewarded resilience and patience over time. The key lies not in avoiding downturns, which is near impossible, but in withstanding them without compromising a sound investment plan.

Lessons from past recessions provide a clear illustration of this principle. Take the global financial crisis of 2008. In the space of just over a year, the S&P 500 fell by more than 50 percent. Financial institutions collapsed, credit markets froze, and the global economy spiralled into recession. The prevailing sentiment was one of panic, with many investors moving to cash or dramatically reducing exposure to risk assets. Yet those who maintained a diversified allocation and continued investing through the turmoil were well positioned to benefit when markets began recovering in 2009. Over the subsequent decade, those same markets delivered some of the strongest returns in modern history.

The COVID-19 crash in March 2020 offered a similar, though more compressed, case study. As countries entered lockdown and global economic activity ground to a halt, equity markets collapsed. Within weeks, valuations plummeted, and investors were confronted with an unprecedented health crisis and an uncertain future. It was a textbook environment for panic selling. But remarkably, the recovery was both faster and stronger than almost anyone anticipated. By the end of the year, most major indices had not only recouped their losses but posted gains. Those who had stayed the course, or rebalanced at the trough, benefited immensely from the rebound.

So why do investors so often struggle to remain invested during these downturns? The answer lies in human psychology. Crashes do not simply test one's financial strategy—they test emotional resilience. Seeing the value of one's investments decline sharply evokes a visceral sense of loss. It activates the same fear responses that kept our ancestors safe from predators—responses that are poorly suited to modern financial markets. The instinct to act, to protect, to flee from danger is powerful. But in the context of investing, it often leads to suboptimal decisions.

The emotional weight of a market crash is compounded by uncertainty. Unlike temporary dips, crashes are often accompanied by legitimate concerns about economic stability, political leadership, or systemic risk. During the dot-com bust, it was the collapse of a speculative bubble. During the 2008 crisis, it was the failure of major financial institutions. In 2020, it was a global pandemic with no clear end in sight. These are not trivial developments, and they justify concern. But what they do not justify is abandoning a well-considered, long-term investment plan based solely on fear.

One of the most effective ways to stay invested during a crash is to have prepared for it in advance. This means constructing a portfolio that reflects one's true risk tolerance and financial goals. Investors who take on more risk than they can emotionally withstand are far more likely to panic during downturns. Conversely, those who know that their portfolio is aligned with their needs, and that they have sufficient liquidity for near-term expenses, can view crashes as uncomfortable but manageable episodes rather than existential threats.

A second key to staying invested is to reframe how one thinks about market declines. Rather than seeing them purely as losses, investors can view them as opportunities to buy assets at reduced prices. This is not an easy shift to make, particularly when fear dominates the headlines, but it is supported by data. Over the long term, markets trend upward, driven by economic growth, innovation, and corporate earnings. Temporary declines, even severe ones, are normal interruptions in this broader trajectory. Those who can invest during these periods, or at the very least continue their regular contributions, benefit from lower entry prices and increased potential for compounding.

Regular, systematic investing—often referred to as pound-cost averaging—can also support psychological resilience. By committing to invest a fixed amount at regular intervals regardless of market conditions, investors avoid the need to make timing decisions. During downturns, the same investment buys more shares, reducing the average cost per unit. This approach not only supports better long-term outcomes but removes emotion from the decision-making process.

Communication and support also play a role in weathering market storms. Investors who work with a trusted adviser, or who are part of a financial planning community, are less likely to make impulsive decisions. Professional advisers provide not only technical guidance but also emotional support—reminding clients of their goals, helping them interpret events in context, and reinforcing the importance of discipline. A well-timed conversation during a market crash can prevent years of regret.

Another practical tool is the investment policy statement. This document outlines an investor's objectives, asset allocation, risk tolerance, and guidelines for decision-making. Having a written plan to refer to during times of stress can serve as an anchor. It reinforces the notion that decisions were made with care and thought, and that short-term volatility does not invalidate long-term strategy. For many, this simple act of revisiting their original plan can restore confidence and perspective.

It is also worth noting that while market crashes are dramatic, they are relatively infrequent. Over the past century, major bear markets have occurred roughly once every decade. Corrections—declines of 10 to 20 percent—are more common, occurring every couple of years. Yet over long investment horizons, these episodes are dwarfed by the periods of growth in between. An investor who remained fully invested in global equities over the last thirty years, despite enduring the 2000 crash, the 2008 recession, and the 2020 pandemic, would have seen their wealth multiply many times over.

That is not to say that staying invested is about doing nothing. It is about doing the right things. It is about rebalancing when appropriate, ensuring liquidity for short-term needs, and reviewing one's financial plan regularly. But it is not about reacting emotionally to headlines, abandoning strategies at the first sign of trouble, or assuming that today's crisis will define tomorrow's world.

Indeed, history teaches that recoveries often begin when sentiment is at its lowest. The media, driven by fear and uncertainty, rarely announces market bottoms. By the time confidence returns, prices have often rebounded significantly. Investors waiting for reassurance may find themselves buying back in after much of the upside has passed. The paradox is that the best opportunities often feel the most uncomfortable.

Staying invested during market crashes is not easy, but it is profoundly rewarding. It requires courage, perspective, and a commitment to long-term thinking. It demands that investors trust in the process, in the power of diversification, and in the resilience of economic systems. Crashes will continue to occur. So will recoveries. The investors who build wealth over time are not those who avoid volatility, but those who endure it with clarity and conviction.

In the end, investing is less about predicting the future and more about preparing for it. A market crash is not a reason to abandon hope—it is a reason to reaffirm purpose. Those who understand this are not merely reacting to markets; they are participating in them with intention, integrity, and foresight. That is what staying invested truly means.

The Importance of Staying the Course

In a world increasingly obsessed with speed, immediacy, and short-term gains, the idea of staying the course may seem almost quaint. Financial news is delivered by the minute, investment apps buzz with real-time alerts, and social media amplifies every market move with urgency. Against this backdrop, the notion of patiently holding a long-term investment strategy might feel countercultural. Yet it is precisely this approach—quiet, methodical, and steadfast—that has consistently proven to be the most effective path to building and preserving wealth. Long-term investors do not win because they avoid volatility or predict markets better than others. They win because they persist.

Staying the course means maintaining commitment to a well-considered investment strategy through all phases of the market cycle—expansions, contractions, corrections, and recoveries. It demands discipline when times are good, and even greater discipline when times are bad. It is grounded not in rigid inaction, but in a deliberate resistance to emotionally charged decisions. This distinction is important. Staying the course is not about ignoring changes in personal circumstances or blindly holding poor investments. It is about resisting the impulse to alter one's strategy in response to noise, fear, or the temptation of quick wins.

The strength of this approach lies in its alignment with how markets behave over time. While prices fluctuate day to day, the broader trend of markets, especially equity markets, has historically been upward. This reflects the cumulative growth of economies, innovation, productivity, and corporate earnings. Setbacks occur frequently—some mild, some severe—but they are transient. Long-term data shows that investors who remain engaged through downturns invariably participate in the recoveries that follow. Over decades, this compounding effect transforms modest, consistent investments into significant wealth.

Consider the performance of major equity indices over the past century. Despite enduring world wars, depressions, oil shocks, inflation crises, political upheaval, and several financial collapses, long-term investors in diversified portfolios have been rewarded. The key variable has not been the ability to anticipate events, but the willingness to endure them without abandoning a sound plan. For example, investors who stayed invested during the 2008 financial crisis—one of the most severe economic shocks since the Great Depression—saw not only a full recovery, but a decade of exceptional returns. Those who exited the market in panic and waited for reassurance often re-entered too late, missing much of the upside.

The benefits of staying the course are not merely financial—they are also psychological. Constantly reacting to market noise is exhausting. The emotional toll of trying to time entries and exits, to chase winners and flee losers, can lead to decision fatigue and anxiety. By contrast, having a stable, well-defined plan provides a sense of clarity and control. It removes the pressure to act on every headline and allows investors to focus on their broader financial goals—whether that is retirement, education, home ownership, or legacy planning.

This approach also helps neutralise the damaging influence of behavioural biases. Humans are not wired for optimal investing. We are prone to herd behaviour, loss aversion, overconfidence, and the recency effect—all of which conspire to undermine rational decision-making. Market downturns trigger fear, and fear drives poor choices: selling at lows, hoarding cash, abandoning long-term positions. Bull markets trigger euphoria, which fuels risk-taking, performance-chasing, and portfolio imbalance. Staying the course acts as a buffer against these biases. It creates a structured environment in which emotions are acknowledged but not allowed to dictate action.

Real-world examples underscore the value of this mindset. Consider two hypothetical investors who began investing £500 per month in a diversified global equity fund in the year 2000. One maintained their contributions consistently for twenty years, through the dot-com crash, the global financial crisis, and the COVID-19 shock. The other halted their investments during downturns and waited for markets to stabilise before resuming. At the end of the period, despite having invested similar amounts, the first investor's portfolio would be significantly larger—not because they picked better funds or timed the markets well, but because they participated in the recoveries without interruption. The second investor, by repeatedly stepping out of the market, missed key periods of growth and undermined the compounding effect.

The importance of compounding cannot be overstated. It is the quiet force that turns small, steady contributions into substantial sums. But compounding only works with time and consistency. Interrupting the process—especially during downturns—has an outsized negative impact. Staying the course preserves the integrity of compounding by ensuring that investments remain in place to generate returns on returns.

Of course, staying the course is not about rigidity. A sound long-term strategy includes room for reassessment based on changes in life circumstances, goals, or financial position. It is appropriate to review asset allocations periodically, to rebalance, and to adapt as one's risk tolerance evolves. But these changes should be driven by planning, not by panic. A thoughtful adjustment to a portfolio in response to entering retirement is very different from selling out of equities because of a market correction. One is strategic, the other reactive.

Staying the course also does not imply neglect. It requires engagement, education, and the occasional reaffirmation of purpose. Investors who understand why they are invested in a particular way—who can articulate their time horizon, risk tolerance, and goals—are more likely to persevere during difficult periods. The act of writing an investment policy statement or engaging in periodic financial reviews strengthens commitment and reduces the likelihood of emotionally charged decisions.

Moreover, working with a trusted financial adviser or planner can enhance the ability to stay the course. Professional guidance provides not just technical expertise, but behavioural coaching. During turbulent periods, an adviser can offer perspective, reframe concerns, and remind clients of their long-term objectives. This partnership often proves invaluable—not because the adviser can prevent losses, but because they help prevent self-inflicted damage through missteps and emotional reactions.

The discipline of staying the course also extends to one's financial habits. It encompasses regular saving, maintaining emergency reserves, living within one's means, and avoiding excessive debt. These behaviours reinforce the stability of the investment strategy and provide flexibility when markets turn volatile. An investor with adequate cash reserves is less likely to sell risk assets at a loss during downturns. Similarly, an investor with manageable expenses can continue making contributions even when markets are down—turning adversity into opportunity.

Ultimately, staying the course is a philosophy as much as it is a tactic. It reflects a belief in the value of patience, the power of compounding, and the resilience of economies and markets over time. It is an acknowledgment that wealth is built not through clever manoeuvres or perfect timing, but through quiet consistency. It does not promise immunity from loss, but it offers the best defence against the self-sabotage that often accompanies market stress.

Investors who embrace this approach are not passive—they are purposeful. They understand that investing is not about reacting to every twist and turn, but about moving steadily toward a defined goal. They trust in the process, accept volatility as a feature rather than a flaw, and measure success not by short-term fluctuations but by long-term progress.

Markets will continue to rise and fall. Headlines will continue to alarm and excite. Fashions in finance will come and go. But the core principles of sound investing remain unchanged. Among these, none is more enduring—or more essential—than the importance of staying the course. For those who commit to this discipline, the rewards are not only financial, but emotional: peace of mind, clarity of purpose, and the quiet confidence that comes from knowing that, over time, patience prevails.

Chapter 7
The Psychology of Wealth - Mastering Investor Behaviour

Behind every investment portfolio, there lies a human mind—complex, fallible, hopeful, anxious, and often prone to error. While modern investing is dominated by spreadsheets, algorithms, and financial models, the reality is that building wealth is as much a psychological endeavour as it is a numerical one. Investors don't operate in neat, controlled environments; rather, decisions unfold in real time, often under pressure, amidst noise, with patchy information and shifting emotions. To grasp the psychology behind wealth is therefore not a mere academic curiosity but a fundamental cornerstone of successful long-term investing.

Emotions have always coloured our relationship with money. Fear, greed, overconfidence, regret, impatience—these impulses have driven markets since their inception. They influence behaviour in ways that can both illuminate and mislead. For most people, emotional investing isn't a calculated choice but a knee-jerk reaction. When markets rise, the thrill of gains often encourages excessive risk-taking. Conversely, when markets stumble, the sting of losses prompts panicked selling. These responses are human—deeply so—but rarely align with sound financial wisdom. All too often, emotional investing means buying high, selling low, and forfeiting the remarkable power of compounding that comes from staying the course.

History offers vivid reminders of these pitfalls. Take the dot-com boom, for instance—an era marked by feverish speculation, as investors threw money at loss-making start-ups boasting astronomical valuations. Enthusiasm ran rampant, and rational caution fell by the wayside. When the bubble finally burst, trillions evaporated, and many latecomers suffered severe capital losses. Similarly, the fear-fuelled sell-off in early 2020, triggered by the unfolding COVID-19 crisis, saw markets plunge and investors flee to cash—only to witness a swift recovery mere months later. Those who let emotions override strategy paid dearly for their haste.

These behavioural missteps are hardly random. They arise from well-documented cognitive biases. Herd behaviour, for example—the impulse to mimic the crowd especially in uncertainty—has evolutionary roots. In ancient times, sticking with the group was often a matter of survival. Yet, in markets, this instinct tends to magnify booms and busts. As more pile into a hot asset class, others feel compelled to follow, inflating bubbles. When panic sets in, the same crowd rushes for the exits, deepening declines.

Loss aversion is another common bias—losses sting more acutely than gains please. This imbalance prompts investors to cling too long to losing positions, hoping for a rebound, while hastily locking in profits on winners. The result? Distorted portfolio choices and a misalignment of risk and reward. Alongside this, confirmation bias leads investors to favour information confirming their existing views, ignoring contrary evidence and thereby entrenching flawed assumptions.

Recognising these biases is the crucial first step, but overcoming them demands discipline—something not innate, but developed. Successful investing hinges less on raw intelligence or market savvy and more on behaviour. Investors who adopt structured, rules-based methods—automating contributions, diversifying carefully, and reviewing results periodically—generally outperform those guided by gut feelings, headlines, or emotional impulses. This discipline provides a stabilising force, helping investors maintain consistency amid market turbulence.

Consistency might be the most underrated virtue in investing. Media stories often celebrate spectacular gains from speculative trades or timing the market, yet most wealth is built steadily, through persistent, regular investment over years. The investor who commits monthly to a diversified portfolio, regardless of market mood, benefits from pound-cost averaging—buying more when prices are low, less when they're high, and sidestepping paralysis born of indecision. Over time, this patient approach outperforms most speculative gambles—not only in returns but reliability.

Today, technology offers valuable tools to support such discipline. Automated investing platforms, recurring contributions, robo-advisers, and goal-based apps make it easier than ever to stick to a plan free from emotional interference. By automating decisions, investors reduce the temptation to react impulsively to short-term market moves. While automation isn't a cure-all, it's a powerful ally against behavioural biases, creating a buffer between intention and impulse and helping investors focus on long-term aims rather than fleeting sentiments.

Yet automation works best when thoughtfully designed. Delegating investment decisions to a system only succeeds if it reflects the investor's values, objectives, risk tolerance, and time horizon. Setting up an automated plan is no substitute for planning itself; it's the disciplined execution of one. Investors must still make choices about asset allocation, account types, tax strategies, and periodic rebalancing. Automation simply ensures these decisions are implemented consistently—come rain or shine in the markets.

The psychological aspect of wealth extends beyond portfolios to the broader, often emotional relationship people have with money. For many, financial goals are about more than numbers—they embody security, freedom, legacy, or self-worth. This emotional weight can either bolster or undermine wealth building. A healthy mindset around money is marked by clarity of purpose, balanced views on risk and reward, and the capacity to defer gratification in pursuit of deeper, more meaningful outcomes.

Cultivating such a relationship requires time and introspection. It involves defining what financial success means on a personal level—not merely in figures, but in life's quality. It demands awareness of emotional triggers, setting clear boundaries around financial choices, and building habits that reinforce positive behaviour. Journaling, working with financial planners, or even mindfulness techniques can aid this process. Those who understand why they invest are far likelier to stay committed to how they invest.

Investor psychology also intertwines with family and intergenerational dynamics. Teaching children about saving, investing, and patience lays the groundwork for lasting financial health, but it raises questions of legacy, communication, and values. Without education and context, wealth can breed entitlement, conflict, or confusion. Wise investors therefore pay attention not only to their own behaviour but to the example they set and the structures they build for future generations.

In essence, mastering investor behaviour is about much more than managing money; it's about managing oneself. It entails recognising emotions, identifying biases, fostering discipline, and employing systems that promote consistency. Crucially, it involves aligning financial decisions with personal meaning, appreciating that money choices reflect one's priorities and shape life's trajectory.

As we proceed to examine the finer points of investor psychology—from the hazards of emotional investing to the benefits of automation and the power of steady habits—we'll return repeatedly to one core idea: investing success isn't about being fearless or flawless. Rather, it rests on being self-aware, purposeful, and prepared. It's about cultivating habits that support sound decisions and acknowledging that discipline often outperforms cleverness. The market will always shift. Emotions will inevitably arise. But equipped with the right mindset and tools, investors can navigate both with clarity—and build enduring wealth in the process.

Emotional Investing and Its Pitfalls

Emotions are an inextricable part of the human experience. They guide relationships, influence career choices, and shape our daily decisions. Yet when it comes to investing, emotions—though entirely natural—can be one of the most consistent sources of self-sabotage. Financial markets are rational in the long term but volatile in the short term, and investors, often driven by psychological impulses rather than objective reasoning, tend to make decisions that feel right emotionally but are misaligned with their best interests. Emotional investing, when left unchecked, incurs not just opportunity costs but actual losses—sometimes severe and long-lasting.

To understand the pitfalls of emotional investing, one must first recognise the mismatch between how financial markets operate and how human psychology is wired. Markets are forward-looking, probabilistic systems that respond to a wide range of stimuli—economic data, corporate earnings, geopolitical events, central bank policies, and investor expectations. They rise and fall on anticipation, not certainty. Investors, on the other hand, crave predictability and control. Faced with volatility and ambiguity, the natural instinct is to seek safety or chase gains. This leads to emotionally charged behaviour: fear during downturns, greed during rallies, and impatience when progress seems slow.

Fear, perhaps the most corrosive emotion in investing, tends to surface most powerfully during market corrections or crises. As prices fall, the visceral discomfort of watching one's portfolio decline can become overwhelming. Investors begin to imagine worst-case scenarios, influenced not only by falling numbers but by sensational media coverage and peer conversations. The instinctive response is to sell—remove oneself from perceived danger, cut losses, and move to cash. Yet history shows that selling during downturns typically locks in losses that might otherwise have been temporary. Markets have always recovered over time, often with surprising speed, and those who sell in fear frequently miss the sharpest stages of a rebound.

The 2008 financial crisis offers a sobering case study. As markets collapsed in response to the subprime mortgage meltdown and subsequent banking failures, investor panic reached fever pitch. Those who exited equities at the depths of the crisis avoided further immediate losses, but they also forfeited the chance to benefit from one of the most powerful bull markets in history. By contrast, those who stayed invested—or continued contributing during the downturn—emerged with significantly stronger long-term returns. The cost of fear was not only the loss incurred from selling low but the lost gains from not participating in the recovery.

On the opposite end of the emotional spectrum is greed. During strong bull markets, the temptation to chase returns becomes intense. Investors see others prospering, hear stories of extraordinary gains, and begin to question the adequacy of their own strategy. This often leads to abandoning disciplined plans in favour of high-risk opportunities that promise outsized rewards. But by the time most people hear about a trend, it is already well underway. Buying into overvalued assets at the peak of a hype cycle often results in losses when the inevitable correction occurs.

The cryptocurrency surge of 2017, and again in 2021, illustrates this dynamic. As Bitcoin and other digital currencies skyrocketed in price, a wave of speculative enthusiasm drew in millions of novice investors. Many were motivated less by conviction in the underlying technology than by fear of missing out. When prices corrected sharply, these same investors, having entered at inflated levels, were left holding assets that quickly lost value. Greed not only inflated the bubble but intensified the fallout, particularly for those who had overextended themselves or invested without a clear understanding of the risks involved.

In between these extremes lies another dangerous emotional pitfall: impatience. Investing is fundamentally a long-term endeavour, but the human mind is conditioned for short-term feedback. We expect immediate results, and when they don't materialise, we grow restless. This can lead to constant tinkering—switching strategies, reallocating funds, reacting to headlines, or second-guessing decisions. Such activity rarely adds value. In fact, studies have shown that the most successful investors are often those who trade the least. Impatience drives overconfidence and unnecessary action, both of which erode returns through transaction costs, tax inefficiencies, and missed compounding opportunities.

These emotional tendencies are exacerbated by the environment in which investors operate. The 24-hour news cycle, financial media, and social platforms create a constant stream of information—much of it designed to provoke emotional reactions rather than support rational decision-making. Alarming headlines, exaggerated claims, and conflicting opinions contribute to a sense of urgency and uncertainty. In this context, maintaining emotional composure becomes not just difficult but a significant competitive advantage.

So how can investors mitigate the risks posed by emotional decision-making? The first step is self-awareness. Recognising emotional triggers—whether it's a market dip, a friend's investment success, or a frightening news report—allows investors to pause and reflect before acting. Building in a buffer between stimulus and response is crucial. That might mean waiting a day before making a trade, discussing concerns with a trusted adviser, or revisiting one's investment policy statement.

Structure also helps. Investors who follow a well-defined financial plan—complete with asset allocation guidelines, risk parameters, and contribution schedules—are less likely to deviate when emotions run high. These structures serve as guardrails, keeping behaviour aligned with long-term goals. Automated investing tools can further reinforce discipline by removing the need for constant decisions. Regular, fixed contributions eliminate timing concerns and help normalise volatility. The more that decision-making is systematised, the less room there is for emotion to distort outcomes.

Another important principle is perspective. Markets are not casinos or battlegrounds; they are mechanisms for allocating capital and distributing returns based on underlying economic activity. Setbacks are part of the process, not signs of failure. Investors who frame downturns as opportunities, rather than threats, are better positioned to respond constructively. This shift in mindset does not eliminate fear or discomfort, but it does reduce their influence over behaviour.

History also provides reassurance. While past performance is no guarantee of future results, long-term market trends demonstrate a clear pattern of resilience. Equity markets, in particular, have recovered from wars, recessions, pandemics, political crises, and financial scandals. Each recovery rewards those who remain patient and penalises those who react emotionally. The challenge is not avoiding emotion—it is learning to navigate it.

This is not to suggest that emotion has no place in investing. On the contrary, emotion is part of what gives money meaning. It reflects our values, our aspirations, our sense of security and responsibility. But when emotion becomes the driver rather than the passenger, the results are often destructive. Mastering the emotional dimension of investing means respecting its power, but not surrendering to it.

Ultimately, emotional investing is costly not just in financial terms, but in psychological ones. It leads to regret, stress, and a diminished sense of control. By contrast, developing the ability to make thoughtful, measured decisions—even when markets are turbulent—produces not only better results, but a greater sense of confidence and clarity. Investors who can manage their emotions are not immune to losses, but they are less likely to compound them through poor timing or impulsive reactions.

In the long run, the markets reward those who show patience, discipline, and consistency. They favour the investor who understands that emotions are a part of the process, but not the compass by which decisions should be made. To master the psychology of wealth is to master, first and foremost, oneself. And in that mastery lies not just better financial outcomes, but a more empowered and resilient approach to life.

Cognitive Biases That Hurt Investing

Investing is often framed as a logical pursuit—an exercise in numbers, data, and strategic reasoning. In theory, rational individuals allocate capital based on expected returns, adjusting for risk and time horizon, all in a measured and consistent fashion. Yet in practice, investment decisions are frequently distorted by a host of invisible forces that have little to do with logic. These are cognitive biases—systematic errors in thinking that cloud judgement and lead investors astray, often without their awareness. They are the mental shortcuts our brains use to simplify complexity, but in the financial world, they tend to simplify at the expense of accuracy and objectivity.

Understanding these biases is critical not just for the academically curious but for anyone who aspires to invest successfully over the long term. Recognising how and why we deviate from rationality allows us to build systems and strategies that protect us from our own worst instincts. While there are many cognitive biases that affect decision-making, several have particularly pernicious effects on investing. These include herd mentality, confirmation bias, anchoring, recency bias, and overconfidence—each undermining rational judgement in subtle yet significant ways.

Herd mentality is perhaps the most socially driven of all biases. It reflects our innate tendency to follow the crowd, especially in uncertain or unfamiliar situations. This behaviour is rooted in evolutionary psychology. In the wild, staying close to the group offered protection. In financial markets, however, it often leads to the amplification of bubbles and panics. When investors see others buying a particular stock or asset en masse, they often feel compelled to join in, fearing they might miss out on potential gains. The fear of being left behind is as emotionally compelling as the fear of loss.

This behaviour was starkly evident during the dot-com boom of the late 1990s. As internet-related companies attracted enormous investor attention, many people piled into stocks with little regard for fundamentals. Valuations soared, driven not by intrinsic value but by momentum and social proof. It was not uncommon for companies with no earnings and no clear path to profitability to be valued in the billions. The euphoria proved unsustainable, and when sentiment turned, the bubble burst spectacularly. The collapse wiped out trillions in market value, and many individual investors suffered severe losses—not because the idea of the internet was flawed, but because their decisions were driven by group behaviour rather than independent analysis.

Herding also manifests during downturns. The 2008 financial crisis offers another cautionary tale. As panic spread and markets declined sharply, many investors sold off their holdings en masse. Despite valuations becoming increasingly attractive, few were willing to go against the prevailing sentiment. The result was a self-reinforcing cycle of selling, which only exacerbated the decline. Those who succumbed to the fear missed the subsequent recovery, which began well before the wider economy stabilised.

Another insidious bias is confirmation bias—the tendency to seek out information that supports our pre-existing beliefs while ignoring or dismissing contradictory evidence. In investing, this bias can be especially damaging. An investor who is enthusiastic about a particular stock may give undue weight to positive news while rationalising or ignoring red flags. They may read analyst reports selectively, follow commentators who echo their views, and disregard alternative perspectives. This echo chamber effect reinforces flawed assumptions and leads to skewed risk assessments.

Confirmation bias often becomes more pronounced in the presence of financial media and digital platforms, where algorithms tailor content to user preferences. If an investor frequently searches for bullish views on technology stocks, they will likely be fed more of the same. This can create a false sense of consensus and conviction, blinding the investor to important counterarguments. Avoiding this trap requires conscious effort—seeking out diverse viewpoints, engaging with sceptical analysis, and being willing to question one's own thesis. The best investors are not those who are always right, but those who are willing to update their beliefs when the evidence changes.

Anchoring is another cognitive distortion that subtly warps judgement. It refers to the human tendency to rely too heavily on the first piece of information encountered when making decisions. In investing, anchors often take the form of previous stock prices, recent highs or lows, or purchase prices. For instance, an investor who bought shares at £100 may be reluctant to sell them at £90, even if all indicators suggest further declines. The £100 purchase price becomes a mental anchor—one that colours the perception of value and influences decision-making, even though the market cares nothing for an investor's entry point.

Anchoring can also affect expectations about future performance. If a stock has risen sharply in recent months, investors may anchor their future return expectations to that past performance, assuming similar growth will continue. This often leads to disappointment and poor outcomes, particularly if the prior gains were fuelled by temporary factors. A more objective approach involves reassessing an asset's value based on fundamentals, not past prices or emotional attachment.

Recency bias compounds the problem by placing disproportionate emphasis on recent events while underweighting long-term trends. This is particularly evident during market volatility. After a sharp correction, investors may become overly pessimistic, extrapolating short-term losses into permanent decline. Conversely, after a period of strong returns, they may become overconfident, assuming the trend will continue indefinitely. Both reactions distort portfolio decisions, leading to overexposure in booms and excessive caution in busts.

The behaviour of investors during the early months of the COVID-19 pandemic illustrates this vividly. As markets plummeted in March 2020, many believed the collapse would be prolonged and severe. The memory of falling prices dominated perception, even as central banks and governments introduced massive stimulus measures. Yet markets rebounded with extraordinary speed. Those who anchored their expectations to the recency of the crash missed one of the most rapid recoveries in financial history.

Overconfidence, a bias that often afflicts both new and experienced investors, is particularly dangerous because it feels like competence. It manifests in an inflated sense of one's ability to pick winners, time markets, or outperform benchmarks. Overconfident investors trade more frequently, take larger positions, and are slower to admit mistakes. They underestimate risk and overestimate their skill, leading to erratic returns and elevated portfolio volatility.

This bias is often reinforced by short bursts of success. An investor who profits from a few fortunate trades may begin to attribute those gains to skill rather than luck. This misattribution encourages riskier behaviour, which often ends poorly. The data on this is clear: investors who trade more frequently tend to earn lower returns, particularly after fees and taxes are accounted for. Humility, not bravado, is a more sustainable investment posture.

So, how can investors guard against these biases? The first defence is awareness. Simply knowing that these patterns exist—and recognising them in oneself—is a powerful step. But awareness alone is not enough. Effective mitigation requires process and structure. Creating a written investment plan, adhering to asset allocation targets, and establishing rules for rebalancing can all help reduce emotional and cognitive interference. Reviewing decisions with a trusted adviser or accountability partner also introduces an external check on bias.

Another helpful practice is maintaining an investment journal. Recording the rationale behind decisions, expectations for outcomes, and emotional state at the time creates a valuable archive. Over time, this journal can reveal patterns—biases that show up repeatedly, blind spots that need correction, or moments of clarity worth emulating.

Ultimately, successful investing is not about eliminating bias altogether—that is unrealistic. It is about recognising that we are fallible and building systems that protect us from those faults. It is about slowing down, reflecting, and approaching decisions with humility and curiosity. It is about embracing the fact that the biggest threat to our portfolio is often not the market, but the mirror.

The psychology of investing is not a peripheral concern—it is central. The most sophisticated strategy, the most advanced tools, and the most detailed analysis will all fall short if the investor cannot manage their own mind. By learning to recognise and overcome cognitive biases, we take a vital step towards better decisions, steadier performance, and ultimately, greater peace of mind in a complex and uncertain world.

Developing Financial Discipline

Financial success is not a product of luck, genius, or a one-time windfall. It is cultivated through consistency, intentional behaviour, and the quiet resolve to stick with sound principles over time. At the heart of this process lies financial discipline—a trait often understated in investment literature but essential for building and sustaining wealth. Discipline is what anchors an investor during market turbulence, tempers exuberance during bull runs, and keeps long-term objectives in focus despite the daily distractions of economic noise and shifting sentiment. Developing financial discipline is less about technical knowledge and more about cultivating behaviours that serve your future self, regardless of short-term discomfort or temptation.

To speak of discipline is to speak of habits, because it is through daily, repeated actions that long-term wealth is built. These actions are often unglamorous: automating savings, contributing to a pension scheme every month, resisting the allure of get-rich-quick schemes, and reviewing a budget that prioritises long-term goals over momentary gratification. While these tasks may lack excitement, they form the backbone of financial resilience. Wealth, at its core, is not about how much one earns, but about how effectively one channels income into productive uses over extended periods.

One of the clearest expressions of financial discipline is the habit of saving before spending. This reversal of the more common "spend first, save what's left" approach reshapes an individual's relationship with money. When saving becomes a non-negotiable, like paying rent or utilities, it shifts from being a passive aspiration to an active priority. This change in mindset is powerful. It establishes the idea that future security is worth present sacrifice and embeds a behaviour that compounds in its effect over years and decades.

Take, for example, the story of a young professional who begins investing £200 per month at the age of twenty-five. Over time, as their income grows, they increase this contribution incrementally, never wavering regardless of market fluctuations. By the time they reach retirement age, their habit—seemingly modest in isolation—has transformed into substantial wealth, thanks to the combined effects of consistency and compounding. Contrast this with someone who starts later, contributes sporadically, or suspends their plan in response to market dips. Despite perhaps having a higher income, their lack of discipline costs them dearly in long-term results.

Discipline is also what keeps investors from abandoning their strategy during times of fear or exuberance. It takes resolve to continue investing during a bear market, when losses mount and negative headlines dominate. Likewise, it requires restraint to avoid overcommitting during speculative booms, when returns appear effortless and optimism runs unchecked. In both scenarios, discipline protects against behavioural errors—buying high and selling low—that erode returns and undermine confidence.

The global financial crisis of 2008 illustrated this powerfully. While many investors fled to cash in a panic, those who maintained their allocations and continued contributing to investment accounts saw their portfolios recover and grow substantially in the years that followed. The same was true during the rapid sell-off in early 2020 amid the onset of the COVID-19 pandemic. Markets rebounded quickly, but only those with the discipline to stay the course benefitted. These examples are not anomalies; they are reminders that volatility is part of investing, and that disciplined behaviour is the antidote to reactive, damaging choices.

But financial discipline extends beyond investing. It permeates all areas of money management, including spending, debt, and goal-setting. Consider debt management. The disciplined individual uses credit judiciously, understanding the cost of borrowing and avoiding high-interest consumer debt that undermines financial progress. They prioritise needs over wants, resist lifestyle inflation, and make conscious decisions about what aligns with their values. Such control is not about deprivation; it is about choosing the life one wants most over the impulse of the moment.

Budgeting, too, becomes an expression of discipline—not as a rigid constraint, but as a framework for intentional living. A disciplined budget is not about tracking every pound obsessively; it is about aligning expenditure with priorities and values. It allows for flexibility and enjoyment while ensuring that essentials are covered, savings targets are met, and financial stress is minimised. It enables people to say "yes" to the things that matter by saying "no" to the things that don't.

Goal-setting plays a central role in sustaining discipline. Abstract ideas like "save more" or "invest regularly" lack the emotional resonance needed to inspire lasting habits. Specific, time-bound goals—buying a home, funding a child's education, achieving financial independence by a certain age—provide motivation and a sense of direction. They turn financial discipline from a chore into a purposeful activity. When actions are connected to aspirations, the effort becomes more meaningful, and adherence becomes more natural.

Accountability further reinforces discipline. Whether it comes through a financial adviser, a partner, or a personal tracking system, being answerable to someone or something creates structure. It reduces the temptation to deviate from the plan and introduces reflection into the decision-making process. Even self-imposed accountability, such as reviewing progress quarterly or writing a personal financial report each year, can deepen engagement and commitment.

Technology can also aid the cultivation of discipline. Automated transfers to investment accounts, budgeting apps that categorise spending, alerts that track savings goals—all serve to remove friction and make disciplined behaviour the path of least resistance. By designing systems that make the desired action easy and the undesired action more difficult, individuals stack the odds in their favour. Automation, when thoughtfully applied, removes the need for daily willpower and replaces it with default settings that reflect long-term intentions.

Yet it must be acknowledged that discipline is not immune to setbacks. Life is unpredictable. Emergencies arise, circumstances shift, and even the most diligent plans may falter. True financial discipline is not perfection—it is resilience. It is the ability to recover from lapses without abandoning the broader path. It is about consistency over time, not flawlessness in execution. A disciplined investor or saver is not someone who never errs, but someone who recommits quickly after being knocked off course.

Financial discipline also evolves. What serves a young professional building their first emergency fund will differ from what is needed by a mid-career executive managing a complex investment portfolio or by a retiree drawing down assets in a tax-efficient manner. As financial lives become more layered, so too must the habits and systems that support them. Ongoing education, reflection, and adaptation ensure that discipline remains fit for purpose as goals and circumstances change.

Perhaps most importantly, financial discipline is not about austerity—it is about agency. It is the practice of aligning money with meaning, using it not as an end in itself, but as a tool to create a life that reflects one's deepest priorities. It offers a sense of control in an uncertain world and a source of confidence amid economic noise. When money is managed with care and clarity, it ceases to be a source of stress and becomes a means of empowerment.

In the end, developing financial discipline is less about restriction and more about liberation. It is the steady, sometimes quiet work of building a foundation that can support not only wealth, but peace of mind. It is the commitment to daily choices—small, repeated, often invisible—that compound into significant results over time. While others chase quick wins or flinch at every market movement, the disciplined investor stands firm, guided not by emotion but by principle. And it is this consistency, more than any brilliant strategy or secret insight, that underpins the creation of lasting financial success.

The Role of Automation in Wealth Building

Wealth building, at its core, is a game of consistency. It is not the occasional bold move that defines financial outcomes, but the quiet, repeated actions executed reliably over long periods. Yet human nature is notoriously inconsistent. We are prone to distraction, emotion, procrastination, and forgetfulness. We overestimate our discipline and underestimate our susceptibility to behavioural traps. This is where automation plays a powerful role. By harnessing technology to perform routine financial tasks, investors can bypass their own limitations and establish a stable framework that steadily builds wealth—regardless of mood, market noise, or motivation.

Automation is not new in the world of finance, but its application to personal investing has accelerated dramatically in recent years. What was once the preserve of institutional asset managers and high-net-worth clients is now available to anyone with a smartphone and a bank account. Direct debit savings, robo-advisory platforms, app-based investing tools, automatic rebalancing, and scheduled portfolio reviews have transformed the way individuals interact with their finances. These technologies are not just convenient—they are transformative. They provide a structural advantage to those who use them wisely.

One of the most foundational uses of automation is the regular transfer of funds from a current account into an investment vehicle. Whether it's a stocks and shares ISA, a pension fund, or a diversified global ETF portfolio, the simple act of automating contributions ensures that investing becomes habitual. It transforms saving from a discretionary act—dependent on willpower or leftover cash—into a systematic priority. This seemingly mundane shift has a profound effect. It turns investment into a default behaviour, rather than a reactive one.

Consider the experience of two individuals with similar income and expenses. One waits until the end of the month to decide how much to invest, factoring in lifestyle spending and discretionary purchases. The other sets up an automated transfer on payday, treating investment like a fixed cost. Over time, the difference is striking. The latter not only contributes more consistently but avoids the emotional burden of deciding each month whether to invest or not. The system does the work, shielding the investor from their own indecision.

This consistency is especially powerful when combined with pound-cost averaging—the practice of investing a fixed amount regularly, regardless of market conditions. By doing so, investors purchase more units when prices are low and fewer when prices are high, smoothing out volatility over time. Automation makes this approach seamless. It eliminates the temptation to time the market, a notoriously difficult feat even for seasoned professionals, and instead instils a rhythm that aligns with long-term compounding.

Beyond regular contributions, automation supports wealth building through portfolio management tools that rebalance investments in accordance with a target allocation. Left unchecked, portfolios can drift significantly as asset classes perform differently over time. Equities may surge, bonds may lag, and what was once a balanced strategy can become risk-heavy without intervention. Automated rebalancing ensures that excess gains are periodically trimmed and underweight areas replenished. This reaffirms the investment strategy and maintains alignment with the investor's original risk tolerance and goals.

Platforms that offer automatic rebalancing do so with precision and without emotion. They do not hesitate in the face of market fear or chase hot sectors in a surge. They follow rules, not reactions. This mechanical consistency helps avoid many of the behavioural pitfalls that afflict manual investors, particularly during periods of volatility. During a downturn, for instance, an automated system may shift funds into equities at lower valuations, a move that might feel counterintuitive for a human observer gripped by uncertainty.

The rise of robo-advisers has extended automation into personalised investment planning. These digital platforms use algorithms to assess an individual's financial situation, risk appetite, and time horizon, then construct and manage a diversified portfolio accordingly. Fees are generally lower than traditional financial advisers, and the experience is designed to be user-friendly and accessible. While robo-advisers are not a substitute for comprehensive financial advice in complex situations, they offer a valuable entry point for those seeking a low-cost, automated way to invest with discipline.

Even beyond investing, automation can streamline broader financial management. Budgeting tools that categorise spending, track goals, and flag anomalies help individuals maintain awareness and control without micromanaging every expense. Savings apps that round up purchases to the nearest pound and invest the spare change allow wealth-building to happen invisibly in the background. Scheduled alerts for bill payments, goal milestones, or contribution limits reinforce good habits and reduce the risk of costly oversights.

The psychological benefit of automation should not be underestimated. Money decisions are emotionally charged. We second-guess ourselves, react to headlines, compare ourselves to others, and fear making the wrong move. Automation acts as a buffer against this noise. It removes the need to decide afresh every month whether to save or invest, reducing decision fatigue and making it easier to adhere to long-term plans. It also provides peace of mind, knowing that progress is being made quietly and reliably—even when life gets busy or uncertain.

That said, automation is not infallible. It is a tool, not a strategy in itself. Poorly designed automation can entrench bad habits or create a false sense of security. For instance, automating investments into a portfolio that lacks diversification or is misaligned with risk tolerance will not yield favourable outcomes simply because it is systematic. Likewise, automation must be reviewed periodically to ensure it reflects changes in income, financial goals, or market conditions. Blind reliance is as dangerous as emotional inconsistency.

Therefore, effective automation begins with intentional design. Investors must first clarify their objectives: what are they saving for, over what time frame, and with what level of risk tolerance? They must then select tools that support these goals, configure systems accordingly, and periodically reassess to ensure alignment. Automation should support decision-making, not replace it. It is most powerful when it executes a well-considered plan, freeing the investor to focus on strategic adjustments rather than tactical execution.

Technology also offers a degree of customisation that supports individual values. For instance, investors can automate contributions into ESG (Environmental, Social and Governance) funds that align with their ethical priorities. Others may choose platforms that allow thematic investing, such as clean energy or innovation, while still maintaining diversification. The convergence of automation and personalisation makes it easier to align wealth-building with broader life goals, enhancing engagement and motivation.

For those concerned about market volatility or economic uncertainty, automation does not require perfection in timing or insight. Its strength lies precisely in its indifference to noise. It continues to execute the plan regardless of headlines, sentiment, or short-term setbacks. This impartiality often outperforms the most carefully timed but inconsistently applied strategies. Over decades, the steady investor who automates contributions and adheres to a diversified portfolio frequently outpaces the reactive investor who chases trends or sits in cash waiting for clarity.

There is also a behavioural elegance in knowing that the most important steps toward financial independence have already been taken care of each month. When your future is being funded on autopilot, the temptation to chase fads, panic during dips, or overcomplicate strategy diminishes. This doesn't make wealth building effortless, but it does make it more sustainable—and sustainability is the essence of long-term success.

In the broader arc of financial behaviour, automation is not a silver bullet but a significant advantage. It compensates for human weakness with mechanical consistency. It transforms intent into action. It simplifies complexity. And most importantly, it creates space—space to think more clearly, to make fewer mistakes, and to focus on what really matters: aligning one's money with one's values, goals, and life ambitions.

The future of wealth building will almost certainly continue to be shaped by technology. Yet the most powerful use of this technology is not to outpace the market, but to outwit ourselves. In that respect, automation is not merely a tool—it is a discipline in disguise. It is the quiet partner that shows up every day, without emotion or ego, building a financial foundation brick by brick. For those willing to use it with care and clarity, the benefits are not just financial—they are profoundly behavioural. And over time, that makes all the difference.

The Power of Consistency

In investing, few principles are as powerful, yet as frequently overlooked, as consistency. While the media spotlights dramatic market moves, high-profile trades, and the fortunes won or lost overnight, the real engine of wealth creation runs quietly in the background. It is the power of regular, disciplined investing—performed not with flair, but with persistence. Investors often search for the next big opportunity, convinced that outsized returns lie in perfectly timed trades or complex strategies. But history, and data, suggest otherwise. Over time, it is not the boldest investor who prospers, but the most consistent.

The appeal of speculation is obvious. It promises quick rewards and taps into the deeply human desire to feel in control, to outsmart the market, and to win. The notion of buying at the bottom and selling at the top is tantalising. It offers a narrative of foresight and mastery. But speculation, by its very nature, relies on prediction—and prediction, especially in financial markets, is perilously difficult. Markets are influenced by countless variables, many of them unforeseeable: geopolitical events, central bank decisions, corporate earnings surprises, and shifts in sentiment. Even professional investors, with access to advanced analytics and vast resources, struggle to consistently beat the market. For individual investors, the odds are even less forgiving.

By contrast, consistent investing removes the need for prediction. It is grounded not in timing but in time. The strategy is simple: contribute regularly, stay invested, and let compounding do the work. Whether markets are soaring or slumping, the investor continues to buy. Over months and years, this discipline builds momentum. During market declines, investments are acquired at lower prices, increasing the number of units owned. During upswings, these units appreciate in value. The result is a smoothing of volatility and the steady accumulation of assets.

This approach, often described as pound-cost averaging, is both elegant and effective. It transforms uncertainty from a threat into an ally. Instead of trying to avoid volatility, the consistent investor embraces it, knowing that downturns provide opportunities to buy more. Crucially, this method requires emotional fortitude—the willingness to invest when others are fearful, and the patience to remain engaged when progress feels slow. But the rewards are substantial.

Consider a hypothetical scenario: two individuals begin investing £300 a month at age thirty. One does so consistently, regardless of market conditions. The other waits for what they believe to be opportune moments, investing only during perceived dips or when headlines suggest a strong outlook. Over a period of thirty years, the consistent investor ends up with a significantly larger portfolio—not because they chose better investments, but because they stayed the course. The market rewarded their persistence with the power of compounding, uninterrupted by hesitation or second-guessing.

This principle is supported by a wealth of empirical evidence. Studies examining investor behaviour regularly show that those who attempt to time the market underperform those who invest steadily. A landmark study by Dalbar Inc., which analysed investor returns in the United States over several decades, revealed that the average equity investor significantly underperformed the market index—not due to poor fund selection, but due to impulsive buying and selling. Investors consistently entered during peaks and exited during troughs, driven by emotion rather than strategy. Those who simply remained invested throughout the same period achieved far better outcomes.

Consistency also provides a powerful counterweight to the emotional highs and lows that define market cycles. During bull markets, when confidence surges and valuations stretch, the disciplined investor maintains their allocation, avoiding the temptation to overextend. During bear markets, when fear dominates and pessimism prevails, the same investor continues to contribute, resisting the impulse to retreat. This equilibrium, difficult as it is to maintain, fosters long-term resilience.

Importantly, the benefits of consistency extend beyond returns. They include clarity, peace of mind, and reduced decision fatigue. Investing, when systematised, becomes a process rather than a performance. The individual no longer has to debate when to invest, how much to contribute, or whether now is the right time. The answer is always the same: invest regularly, as planned. This removes guesswork and the emotional strain that often accompanies financial decisions. It allows the investor to focus on broader goals—home ownership, education, retirement—rather than short-term fluctuations.

Real-world examples reinforce the effectiveness of this approach. During the global financial crisis of 2008, many investors panicked and withdrew from the market, locking in losses. Yet those who continued their monthly contributions, despite the economic chaos, ended up purchasing shares at significantly depressed prices. When the market recovered, these investments rebounded handsomely, accelerating portfolio growth. The discipline to stay invested, to remain consistent in the face of adversity, proved more valuable than any forecast or tactical adjustment.

A similar pattern played out in the early months of the COVID-19 pandemic. As markets tumbled in March 2020, fear spread rapidly. Yet within weeks, a sharp recovery began. Investors who remained committed to their contribution schedules, or who increased their investments during the downturn, experienced some of the fastest gains in recent history. Those who paused or attempted to time the rebound often re-entered after prices had already risen, missing key gains.

The consistent investor is not passive—they are purposeful. Their strategy is not rooted in inertia but in conviction: the belief that markets, while unpredictable in the short term, reward patience and participation over time. They understand that investing is not a sprint or a series of high-stakes bets, but a cumulative effort. Each monthly contribution, however small, is a brick laid in the foundation of long-term financial security.

This philosophy also cultivates humility. It acknowledges the limitations of human foresight and opts instead for a methodical approach that does not require clairvoyance. By committing to regular action rather than perfect timing, the investor accepts uncertainty while still making progress. This humility is not a weakness—it is a strength. It allows for mistakes without derailing the plan, and it creates space for adaptation without abandoning discipline.

The digital age has made it easier than ever to be consistent. Automation tools, investment apps, and direct debit systems enable individuals to invest regularly with minimal effort. Once configured, these systems operate quietly in the background, executing the strategy without requiring daily attention. This reduces friction and increases adherence, turning good intentions into tangible results. The less reliant an investment plan is on willpower, the more likely it is to succeed.

That said, consistency must be underpinned by quality. Regular investing into poorly chosen assets or misaligned portfolios will not produce favourable outcomes. The initial strategy must be sound—diversified, cost-efficient, aligned with personal goals—and reviewed periodically to ensure continued relevance. But once established, it is consistency that amplifies its effectiveness.

In personal finance, as in many areas of life, it is not the occasional act of brilliance that defines outcomes but the quiet, repeated act of commitment. Regular investing is not glamorous. It rarely features in headlines or garners accolades. But it works. It works not by avoiding risk, but by absorbing it systematically. It works not by predicting the future, but by participating in it consistently. And most importantly, it works not because of what markets do, but because of what the investor does—month after month, year after year.

In the final analysis, the power of consistency lies in its ability to transcend both noise and ego. It strips away the illusion of control and replaces it with action. It favours process over prediction, progress over perfection. For those seeking to build wealth sustainably, it offers a simple yet profound truth: show up, invest regularly, and stay the course. Everything else is secondary.

Chapter 8
The Role of Passive Investing - Why Simplicity Works Best

In a financial environment awash with complexity, ceaseless noise, and an ever-present pressure to act, passive investing quietly asserts itself as a surprisingly effective alternative. The premise is straightforward—build long-term wealth by holding broadly diversified, low-cost investments, without the futile attempt to outsmart the market. It's a notion that runs counter to the usual investing drama, yet this very simplicity, combined with the discipline it demands, is precisely why it holds such enduring power.

At its heart, passive investing is a strategy rooted in restraint. It resists the temptation to chase fleeting trends, ignore sensational headlines designed to provoke knee-jerk reactions, and avoid the emotional turbulence that too often defines active trading. Instead, it adopts a long-term, rules-based method for accumulating wealth—one grounded firmly in empirical evidence and tested by time. The aim is not to outpace the market but to capture its returns steadily, efficiently, and with minimal fuss.

To truly grasp passive investing, it helps to place it alongside its counterpart. Active investing entails frequent buying and selling, guided by analysis, forecasts, or intuition. It's dynamic, labour-intensive, and predicated on the belief that superior skill or information can generate above-average returns. Passive investing, on the other hand, seeks to replicate the performance of a market index—be it the FTSE All-Share, the S&P 500, or a global equities benchmark—by holding either every constituent or a representative sample. The passive investor doesn't try to outwit the market; they simply participate broadly and continuously.

This isn't just academic theory. A wealth of research shows that most active fund managers struggle to outperform their benchmarks consistently over time—particularly once fees, taxes, and transaction costs are factored in. The oft-cited S&P Dow Jones Indices report, updated regularly, underscores this reality: the majority of active funds underperform their indices across multiple years. Sure, some managers may best the market in any single year, but very few manage this feat consistently or predictably.

Index funds—the backbone of passive investing—present a compelling alternative. These funds aim to mirror an index's performance by holding its component securities. Without the need for costly analyst teams or complex trading tactics, they typically charge far lower fees than active funds. At first glance, the difference in cost—say, 0.5% to 1% annually—may seem modest, but stretched over decades, its impact is profound. Lower expenses mean investors keep more of their returns, compounding wealth rather than seeing it eroded by fees. This is one of the most overlooked yet powerful advantages in wealth creation.

Furthermore, index funds provide broad diversification. By encompassing a wide variety of assets—spanning sectors, regions, and company sizes—they mitigate the risk tied to any single holding. This diversification smooths out returns and cushions against the volatility of individual stocks. It also reduces the burden of constant monitoring and tinkering, freeing investors from the stress and time demands that come with more concentrated or actively managed portfolios.

Passive investing also stands firm against behavioural pitfalls. Active traders are frequently swayed by emotion—fear in downturns, greed in rallies, impatience in the lulls—which leads to overtrading. This behaviour not only racks up transaction fees and tax bills but often results in buying high and selling low. In contrast, passive investors, by sticking to a steady plan, limit the chances of falling into these traps. By removing the necessity of constant decision-making, they sidestep many costly mistakes made under pressure.

Picture an investor who, over two decades, faithfully contributes to a low-cost global index fund. They don't attempt to time the market, shuffle sectors, or chase the latest fads. Instead, they automate contributions and glance at their portfolio only occasionally. Meanwhile, another investor tries to predict economic shifts, central bank moves, and earnings surprises—buying and selling in response.

Despite their efforts, this active investor's returns are often diminished by higher fees, poorly timed trades, and missed market rebounds. Meanwhile, the passive investor enjoys uninterrupted compounding, a balanced risk profile, and less stress.

Now, this isn't to say passive investing requires no effort or is a magic bullet. It demands discipline—particularly the discipline to do less rather than more. It calls for a long-term mindset, tolerance for market fluctuations, and a readiness to accept market returns instead of chasing elusive outperformance. For many, this proves psychologically difficult. The urge to "do something" during downturns can be overwhelming. Likewise, the fear of missing out during bull runs is hard to resist. Yet the passive investor understands that consistency—not cleverness—is the surest route to financial independence.

Implementing a passive strategy involves some clear steps. First, the investor must define their financial goals, time horizon, and appetite for risk. These factors guide the right mix of equities, bonds, and other assets. Next comes the selection of a handful of diversified index funds or ETFs that provide exposure to these areas—a global equity fund, a bond index, perhaps a regional or thematic fund. Once selected, the investor sets up regular contributions—monthly or quarterly—and commits to infrequent portfolio reviews, mainly for rebalancing.

Rebalancing, when done passively, is straightforward. If equities outperform and grow too large a share, the investor might trim them slightly and shift proceeds back into bonds, preserving the original risk balance. This approach prevents the portfolio from drifting into excessive risk or undue caution. And crucially, it can be automated, further reducing emotionally driven decisions.

The essence of passive investing is not laziness but intention. It is a deliberate choice to favour long-term growth over short-term noise, to embrace markets rather than outsmart them, and to recognise that wealth builds not through frenetic activity but through quiet, persistent commitment. In many ways, it's as much a philosophy as it is a financial tactic—an acceptance that the world's complexity, markets' efficiency, and the value of time make speculative manoeuvres both risky and inefficient.

No wonder this philosophy has gained momentum. As investing becomes more accessible, many realise that simplicity is not a concession but a strength. With digital platforms, low-cost brokerages, and intuitive tools, barriers to entry have never been lower. Passive investing empowers individuals to take part in wealth creation with confidence, even without formal finance training.

Perhaps above all, passive investing allows people to live their lives. Rather than monitoring screens, analysing economic indicators, or second-guessing every move, passive investors can focus on careers, family, health, and personal growth, secure in the knowledge that their financial future is quietly and efficiently cared for.

In a culture that often equates complexity with sophistication and busyness with wisdom, passive investing offers a radical counterpoint. It suggests that sometimes the smartest move is to do less, to trust in process, and to let time and markets work their magic. It invites a redefinition of success—not as beating others, but as meeting one's own goals with clarity and calm. And in doing so, it reclaims the idea that investing can be both elegantly simple and profoundly effective.

What is Passive Investing?

Passive investing is perhaps one of the most counterintuitive yet consistently effective approaches to wealth accumulation. At a glance, it appears to run against much of what conventional thinking associates with successful investing: activity, analysis, and agility. Yet it is precisely by embracing simplicity and rejecting the instinct to outmanoeuvre the market that passive strategies have repeatedly demonstrated their strength over time.

To understand passive investing, one must begin by distinguishing it from its more traditional counterpart—active investing. The active approach is predicated on the belief that with sufficient research, insight, and timing, an investor can identify mispriced assets and capitalise on inefficiencies in the market. This leads to frequent buying and selling, continuous monitoring, and an ongoing attempt to beat market averages. In contrast, passive investing is rooted in the recognition that markets are, more often than not, efficient over the long term. Rather than seeking to outperform them, passive investors aim to match broad market returns by investing in diversified index funds or exchange-traded funds (ETFs) that mirror the performance of a specific index, such as the FTSE 100 or the MSCI World.

The buy-and-hold strategy at the heart of passive investing relies on time and compounding, not prediction or perfect timing. It is an approach that requires patience, not performance chasing. Once invested in a diversified portfolio, the passive investor makes minimal changes, choosing instead to let the market work on their behalf. This method benefits from lower costs, reduced tax liabilities, and, critically, a behavioural advantage: it removes the emotional temptations to react to market noise.

Empirical evidence overwhelmingly supports the efficacy of passive investing. Over the past several decades, the majority of actively managed funds have underperformed their benchmark indices. Research from Standard & Poor's consistently shows that, across multiple time horizons and asset classes, most active fund managers fail to beat the market after fees are taken into account. This underperformance is not limited to any single region or investment style. It is a widespread and persistent reality. Even in markets where inefficiencies are thought to be more common—such as emerging markets or small-cap equities—passive strategies have proven competitive.

The advantage of passive investing is not merely theoretical. It can be seen in the practical outcomes of real investors. Consider a hypothetical case: two investors start with the same capital. One adopts an active strategy, shifting between sectors, timing entries and exits, and following market commentary closely. The other chooses a simple index fund, holds through bull and bear markets, and makes no attempt to intervene. After twenty years, the passive investor typically ends up with a larger portfolio—not because they made superior investment choices, but because they avoided the drag of fees, taxes, poor timing, and stress-driven decisions.

This is not to imply that all active investing fails or that all passive investing succeeds. There are skilled active managers who do outperform, and some passive investors who deviate from discipline. However, the burden of proof and performance in active investing is heavy. It requires not just being right, but being right consistently—something very few achieve. In passive investing, by contrast, success is statistically more likely, provided the investor adheres to the principles of diversification, cost control, and patience.

At the heart of passive investing lies a deeper understanding of human behaviour. Investors are not cold, rational calculators. They are emotional, impulsive, and often driven by narratives rather than data. This leads to harmful behaviours such as panic selling during market downturns or exuberant buying during rallies. Passive investing mitigates these tendencies by removing the need for constant decision-making. By committing to a long-term strategy and reducing the frequency of transactions, passive investors are less likely to be swayed by emotion and more likely to stay the course.

The psychological relief this affords should not be understated. Active investing can feel like a full-time job. It demands attention, interpretation, and fast response. For the average investor with a career, a family, and competing priorities, this level of involvement is not only impractical—it is unnecessary. Passive investing allows one to participate in the market's long-term growth without being consumed by it. It offers the freedom to focus on life while quietly building financial security in the background.

Critics of passive investing often argue that it leads to mediocrity—that by settling for average market returns, investors forfeit the possibility of doing better. But this overlooks two key realities. First, average market returns over time are historically strong, particularly when compounded over decades. A globally diversified portfolio has delivered real, inflation-adjusted gains for generations. Second, the vast majority of those who attempt to do better end up doing worse, often significantly so. In this context, achieving market returns is not mediocrity—it is prudence.

Moreover, passive investing is not about surrendering control. It is about choosing where control is most effective. Instead of attempting to control the market, which is impossible, the passive investor controls their costs, behaviour, and asset allocation. These are the levers that have the most influence on outcomes, and they are entirely within one's grasp.

Setting up a passive investing strategy involves some initial decisions: selecting appropriate index funds or ETFs, determining asset allocation based on risk tolerance and goals, and automating regular contributions. Once in place, this system requires little ongoing management. Periodic rebalancing may be necessary to maintain target allocations, and life events may warrant adjustments. But beyond that, the primary requirement is consistency.

There is also a values-based dimension to passive investing that is often overlooked. Simplicity, transparency, and accessibility are its hallmarks. The absence of opaque strategies, hidden fees, or speculative positioning makes it easier for investors to understand what they own and why. This transparency builds trust in the process and encourages long-term commitment. It is a philosophy of investing that aligns with clarity, not complexity; process, not prediction.

This is particularly relevant in a digital age where information is abundant but wisdom is scarce. Investors are bombarded with conflicting advice, attention-grabbing forecasts, and endless options. Passive investing cuts through the noise. It offers a grounded, evidence-based alternative to the financial theatre that surrounds much of active trading. It invites investors to step back from the frenzy and instead build a robust foundation quietly and efficiently.

The broader economic impact of passive investing also deserves mention. By anchoring capital in broad market indices, passive investors support the broader functioning of capital markets. They provide liquidity, reduce speculative froth, and foster a longer-term orientation in corporate governance. As passive ownership grows, it has the potential to stabilise markets and temper the short-termism that often afflicts listed companies.

Yet for all its advantages, passive investing is not a panacea. It must be approached with the same thoughtfulness as any other strategy. Investors must choose funds wisely, avoid overconcentration in any one region or sector, and resist the temptation to chase the latest thematic index without due diligence. Passive does not mean passive in thought—it means deliberate in action.

In embracing passive investing, individuals are not abdicating responsibility. They are recognising that, in a probabilistic and volatile world, humility and discipline often outperform hubris and speculation. The buy-and-hold strategy is not a bet on inertia, but a calculated decision to trust in long-term economic progress, diversification, and the quiet, compounding force of time. For those willing to adopt it, the rewards are substantial—not just in financial terms, but in peace of mind and freedom from the constant churn of reactive decision-making.

Passive investing is, ultimately, a testament to the power of simplicity. In a financial world that too often confuses activity with achievement, it reminds us that sometimes the smartest move is to stand still, to stay invested, and to let markets do what they have always done over time: reward those who remain patient, disciplined, and consistent.

Why Index Funds Outperform Most Investors

The allure of beating the market has long captured the imagination of investors. From financial professionals armed with sophisticated tools to individual traders chasing the next big win, the drive to outpace average returns remains deeply ingrained in investment culture. Yet despite this fervent pursuit, the data tells a different story—one that consistently favours the steady, unassuming strategy of index investing. Index funds, often dismissed for their simplicity, have not only held their own but routinely outperformed the majority of active investors over the long term. The explanation lies not in complexity or innovation, but in three enduring advantages:

lower costs, inherent diversification, and a structure designed to reduce behavioural missteps.

An index fund is designed to replicate the performance of a specific financial market index, such as the S&P 500, the FTSE 100, or a global stock market benchmark like the MSCI World Index. Rather than trying to select winning stocks or anticipate market movements, index funds mirror the entire market—or at least a representative slice of it. The idea is straightforward: by owning the market, investors ensure they receive market returns, minus a minimal fee. Over time, this simple approach proves exceedingly difficult to beat.

One of the most significant reasons index funds outperform most investors is their cost efficiency. Active investment management is expensive. It requires teams of analysts, researchers, and fund managers, all drawing salaries and incurring operational expenses. These costs are passed on to the investor in the form of higher annual fees. In contrast, index funds are managed passively, requiring little more than periodic adjustments to ensure the fund continues to track its benchmark. As a result, their expense ratios are typically a fraction of those charged by actively managed funds.

This fee difference, while seemingly minor, has a profound impact when compounded over decades. A fund charging 0.75% annually will consume a significantly greater portion of a portfolio's returns than one charging 0.10%. In fact, studies consistently show that fees are one of the most reliable predictors of future fund performance—not because lower fees guarantee higher returns, but because they create less of a hurdle for the fund to overcome. The investor in a low-cost index fund retains more of their gains, allowing compounding to work more effectively over time.

Closely related to the advantage of cost is the benefit of diversification. Index funds spread investments across a wide array of securities, offering broad exposure to entire markets or sectors. A fund tracking the S&P 500, for instance, includes 500 of the largest companies in the United States across a variety of industries. This diversification reduces the risk associated with any single company or sector underperforming. By contrast, many actively managed funds or self-directed portfolios are more concentrated, often based on convictions about specific stocks, industries, or regions.

Diversification does not eliminate risk, but it smooths the investment experience. It lowers the probability of catastrophic loss due to the failure of a single asset and increases the likelihood that an investor will achieve average market returns. When coupled with a long-term investment horizon, diversification enhances resilience during periods of volatility and provides exposure to the companies and sectors that will drive future growth—many of which cannot be predicted in advance.

Beyond cost and diversification, index funds offer a structural advantage that helps investors sidestep common behavioural pitfalls. One of the great paradoxes of investing is that while markets tend to rise over the long term, individual investors often underperform the very assets they invest in. This performance gap is largely attributable to poor timing—buying high during exuberant periods and selling low during times of fear. Active management, whether by professionals or individuals, invites this kind of behaviour. The temptation to chase trends, react to news cycles, or overhaul portfolios in response to short-term volatility is ever-present.

Index funds, by contrast, foster discipline. Their passive nature removes the impulse to make constant adjustments. Investors in index funds are less likely to engage in performance-chasing or panic-driven selling, simply because the strategy is not built around market timing or tactical shifts. This behavioural insulation is subtle but powerful. It encourages a focus on the long term, reducing the impact of emotionally charged decisions that so often erode returns.

There is also an intellectual humility embedded in index investing that aligns with the evidence on market efficiency. Decades of research in financial economics suggest that markets quickly incorporate available information into asset prices. This makes it extremely difficult for any investor to consistently identify mispriced securities and exploit them for profit. While some active managers do outperform, distinguishing skill from luck is notoriously difficult, and very few sustain outperformance over long time horizons. By acknowledging the challenge of beating the market, index investors opt to capture its gains rather than gamble on superior foresight.

This approach is not only sensible—it is profoundly empowering. It removes the need to decipher economic forecasts, pick the next star stock, or determine the optimal entry and exit points. Instead, the investor adopts a philosophy grounded in consistency, transparency, and alignment with long-term goals. The simplicity of the method belies its strength: rather than trying to do better than the market, the index investor avoids doing worse.

Consider real-world data. In the United Kingdom, the Financial Conduct Authority has repeatedly highlighted the underperformance of actively managed funds relative to benchmarks. Similarly, research from Morningstar shows that only a minority of active funds outperform comparable passive alternatives after fees over ten- and fifteen-year periods. In the United States, the SPIVA (S&P Indices Versus Active) Scorecard reports that over 85% of actively managed large-cap equity funds underperform their benchmarks over a twenty-year span. These findings are not anomalies—they are consistent across geographies and time periods.

Practical applications further illustrate the merit of index investing. A young professional aiming to save for retirement can set up automatic contributions into a low-cost global index fund via a workplace pension or individual savings account. With minimal intervention, their wealth accumulates steadily, shielded from the drama of financial headlines. Similarly, a retiree seeking to preserve capital while generating income can allocate funds across bond and equity indices, maintaining diversification and managing risk without the need for constant portfolio adjustments.

Even institutional investors increasingly incorporate index funds into their strategies. Sovereign wealth funds, university endowments, and pension schemes often allocate a significant portion of their assets to passive vehicles, recognising the difficulty of achieving consistent outperformance through active management alone. Their embrace of indexing underscores its legitimacy not only for the novice investor but for the most sophisticated participants in the market.

It is important to recognise that index investing is not without its critics. Some argue that passive investing may distort markets by channelling capital indiscriminately, or that it reduces price discovery. Others suggest that it creates a "herding" effect, where too many investors crowd into the same securities. While these concerns merit consideration, they are more theoretical than practical in the current landscape. Passive investing still represents a minority of global assets under management, and markets continue to exhibit robust price discovery and volatility.

Moreover, index investing is adaptable. Investors can tailor their exposure through different indices—broad market, sector-specific, international, or even ESG-focused—allowing for personalisation while retaining the core benefits of low cost and diversification. This flexibility ensures that the strategy remains relevant across a wide range of financial goals and risk appetites.

Ultimately, the strength of index funds lies in their alignment with investor interests. They are designed not to impress, but to deliver. They do not promise extraordinary returns, but they consistently outperform most alternatives. They do not rely on market insight or flawless execution, but on principles that are accessible, repeatable, and supported by evidence. For those who prioritise long-term success over short-term excitement, index funds offer a compelling and well-proven path to wealth accumulation.

In a marketplace often characterised by noise, complexity, and unnecessary costs, index funds provide a refreshing antidote. They represent the quiet triumph of rationality over hype, structure over speculation, and patience over performance-chasing. For most investors, they are not just a good option—they are the best one.

The Dangers of Overtrading

In investing, more activity does not equate to better results. In fact, frequent trading—commonly known as overtrading—is one of the most insidious threats to long-term wealth accumulation. It undermines compounding, increases costs, magnifies emotional errors, and encourages the illusion of control where none exists. Yet in the modern financial landscape, with real-time data, low-cost trading platforms, and an ever-present stream of market commentary, investors are increasingly seduced by the idea that success comes from constant action. The reality, however, is that excessive buying and selling rarely enhances returns. More often, it quietly erodes them.

Overtrading is not simply a matter of how many transactions an investor executes, but of why those trades are made. At its heart lies a psychological tension: the desire to be seen as proactive, decisive, and in control. This is understandable. Financial markets can feel overwhelming, and doing nothing in the face of volatility or opportunity seems counterintuitive. But many of these reactions are not based on strategy—they are responses to emotion: fear, greed, boredom, or the compulsive need to respond to every fluctuation.

The costs of overtrading are both direct and indirect. The most visible cost is transactional. Every trade incurs a fee, however small. These costs accumulate rapidly when trading becomes habitual. Even with the advent of low-commission platforms, spreads between bid and ask prices still represent a hidden tax on activity. For active traders moving in and out of positions frequently, these seemingly minor frictions can compound into significant performance drag over time.

Then there is the matter of tax. In jurisdictions with capital gains taxes, realising profits through frequent trades crystallises tax liabilities more quickly than long-term investing. This reduces the amount of capital left to reinvest and compound. Tax-efficiency, often overlooked in discussions of investing, is a critical determinant of net returns. Investors who hold positions over long periods defer these tax events and benefit more fully from compounding. Those who trade frequently disrupt this cycle and pay the price.

Beyond fees and taxes lies a subtler, yet more damaging consequence: the erosion of investment returns through poor timing. Multiple studies, including those by Morningstar and Dalbar, have highlighted a persistent gap between fund performance and investor performance. In simple terms, the average investor earns less than the funds they invest in—because they tend to buy high and sell low. This behaviour is often driven by attempts to outmanoeuvre short-term market movements. The more frequently an investor trades, the greater the likelihood they will mistime the market.

A striking example of this can be seen in the aftermath of the 2008 financial crisis. Investors who sold during the depths of the market collapse—believing they were avoiding further losses—often missed the early stages of the recovery, which delivered some of the strongest returns in modern history. Similarly, during the COVID-19 crash in early 2020, markets fell sharply only to rebound with unprecedented speed. Those who panicked and sold struggled to re-enter before the rebound gained pace, while those who remained invested benefitted from the rapid recovery. Frequent traders, attempting to anticipate each move, were more likely to miss the turn.

Overtrading is also fuelled by the cognitive bias of overconfidence. Many investors, especially those with some experience or early success, begin to believe they possess an edge—an ability to read the market or time entries and exits with accuracy. This belief is rarely borne out in practice. Markets are complex, and short-term movements are largely driven by a mixture of noise, sentiment, and randomness. The more one trades on perceived insights, the more one exposes themselves to this randomness, mistaking luck for skill.

There is also an element of addiction in overtrading. For some, the act of trading becomes a form of stimulation. The rush of making decisions, the dopamine hit of a successful trade, and the validation of being right create a powerful feedback loop. Over time, this can lead to compulsive behaviour, where trading is driven more by emotional satisfaction than by sound financial reasoning. In such cases, investing ceases to be about long-term goals and becomes a form of speculation—or worse, entertainment.

Real-world data continues to reinforce the dangers of excessive trading. A well-known study by Brad Barber and Terrance Odean analysed brokerage accounts over several years and found that investors who traded the most earned significantly lower returns than those who traded less frequently. The most active traders, despite their confidence and effort, consistently underperformed. The study's conclusion was stark: "Trading is hazardous to your wealth."

By contrast, the most successful investors—those whose names are invoked with reverence—are known not for their hyperactivity but for their patience. Warren Buffett famously described his ideal holding period as "forever," and he has repeatedly emphasised the value of buying quality businesses and allowing them to grow over time. His success stems not from identifying short-term price movements, but from understanding long-term value and resisting the impulse to act unnecessarily. The same principle applies to ordinary investors. Long-term investing, underpinned by a disciplined strategy and minimal interference, tends to outperform reactive trading.

That is not to suggest that all buying and selling is inherently flawed. There are legitimate reasons to adjust a portfolio: rebalancing, responding to life events, or correcting genuine mistakes. However, these actions are purposeful, infrequent, and grounded in a broader plan. Overtrading, by contrast, is characterised by impulsivity and the absence of clear strategy. It is not responsive—it is reactive.

One of the most effective antidotes to overtrading is automation. By setting up automatic contributions, predetermined rebalancing schedules, and rule-based strategies, investors can remove the temptation to trade based on emotion. Automation instils discipline, reduces the influence of daily noise, and ensures that decisions are made according to plan rather than panic. It shifts the emphasis from performance to process—a subtle but transformative shift.

Education also plays a vital role. Understanding the long-term behaviour of markets, the impact of compounding, and the historical patterns of investor psychology helps contextualise short-term volatility. It builds confidence in staying the course and resisting the urge to intervene unnecessarily. A well-informed investor is less likely to be swayed by headlines or short-term trends and more likely to focus on their overarching goals.

Advisers and financial planners can reinforce this discipline by acting as behavioural coaches. Their role is not merely to recommend products, but to help clients stay aligned with their objectives, especially when fear or excitement threatens to derail their plan. They provide perspective, remind investors of the bigger picture, and discourage reactive decisions that may feel urgent but are often misguided.

Ultimately, the most powerful lesson about overtrading is that restraint is a strength, not a weakness. In a world that glorifies action and rewards immediacy, the discipline to remain still can be remarkably effective. Investing is not a performance—it is a practice. It rewards patience, clarity, and consistency far more than hustle and hyperactivity. By resisting the lure of constant trading, investors not only preserve their capital but reclaim their time, focus, and peace of mind.

Financial success is not about making brilliant decisions every day. It is about making a few good decisions, sticking to them, and allowing them to unfold over time. The paradox of investing is that doing less often results in having more. The dangers of overtrading lie not just in lost returns, but in lost opportunity—the opportunity to let wealth grow undisturbed, to benefit from the quiet force of compounding, and to enjoy the freedom that comes from a strategy that does not demand constant attention.

For most investors, the best course is not to outsmart the market, but to outlast it. That requires endurance, not excitement. It requires a plan, not a prediction. And above all, it requires the discipline to know when not to act.

How to Set Up a Passive Investment Strategy

Passive investing is not merely a financial tactic; it is a philosophy that champions simplicity, patience, and long-term thinking. While the investment industry often markets complexity—trading strategies, market timing models, proprietary funds—the passive approach is refreshingly straightforward. At its core, it is about capturing market returns through low-cost, diversified instruments and allowing compounding to work over time with minimal interference. Yet despite its simplicity, building an effective passive investment strategy requires thoughtful planning and an appreciation of a few key principles that underpin its success.

The first step in constructing a passive investment plan is to establish a clear understanding of personal financial goals. Investing should never be an isolated exercise; it must serve a broader purpose. These goals might include building a retirement fund, creating a safety net for one's family, saving for a child's education, or attaining financial independence. The clarity of purpose provides a framework for all future decisions—what to invest in, how much risk to assume, and over what time horizon to evaluate progress. Without this anchor, even the most efficient investment strategy risks becoming a mechanical routine devoid of meaning or consistency.

With objectives clearly defined, attention turns to time horizon and risk tolerance. These two factors determine the appropriate asset allocation—the blend of equities, bonds, and possibly other asset classes in a portfolio. A younger investor with decades before retirement can afford greater exposure to equities, absorbing short-term volatility in exchange for higher long-term growth potential. Conversely, someone nearing retirement might prioritise capital preservation and income, favouring bonds or cash-equivalents. There is no single formula; each allocation must reflect not only financial circumstances but also psychological comfort. A well-designed portfolio must be sustainable in both market turbulence and peace of mind.

Passive investing is most commonly executed through index funds and exchange-traded funds (ETFs). These instruments are constructed to track the performance of a specific index, such as the FTSE All-Share, the MSCI World, or the Bloomberg Global Aggregate Bond Index. Their appeal lies in their simplicity and efficiency—they offer broad market exposure at a fraction of the cost of actively managed funds. Choosing a mix of index funds that reflect the desired asset allocation ensures diversification and keeps the strategy aligned with long-term objectives.

Consider a practical example. A thirty-year-old professional might decide on an 80/20 allocation—eighty percent equities and twenty percent bonds. Within the equity portion, they might select a global stock index fund and a domestic equities fund to balance international and home-market exposure. For the bond portion, a total bond market index fund might provide sufficient diversification. By holding just three funds, this individual captures a vast swath of global capital markets, spreading risk across thousands of companies and government issuers with a strategy that requires little maintenance.

Once the funds are selected, automation becomes a critical ally. The cornerstone of passive investing is regularity—investing fixed amounts at consistent intervals regardless of market conditions. This can be achieved by setting up monthly direct debits into investment accounts. This process, often referred to as pound-cost averaging, reduces the emotional component of investing by removing the decision of *when* to invest. Contributions continue automatically through market highs and lows, ensuring consistent accumulation and reducing the temptation to react to short-term volatility.

Alongside automation, cost awareness is essential. Even within the passive universe, fund fees can vary. While all index funds are generally cheaper than their actively managed counterparts, differences in expense ratios still matter. A fund charging 0.40% annually may not sound expensive, but compared to one charging 0.10%, the impact over a few decades of compounding is substantial. Every basis point saved contributes directly to net returns. Investors should pay attention not only to fund fees but also to account charges, platform fees, and the bid-ask spread in ETFs.

After the structure is in place, the focus should shift to maintenance—not active tinkering, but thoughtful oversight. The primary maintenance task is periodic rebalancing. Over time, market movements will cause the asset allocation to drift. Equities may outperform and grow beyond their intended weight, increasing portfolio risk. Rebalancing involves selling some of the outperforming assets and reinvesting in underrepresented ones to restore the original allocation. This discipline not only keeps the portfolio aligned with risk preferences but also encourages a counter-cyclical behaviour: buying low and selling high.

This act of rebalancing, however, must be guided by rules rather than impulse. Many investors choose to rebalance once or twice a year or when allocations deviate beyond pre-set thresholds. The key is to systematise it. Reacting emotionally—especially during market corrections—can lead to ill-timed trades and loss of discipline. A rule-based approach ensures that decisions are made methodically, not emotionally.

Tax considerations must also be accounted for, particularly for investors building substantial portfolios. Using tax-advantaged accounts, such as ISAs or pensions in the UK, can dramatically enhance long-term returns by shielding gains and income from tax. Investors with taxable accounts should also be aware of capital gains liabilities and strategies such as tax-loss harvesting, where losses are deliberately realised to offset gains and reduce overall tax exposure. Though passive investing emphasises simplicity, tax optimisation remains an area where strategic thought can add genuine value.

Perhaps the most underestimated component of a successful passive strategy is behavioural resilience. Markets will fluctuate—sometimes violently. Economic headlines will stir anxiety or greed. Friends will share stories of spectacular gains from speculative trades. Temptations will arise to adjust the portfolio, chase hot sectors, or abandon the plan altogether. Yet the essence of passive investing is to *not* react. The structure is built for endurance, not excitement. It is designed to withstand crises, bubbles, corrections, and booms. The investor's job is to trust the process and let time do the work.

This is easier said than done. But anchoring the strategy in personal goals—reminding oneself why the portfolio exists—can provide the necessary perspective. Viewing investing not as a daily scorecard but as a long-term effort to support meaningful life outcomes creates emotional distance from market fluctuations. In this way, passive investing is not merely a financial discipline but a psychological one. It rewards those who can delay gratification, remain consistent, and stay grounded amidst uncertainty.

Passive strategies are not just for the financially sophisticated. In fact, their greatest strength is that they are accessible to anyone, regardless of income, education, or financial background. With as little as a few hundred pounds, an individual can gain exposure to global markets, benefit from professional fund structures, and begin building wealth incrementally. This democratisation of investing is one of the quiet revolutions of our time—empowering people not through complex products or secret insights, but through simplicity, discipline, and transparency.

For retirees or those approaching financial independence, the strategy evolves but the philosophy remains intact. Income-producing index funds, such as those focused on dividend-paying stocks or bonds, can provide regular cash flow. The focus shifts from accumulation to withdrawal planning, but the need for diversification, cost control, and behavioural consistency remains. Passive investing scales gracefully with life's stages—requiring only that the investor adjusts allocation in accordance with changing needs, not that they abandon the principles that brought them success.

In an industry often defined by overcomplication and salesmanship, the passive investor quietly reclaims agency. They choose to engage with markets on their own terms, guided by evidence rather than marketing, and clarity rather than noise. Their wealth is not the product of frantic trades or contrarian bets, but of steady compounding, efficient structure, and the conviction to do less, not more.

To set up a passive investment strategy, then, is to take control—not by trying to predict markets, but by aligning capital with intention. It is about building a process that serves your life, not the market's cycles. It is about embracing the discipline of simplicity and the power of patience. And above all, it is about trusting that slow, steady progress, anchored in structure and guided by purpose, will ultimately lead not only to financial success but to greater freedom, stability, and peace of mind.

Letting Your Investments Work for You

The essence of passive investing lies in a liberating idea: that with the right structure and habits in place, your money can grow quietly and consistently, largely without your daily intervention. This concept—letting your investments work for you—is not about financial laziness or neglect, but about intelligent design and behavioural restraint. It represents a radical shift in mindset, from labouring over decisions to empowering your capital to compound over time. Achieving financial success with minimal effort is not only possible—it is, for many, the most sustainable path to long-term prosperity.

In the fast-paced and often hyper-analytical world of personal finance, there is a persistent narrative that effort and expertise are prerequisites for investment success. Media pundits analyse markets with surgical precision, influencers share trade-by-trade breakdowns, and financial platforms inundate users with real-time data and news. Against this backdrop, doing less can feel countercultural—even irresponsible. Yet the data consistently shows that investors who embrace simplicity and consistency tend to outperform those who trade frequently or tinker endlessly with their portfolios.

Letting your investments work for you begins with clarity. It requires recognising that wealth is built not through relentless hustle, but through the compounding of returns over time. Compound interest, often described as the eighth wonder of the world, operates best when it is left undisturbed. By reinvesting earnings and allowing growth to accrue upon growth, investors create a self-reinforcing cycle that accelerates wealth accumulation. The only real ingredient this mechanism demands is time—and the patience to avoid interfering unnecessarily.

Consider an investor who sets aside £300 per month into a globally diversified index fund. Without attempting to time the market, pick stocks, or outmanoeuvre economic cycles, they continue this practice steadily over 30 years. Assuming a modest average return, their portfolio grows to a substantial sum—thanks not to brilliance or effort, but to consistency and discipline. The investor has, in effect, built a financial machine that runs on autopilot. Their role is not to drive it every day, but to fuel it regularly and avoid sabotaging its progress.

What makes this strategy so compelling is its accessibility. You don't need a degree in finance, insider connections, or a sixth sense for markets. You need a plan, a structure, and the humility to let that structure do its work. This approach is not about foregoing responsibility—it's about placing your energy where it truly counts: setting clear goals, selecting appropriate investments, and sticking to the plan. By automating contributions, using low-cost index funds, and rebalancing occasionally, you establish a system that minimises the need for constant decision-making while maximising long-term output.

The psychological benefits of this approach are just as important as the financial ones. Investing can be emotionally taxing. Market downturns spark fear. Booms trigger envy or greed. News headlines provoke anxiety. Every price movement invites a reaction. But when your strategy is designed to operate in the background, these emotional triggers lose much of their power. You stop viewing your portfolio as something to manage reactively and begin to see it as an ongoing, stable asset that is quietly aligned with your broader life aspirations.

This detachment does not imply apathy. Rather, it enables greater focus on what really matters: your career, your relationships, your health, and your contributions to the world. Money becomes a tool that works for you, rather than a constant source of attention or stress. It supports your life, rather than dominating it. When your investments are structured to grow autonomously, you are freed from the need to micromanage and are better able to pursue a richer, more meaningful existence.

Real-world examples abound. Many of the wealthiest individuals do not spend their time watching stock tickers or making daily trades. They've constructed portfolios of durable assets—equities, property, income-generating instruments—that appreciate over time with minimal interference. Their secret is not aggressive trading but leverage of time, diversification, and consistency. For instance, Jack Bogle, the founder of Vanguard and a pioneer of index investing, emphasised repeatedly that successful investing is about "staying the course." His own strategy was disarmingly simple: invest in low-cost index funds and let the market do the heavy lifting.

This philosophy also explains the rising popularity of target-date funds, especially in workplace pensions. These funds automatically adjust asset allocation based on the investor's time horizon, gradually becoming more conservative as retirement approaches. The investor chooses a fund aligned with their expected retirement year and makes regular contributions. The fund takes care of the rest—managing risk, diversifying across markets, and maintaining balance. It's a prime example of investments working for the individual with minimal oversight.

Technology has only strengthened this capability. Robo-advisers, digital investing apps, and automatic savings tools now make it easier than ever to implement a hands-off strategy. You can schedule deposits, allocate funds according to your goals, and even set parameters for automatic rebalancing. These systems, while requiring a bit of initial setup, then perform with quiet reliability, often outperforming more complex, human-led efforts. The investor's task becomes less about decision-making and more about stewardship—ensuring that their goals remain in sight while the system does its job.

There are, of course, moments when some intervention is required. Life changes—such as marriage, career shifts, inheritance, or children—may warrant revisiting your plan. But these are strategic adjustments, not day-to-day reactions. They reaffirm the idea that your investments are partners in your life goals, not puzzles to be solved every week.

One of the subtler advantages of this approach is behavioural. The less you interfere with your investments, the less likely you are to make costly errors. Research in behavioural finance consistently shows that investors harm their own returns by buying and selling at inopportune times—buying high out of excitement, selling low out of fear. By building a system that limits the opportunity or temptation to act rashly, passive investors often achieve better outcomes simply by getting out of their own way.

It's worth noting, too, that letting your investments work for you doesn't mean setting them up blindly. It means making conscious, informed choices early on—choices about risk tolerance, diversification, fees, and tax efficiency—and then allowing those choices to mature. This foundation is not rigid; it can evolve with your circumstances. But the key is that change should be intentional, not impulsive.

Critically, this model challenges a pervasive cultural assumption: that financial success must be hard-earned through constant toil. Passive investing suggests something more empowering—that once a thoughtful structure is in place, it can carry you forward with minimal friction. This doesn't diminish the value of discipline or learning. On the contrary, it reinforces them. Discipline lies in resisting needless change. Learning is about refining strategy, not reinventing it monthly.

In personal finance, complexity often masquerades as sophistication. But simplicity, when grounded in sound principles, is not simplistic—it is elegant, effective, and liberating. Letting your investments work for you is the financial equivalent of designing a well-run machine. You do the important work of designing and calibrating it, then trust it to operate. You don't need to be at the controls every moment; you simply need to make sure it's still aligned with your destination.

Financial independence, for many, is not about amassing enormous wealth. It's about freedom—freedom from worry, from dependency, and from the tyranny of constant financial decision-making. A passive investment strategy, once established, becomes a silent engine powering this freedom. It doesn't shout. It doesn't demand. It simply performs.

This is the quiet triumph of thoughtful investing. With time, patience, and structure, your money begins to serve you—not the other way around. And in doing so, it delivers not just financial returns, but the rarest of commodities: peace of mind.

Chapter 9
The Power of Automation - Set and Forget Wealth Building

In today's personal finance landscape, where complexity and speed often dominate, simplicity and steady habits have become surprisingly scarce virtues. Everywhere you turn—whether it's the relentless churn of financial news or the ceaseless commentary on social media—there's a strong pull to overanalyse, react on impulse, or endlessly second-guess decisions that, by their nature, are meant to unfold over years, if not decades. Yet, amidst this whirlwind, automation quietly offers a remedy. It equips investors with a framework that builds wealth not through dramatic timing or constant vigilance but through systems that hum along reliably, free from the distractions of emotion. Automation doesn't merely streamline investing; it fundamentally changes it—cutting through behavioural traps, fostering discipline, and making sustained wealth accumulation something both achievable and, dare I say, sustainable.

At its essence, automation involves shifting responsibility from the fallible human hand to technology. This might sound straightforward, even mechanical, but its consequences run deep. Human beings are, frankly, prone to errors when managing money. We fall prey to fear, greed, overconfidence, and shortsightedness. Behavioural finance has documented time and again how investors often sabotage their own returns with poorly timed decisions. Automating critical aspects of investment behaviour lets us sidestep these pitfalls, crafting a process that marches on regardless of market mood swings or personal whims.

One of the simplest yet most effective expressions of automation is dollar-cost averaging. Instead of dumping a lump sum into the market all at once, this approach involves investing a fixed sum at regular intervals, no matter what's happening on the ticker. The beauty lies in its counterintuitive logic: buying more when prices dip and less when they climb, smoothing out volatility over the long haul. It's no crystal ball—profits aren't guaranteed, nor does it shield you from losses—but it imposes a rhythm that cuts through the paralysis of "timing the market." Combine this with automated payments, such as direct debits to an investment account, and you have a remarkably efficient wealth-building tool.

Look at automated pension contributions as a larger-scale example. Workplace retirement schemes have long leaned on automation to encourage consistent saving. Contributions are deducted from pay before you even see the money—out of sight, out of mind, as the saying goes. This taps into a psychological truth: we don't miss what we don't see. Saving becomes the default, rather than a chore. Over decades, those steady investments, channelled into diversified funds, can grow into impressive portfolios—all achieved with minimal effort or ongoing thought from the investor.

But automation isn't just about regularity; it's about alignment. Portfolios naturally drift as markets move. What started as a balanced 70% equities and 30% bonds mix might skew heavily towards equities after a bull run, pushing risk beyond what the investor is comfortable with. That's where rebalancing comes in—returning the portfolio to its intended allocation and maintaining the desired balance of risk and reward.

Today, many platforms and robo-advisors automate this rebalancing process, taking emotion out of the equation. This guards against the all-too-common trap of chasing hot performers or hesitating to trim winners out of fear. Instead, rules-based automation enforces discipline, ensuring portfolios stay true to their original purpose rather than market fads.

Thanks to advances in technology, all of this is more accessible than ever. Investing apps, digital advisory services, and financial automation tools have opened the door to wealth-building for a far broader audience. Gone are the days when you needed costly advisers or deep expertise in portfolio theory. Whether it's setting up recurring payments, spreading funds across low-cost ETFs, or enabling automatic rebalancing, the infrastructure exists to support investors at every level. These tools aren't merely convenient; they're empowering. They lighten the cognitive load, remove barriers to entry, and encourage steady engagement without demanding obsessive focus.

Robo-advisors are a particularly interesting fusion of automation and personalisation. By analysing your risk appetite, objectives, and timeframe, they craft tailored portfolios managed and rebalanced automatically. Their fees tend to be lower than traditional advisory models, and their user-friendly interfaces favour clarity over technical jargon. For anyone who might otherwise feel overwhelmed by financial decisions, this offers structure, reassurance, and peace of mind—all running on autopilot.

Yet the true power of automation goes beyond mere mechanics. It lies in what it frees up for the investor. When your investment routine runs itself, the mental energy once devoted to market speculation, doubt, and news-cycle noise can be redirected toward what matters most—whether that's family, career, health, or simply enjoying life. Financial well-being becomes less a daily worry and more a quiet background process supporting broader life goals.

Crucially, automation brings consistency—arguably the cornerstone of successful investing. Doing the right thing repeatedly, over time, is where the real magic happens. Automation strips away the unpredictability of human nature, making disciplined action effortless. No need to summon willpower each month to transfer money, pick funds, or wrestle with market conditions. The system does the work, reliably and without fail. And, as countless examples demonstrate, compounding returns over time is the engine driving wealth.

Consider a typical couple who start investing modestly in their thirties, automating pension payments and channeling savings monthly into diversified index funds. They don't make headlines, don't trade actively, and rarely obsess over their balances. Yet by their sixties, they've amassed a substantial nest egg—outperforming many who earned more or spent endless hours managing their portfolios. Their advantage? A system that kept working day after day, year after year, without fuss or deviation.

That said, automation is no cure-all. It demands thoughtful setup and periodic review to ensure it remains aligned with changing financial situations and goals. Left unattended for decades, an automated plan can drift or become outdated. But paired with intentional check-ins, it forms a rock-solid foundation for effective investing.

There's also a subtle psychological shift that occurs when investors begin to see automation not as a shortcut, but as a strategy. It reframes what it means to be financially responsible. Wealth-building no longer hinges on constant vigilance or exceptional intellect. Instead, it becomes a matter of design: crafting a system that quietly works on your behalf. It's about placing trust—not in fickle markets or pundits, but in process. Designing a life where financial decisions serve you unobtrusively, rather than demanding your constant attention.

This philosophy upends the traditional idea that success requires relentless effort. In most walks of life, more effort yields better results. Investing, however, often rewards the opposite: too much effort leads to overthinking, overreacting, and ultimately, underperformance. Automation flips this script. It values restraint. It elevates structure above spontaneity. It invites us to swap impulse for intention.

Looking ahead, as technology continues to evolve, the case for automation in wealth-building only grows stronger. Advances in machine learning, smoother user experiences, and tighter integration between banking and investing will make it ever easier to adopt robust, automated strategies. The investor's role won't vanish—it will transform. From decision-maker to architect. From trader to steward.

Ultimately, the greatest gift automation offers is freedom. Freedom from anxiety, indecision, and the relentless noise of markets and media. Freedom to live fully, secure in the knowledge that your money is growing quietly, steadily, and in line with your values and aspirations.

To automate wisely is to acknowledge our own limitations and design around them. It is to entrust our financial future not to predictions but to process. And in stepping away from the noise, we make space for something far more potent: the slow, steady, silent build-up of wealth. Let the systems do the heavy lifting—so you can focus on the life you're truly building.

The Benefits of Automated Investing

Investing, at its most effective, is not about reacting swiftly to market movements or attempting to outmanoeuvre volatility through sheer insight. Instead, it is about adhering to a well-constructed strategy with patience and consistency over the long term. Yet this ideal often clashes with reality. The human mind, wired for survival and quick reactions, is poorly equipped for the emotional and cognitive demands of investing. Fear, greed, overconfidence, loss aversion, and the constant noise of financial media all conspire to derail even the most well-intentioned investor. This is where automation offers a powerful solution: by removing human error from the investment process, it creates a more stable, disciplined, and ultimately successful approach to building wealth.

At its essence, automated investing refers to the use of systems—digital tools, scheduled processes, and algorithm-driven platforms—that make investment decisions or execute transactions without requiring manual intervention each time. The primary advantage is that it bypasses the emotional and behavioural biases that so often hinder rational financial behaviour. Rather than relying on the investor to act consistently, automation ensures that beneficial habits are carried out regularly, even when the market feels chaotic or the investor is tempted to act otherwise.

Human error in investing is rarely technical; it is psychological. Decades of behavioural finance research, particularly the work of Daniel Kahneman and Amos Tversky, has shown how cognitive biases influence decision-making. Investors frequently chase past performance, panic during downturns, or become paralysed by information overload. Consider the investor who exits the market during a crash, locking in losses, and then waits too long to re-enter, missing the rebound. Or the one who pours money into a "hot" sector at its peak, only to see it decline shortly thereafter. These are not isolated incidents—they are patterns. And they are driven more by emotion than logic.

Automated investing helps eliminate these patterns by embedding decisions into a pre-defined structure. Instead of having to decide each month whether to invest, how much to contribute, or which assets to buy, these steps are handled automatically. Scheduled contributions, portfolio allocations, and even rebalancing routines can be programmed to occur at regular intervals. This does not simply reduce the burden of decision-making; it removes the window of opportunity for behavioural missteps. The fewer moments of emotional vulnerability, the greater the chance of staying on track.

A compelling example lies in the use of direct debits to fund investment accounts. A young professional might automate a monthly transfer from their current account to a stocks and shares ISA, with the money allocated to a low-cost global index fund. Once set, this process continues silently, regardless of headlines, sentiment, or market volatility. Over years, these contributions accumulate, and the compounding effect begins to take hold. The investor is not required to monitor the market or adjust their behaviour; the system does the work. What they avoid—missing a contribution during a period of uncertainty or delaying investment due to fear—is as important as what they gain.

Another advantage of automation is its role in maintaining investment discipline through rebalancing. Over time, a portfolio's asset allocation can drift as different sectors or asset classes perform unevenly. Without intervention, a portfolio that began with 70% equities and 30% bonds might shift to a riskier composition, especially during a sustained equity rally. Rebalancing restores the intended allocation, typically by selling portions of overperforming assets and reallocating to underrepresented areas. This process can be emotionally difficult—selling what is rising in value to buy what is lagging. But when done automatically, according to preset rules, it becomes a rational, unemotional task. This not only maintains the investor's risk profile but encourages a counter-cyclical approach that enhances long-term performance.

Automation also addresses a common source of inertia in personal finance: the belief that investing requires expertise or constant attention. Many individuals delay investing altogether because they feel unqualified, overwhelmed, or unsure where to begin. Automated platforms—particularly robo-advisors—lower this barrier significantly. With a few simple inputs (goals, risk tolerance, time horizon), these platforms can construct diversified portfolios and manage them on the investor's behalf. For a modest fee, they deliver institutional-quality strategies to everyday investors, removing the need for deep knowledge or frequent decision-making. This democratises access to smart investing, enabling more people to benefit from capital markets without becoming financial experts.

There is also a time-saving benefit that should not be overlooked. Time is a scarce and valuable resource. Constant portfolio monitoring, reading financial news, analysing economic data—these tasks consume energy and attention. Automation gives this time back. With systems in place, the investor can focus on their career, family, health, or personal growth, knowing that their financial plan is progressing in the background. This sense of detachment is not careless—it is intentional. It reflects a trust in process rather than performance-chasing.

Of course, automation does not eliminate all risk. Markets still fluctuate. Economic downturns still occur. But what automation offers is protection against self-inflicted harm. It ensures that the investor does not compound market risk with behavioural risk. By following a consistent, rule-based approach, the investor can withstand volatility more effectively and benefit from the market's long-term upward trend.

An illustrative example can be found in retirement savings. Automatic enrolment in workplace pension schemes has significantly increased participation rates. Before automation, many employees failed to opt into pension plans, often citing procrastination or a lack of understanding. With automatic enrolment and default contribution rates, participation became the norm rather than the exception. This simple structural shift led to a measurable increase in retirement preparedness—not because people changed their financial habits, but because the system changed around them.

The same principle applies across the investing spectrum. Whether it's setting up a monthly investment plan, enabling automatic dividend reinvestment, or configuring rules-based rebalancing, each act of automation strengthens the investor's position—not through superior insight, but through superior structure.

Importantly, automation also fosters better behaviour over time. Investors who see consistent progress, even if incremental, are more likely to stay engaged and committed. This creates a positive feedback loop. Regular contributions lead to visible growth. Visible growth reinforces commitment. Commitment leads to continued contributions. Automation sets this cycle in motion and sustains it through both good and difficult times.

There is also a psychological relief in knowing that something is being done. Money is being invested. Wealth is being built. Progress is happening, even when life becomes busy or unpredictable. This alleviates stress and reduces the tendency to react impulsively during periods of uncertainty. In a very real sense, automation is not just a financial tool—it is a form of emotional insurance.

For those who are sceptical of relinquishing control, it is worth remembering that automation can be adjusted. It is not rigid or irreversible. Contributions can be increased or paused. Portfolios can be re-evaluated. But the default action is always the right one: to continue. This bias towards action—structured, not reactive—is what sets automation apart from traditional, discretionary investing.

Ultimately, the benefits of automated investing are both practical and psychological. It enforces discipline, reduces errors, and encourages consistency. It removes the emotional weight of financial decision-making and replaces it with clarity and structure. And it empowers investors to focus less on trying to outsmart the market and more on building a sustainable, purpose-driven financial life.

Letting automation take the reins is not about doing less; it is about doing what matters most, more reliably. In an environment where every decision can be coloured by emotion or distraction, automation acts as a safeguard. It replaces fragile willpower with durable systems. It transforms good intentions into measurable outcomes. And over time, it is often this quiet, methodical approach that leads to the most meaningful financial success.

Dollar-Cost Averaging (DCA)

Investing, for many, is as much a psychological discipline as it is a financial one. Markets move with volatility, investors respond with emotion, and the combination often leads to poor decisions and missed opportunities. Amid this uncertainty, Dollar-Cost Averaging (DCA) offers a rational, systematic approach that simplifies the investment process, reduces emotional friction, and, most importantly, minimises timing risk. At its core, DCA is the practice of investing a fixed amount of money at regular intervals—regardless of market performance. This consistency brings discipline to investing and helps to even out the inevitable fluctuations in asset prices over time.

The basic mechanics of DCA are straightforward. Instead of trying to time the market—investing a lump sum at what may or may not be an advantageous moment—the investor commits to investing a set amount at regular intervals. When prices are high, that fixed contribution purchases fewer shares or units. When prices are low, it purchases more. Over time, this strategy smooths out the average cost per unit, hence the name. It avoids the pitfall of investing everything just before a downturn and reduces the emotional burden of wondering whether now is the "right" time to invest.

The elegance of DCA lies in its simplicity, but its benefits go far deeper than mechanical regularity. One of the most important is psychological protection. Investors are often paralysed by the fear of making a mistake. When markets are soaring, they worry about buying at the top. When markets are falling, they hesitate for fear of further declines. This indecision can lead to long delays in entering the market or worse—reactive behaviour such as buying at peaks and selling in panics. DCA cuts through this hesitation. By automating the investment process and detaching it from the investor's mood or market sentiment, it promotes consistency and emotional detachment.

Consider a hypothetical investor who begins investing £500 per month into a diversified index fund. Over the course of a year, the fund's value fluctuates—sometimes rising, sometimes falling—but the investor maintains their monthly contributions. When the fund drops, their £500 buys more units. When it rises, it buys fewer. The result is an average price that reflects the full range of market conditions. While others may be trying (and often failing) to buy at the lowest point or avoid downturns entirely, the DCA investor steadily accumulates assets at a blended cost, without the stress of timing decisions.

Real-world data supports the wisdom of this approach. While lump-sum investing may, over long timeframes, statistically yield slightly higher returns in upward-trending markets, the difference is often marginal—and it comes with higher psychological strain. For investors who are risk-averse, hesitant, or operating with uncertain market timing, DCA offers a more tolerable path into the market. It enables participation without pressure and builds confidence through gradual exposure.

Moreover, DCA aligns well with the way most people earn and save. Salaries are typically paid monthly. Expenses follow regular cycles. By synchronising investments with income—investing a fixed portion each month—individuals integrate investing into their financial routine. It becomes habitual rather than occasional. This routinisation is key to long-term success. It ensures that wealth-building becomes a consistent effort, not a sporadic activity dictated by whim or surplus cash.

There is also an inherent humility in the DCA approach—a recognition that the future is unknowable and that even the most experienced investors cannot reliably predict short-term market movements. Rather than betting on direction or trying to outguess the next market shift, DCA assumes that markets will fluctuate, sometimes wildly, and that the best course is not to react, but to continue. This humility, far from being a weakness, is a strategic strength. It replaces hubris with process and overconfidence with discipline.

This approach is particularly effective during periods of heightened volatility. When markets are unpredictable, and sentiment swings between fear and euphoria, DCA provides a calming structure. It removes the need to constantly interpret events or assess whether prices are "too high" or "low enough." In downturns, it turns adversity into advantage—buying more units when prices are depressed. In rallies, it continues to participate without overextending. Over time, the investor builds a portfolio that reflects a wide range of market conditions and benefits from the natural ebb and flow of prices.

One of the most illustrative real-world scenarios for DCA was the 2008 global financial crisis. Investors who attempted to time the bottom often found themselves paralysed by uncertainty, waiting for the dust to settle. By the time they felt confident enough to re-enter the market, prices had often already rebounded. In contrast, investors who maintained regular contributions throughout the downturn acquired assets at significantly lower valuations. When the recovery began, they were well-positioned to benefit. Their returns were not the result of foresight, but of consistency. DCA allowed them to buy into the market at its weakest points—not by design, but by process.

Likewise, during the COVID-19 market shock in early 2020, DCA again demonstrated its strength. Those with automated contributions continued investing through the sharp decline and subsequent rapid recovery. While others debated whether to sell, wait, or buy, DCA investors stayed the course. The speed of the rebound meant that many who paused contributions missed a significant portion of gains. Meanwhile, automated investors were rewarded for their steadfastness.

It is worth noting that DCA does not promise immunity from loss. Like any investment strategy, it is subject to market risk. If the market experiences a prolonged downturn or an asset class underperforms significantly, DCA will not prevent losses. What it does offer is a structured, psychologically sustainable way to participate in markets without succumbing to the pressures of timing. It provides a framework that emphasises process over prediction, which is precisely where many investors falter.

Furthermore, DCA complements other long-term strategies such as passive investing and portfolio diversification. By investing regularly into a diversified set of low-cost index funds, the investor not only benefits from price averaging but also from broad exposure to the market. This synergy creates a strategy that is low-maintenance, cost-effective, and behaviourally robust—well-suited to individual investors who want to build wealth without constant oversight or anxiety.

From a practical standpoint, implementing DCA has never been easier. Most investment platforms and pension providers offer options to set up recurring contributions. These can be aligned with salary dates and tailored to individual cash flow. Once established, the system runs automatically, removing the need for manual transfers or investment decisions each month. This automation amplifies the behavioural benefits of DCA, reducing friction and making consistency almost effortless.

There is also a philosophical resonance to DCA that appeals to many long-term investors. It reflects a commitment to steady progress rather than speculative leaps. It embodies a belief in the market's long-term potential and a willingness to weather its short-term storms. It is less about trying to win and more about ensuring you stay in the game. And over decades, staying in the game—compounding, accumulating, and avoiding costly errors—is often the most decisive factor in financial success.

Ultimately, Dollar-Cost Averaging is not a flashy strategy. It will not produce overnight riches or headlines. But what it lacks in drama, it makes up for in durability. It respects both the realities of the market and the psychology of the investor. It provides a method for building wealth that is resilient, accessible, and adaptable. For those who seek financial stability and growth without the burden of constant decision-making, DCA offers a powerful, evidence-based alternative. It shifts the question from "when should I invest?" to "how consistently can I invest?"—and in doing so, it aligns the process of wealth-building with the rhythm of real life.

Automated Retirement Contributions

Building a financially secure retirement is among the most important and long-term commitments an individual can make. Yet for many, it remains an intimidating, often delayed undertaking. This reluctance isn't always due to a lack of awareness; more often, it's the result of behavioural inertia, short-term financial pressures, or the psychological distance between today and a far-off future. One of the most effective solutions to these challenges is automated retirement contributions—an understated, highly efficient strategy that fosters consistent investing habits, reduces emotional interference, and helps grow wealth with minimal effort over time.

At its core, automating retirement contributions means systematically directing a portion of one's income into retirement accounts without needing to take action each time. This could involve employer-sponsored pension schemes, personal pensions, or self-invested personal pensions (SIPPs), depending on the individual's circumstances. The key characteristic is that contributions occur regularly, typically monthly, and are deducted directly from earnings or bank accounts. This ensures participation in long-term investing without the need for constant decision-making or willpower.

The behavioural benefits of automation are as important as the financial ones. Numerous studies in behavioural economics, including those led by Richard Thaler and Shlomo Benartzi, have demonstrated that default options and automated behaviours significantly increase retirement savings. Their research on the 'Save More Tomorrow' programme, for instance, showed that when employees were enrolled automatically in retirement contribution increases, participation rates soared. Most importantly, employees continued contributing at higher levels over time, primarily because the process required no ongoing effort or choice.

This behavioural insight speaks to a simple truth: people are more likely to do what is easy and automatic than what is effortful and optional. When contributions happen in the background—before money reaches a spending account—they are less likely to be missed or deferred. Automation eliminates the mental burden of deciding whether or how much to save each month. It turns investing into a background process, quietly and efficiently working in favour of the individual's long-term financial security.

The compounding effect of early and consistent contributions is profound. Consider a 25-year-old who begins investing £300 per month into a pension fund, set to increase by a modest amount in line with inflation. With consistent contributions, a well-diversified investment strategy, and the benefit of tax relief, that individual could potentially build a retirement portfolio worth several hundred thousand pounds by the time they reach their sixties. They may never have made a single active investment decision, but by setting up automated contributions early, they allowed time and the markets to do most of the heavy lifting.

Tax efficiency is another key advantage of automated retirement contributions. In the UK, pension contributions benefit from tax relief at an individual's marginal rate, effectively boosting the value of each pound invested. For basic-rate taxpayers, this means that a £100 contribution only costs £80 in net income; for higher-rate taxpayers, the net cost is even lower. By automating contributions, individuals ensure they consistently take advantage of this relief—something that many who rely on ad hoc investing often overlook or forget to claim in full. Additionally, workplace pensions frequently come with employer matching contributions, further amplifying the value of regular saving. Missing out on these matches due to inconsistent contributions is one of the most easily avoidable wealth-building mistakes.

Automated contributions also help smooth out the volatility of market timing. Since money is being invested regularly, the investor benefits from pound-cost averaging—buying more units when markets are low and fewer when they are high. This approach naturally distributes investment risk across time and reduces the likelihood of committing all funds at a market peak. Over decades, this disciplined accumulation can lead to a substantial portfolio built through hundreds of small, consistent investments rather than a few speculative decisions.

One of the most powerful aspects of automating retirement contributions is how it aligns personal finance with broader life rhythms. Salaries tend to be paid on a monthly cycle. Bills and essential spending occur on a regular basis. By linking investment to this cadence, saving becomes part of the flow rather than an additional burden. It requires no extraordinary motivation. It does not rely on surplus income. It simply happens. And because it happens consistently, it becomes a habit—quietly accumulating wealth without fanfare.

For many, this strategy also relieves the anxiety associated with investing. The pressure to time the market or choose the perfect moment to invest can lead to paralysis. The emotional rollercoaster of market cycles—particularly during downturns—can deter even the most financially literate from sticking to their plans. But when retirement contributions are automated, the investor is shielded from these psychological traps. They contribute whether the market is up or down, in fear or in euphoria. This removes the temptation to pause contributions in turbulent periods—pauses that often result in missing recoveries and long-term gains.

Moreover, automating retirement savings fosters a powerful psychological shift. The individual begins to view themselves not merely as someone who *should* invest but as someone who *is* investing. Identity follows action. Over time, the habit of regular contributions builds a sense of financial agency and responsibility. The investor begins to take quiet pride in their discipline. They are no longer at the mercy of short-term impulses or uncertain markets; they are working with a system designed to support long-term goals.

In practical terms, setting up automated retirement contributions has never been more accessible. Most employers in the UK now offer auto-enrolment pension schemes, where employees are automatically enrolled and contribute a minimum percentage of their salary, often supplemented by employer contributions. Those who are self-employed or earning outside traditional structures can establish direct debits into personal pensions or SIPPs, with options to increase contributions as their income grows.

Importantly, automation doesn't mean rigidity. Contribution levels can be reviewed and adjusted annually or in response to major life changes. Many pension providers now offer tools to project retirement income, helping individuals understand how their contributions translate into future security. Some platforms allow users to set contribution escalation features, automatically increasing contributions in line with salary rises or inflation. These adjustments maintain alignment with personal circumstances while preserving the core benefit of consistent, automated investing.

There's also an important intergenerational dimension to automated retirement planning. Parents who automate their own contributions model positive financial behaviour for their children. They demonstrate that investing is not a matter of wealth, luck, or timing, but of structure and consistency. In a world where financial literacy is increasingly essential yet seldom taught formally, such examples are invaluable.

While retirement planning is often framed as a distant goal, automation brings it into the present. It turns an abstract future need into a concrete, monthly action—small, manageable, and quietly transformative. It reflects a deeper principle: that building a life of financial independence is not about brilliance or timing, but about consistency, patience, and trust in the process.

In many ways, automated retirement contributions exemplify the best of modern investing. They combine behavioural insight, technological convenience, and financial efficiency into a strategy that works not just for the mathematically inclined or market-savvy, but for anyone willing to take the first step and let time do the rest. By starting early, setting up contributions, and letting them run in the background, individuals give themselves the greatest gift of all—peace of mind. Peace in knowing that while they live their life, their financial future is steadily taking shape, month by month, without needing them to chase returns or beat the market. That is the quiet power of automation—and its enduring legacy for the financially prepared.

Rebalancing Strategies for Long-Term Growth

The discipline of investing is often portrayed as a quest for the best opportunities—finding the next growth stock, timing market peaks and troughs, or chasing superior returns. Yet, much of successful wealth accumulation comes not from aggressive moves or dazzling insights but from a quieter, more deliberate act: maintaining alignment. This is where portfolio rebalancing plays a crucial role. Though often overlooked, rebalancing is fundamental to long-term investment success. It ensures that your financial strategy remains in harmony with your objectives, risk tolerance, and evolving life circumstances—regardless of how the markets behave.

At its essence, rebalancing is the act of returning your portfolio to its target asset allocation. When an investment plan is first created, it is usually structured around a deliberate balance of equities, bonds, cash, and possibly alternative assets. This mix reflects your goals, time horizon, and comfort with risk. But markets are dynamic, and over time, the performance of different asset classes causes your portfolio to drift. Equities may outperform, increasing their share of your holdings beyond what is appropriate for your risk profile. Conversely, bonds might decline or stagnate, leaving your portfolio exposed to greater volatility than you intended.

This gradual drift can significantly alter the risk and return characteristics of your portfolio. What began as a balanced plan—say, 60 percent equities and 40 percent bonds—may quietly become a much more aggressive allocation, such as 75/25, if equities have enjoyed a sustained rally. While this might seem beneficial in times of market strength, it also leaves you more vulnerable to sharp downturns. Conversely, if equities underperform, your portfolio may become overly conservative, limiting its growth potential and undermining your ability to meet long-term objectives. Rebalancing counters this drift by periodically adjusting allocations back to their original—or revised—targets.

The logic of rebalancing is both mathematical and behavioural. Mathematically, it enforces a discipline of buying low and selling high. If equities rise and exceed their target allocation, rebalancing involves selling some of those gains and reallocating to bonds or other underweight assets. This process captures profits and redistributes them to areas with greater upside potential. Behaviourally, it reduces the risk of performance-chasing and emotional investing. It encourages decisions based on a plan, not on sentiment. Rather than succumbing to euphoria when markets soar or panic when they fall, the rebalancing investor remains grounded in a clear structure.

There are several approaches to rebalancing, each with its advantages depending on personal preferences and circumstances. The most straightforward is time-based rebalancing. This involves reviewing and adjusting your portfolio at regular intervals—typically quarterly, semi-annually, or annually. This method imposes a rhythm on your investment maintenance, ensuring that the portfolio is not left to drift indefinitely. While it may result in occasional rebalancing when changes are minimal, its strength lies in predictability and ease of execution.

Another method is threshold-based rebalancing, where changes are triggered only when allocations deviate beyond a predetermined range—say, five or ten percentage points from the target. This approach is more responsive to actual market movement and can reduce unnecessary trades, which helps minimise costs and tax consequences. However, it requires more frequent monitoring and a willingness to act when thresholds are breached, which may be psychologically difficult during volatile periods.

A third, increasingly popular approach involves hybrid rebalancing—combining time and threshold elements. For instance, an investor may commit to reviewing the portfolio semi-annually but only making adjustments if deviations exceed certain limits. This method balances the benefits of regular oversight with the efficiency of threshold-based decisions.

Regardless of the method chosen, rebalancing should be framed not as a tactical move, but as a structural safeguard. It is not about reacting to market conditions, but about preserving the strategic intent of your investment plan. Rebalancing does not require forecasts, intuition, or market calls. It requires discipline—a commitment to the principles on which your portfolio was built.

This discipline is particularly valuable during periods of heightened market volatility. When asset prices swing wildly, the temptation to abandon your plan in favour of perceived safety—or opportunity—can be overwhelming. Rebalancing provides a clear rationale for action that is grounded in logic rather than emotion. If equities decline sharply and fall below their target weight, rebalancing will direct you to buy more—not because you believe a recovery is imminent, but because your allocation has shifted. This often means buying when others are selling, a counterintuitive but historically rewarding behaviour.

Consider the aftermath of the 2008 financial crisis. Investors who had a disciplined rebalancing strategy were able to purchase equities at significantly reduced valuations, even as the broader market was gripped by fear. As markets recovered over the following decade, those investors benefited disproportionately—not because they had superior foresight, but because they maintained structural discipline. The same pattern played out during the COVID-19 downturn in early 2020. While many investors hesitated or exited the market, those with automated or scheduled rebalancing strategies restored their allocations and were thus positioned to capitalise on the rapid rebound.

Rebalancing is not only about mitigating risk—it also plays a role in maximising long-term returns. By ensuring that your portfolio consistently reflects your intended risk profile, it prevents overexposure to any one asset class, particularly during speculative bubbles. This helps avoid painful reversals that can set back progress by years. At the same time, by reinvesting gains into lagging areas, it increases the likelihood of capturing value when market trends rotate. Over a long horizon, this reallocation contributes meaningfully to compounded growth.

It's important to acknowledge that rebalancing comes with trade-offs. Selling high-performing assets may generate capital gains and associated tax liabilities, especially in taxable accounts. It may also involve transaction fees or administrative complexity. However, these costs must be weighed against the benefits of controlled risk exposure and disciplined investment behaviour. Many modern platforms mitigate these concerns through tax-efficient fund structures, fractional share capabilities, and automated rebalancing features that reduce administrative burden.

For those using tax-advantaged accounts, such as pensions or ISAs in the UK, rebalancing can be executed without incurring tax liabilities. This makes it particularly attractive to conduct strategic shifts within these vehicles, preserving the long-term integrity of the portfolio without penalty. For larger, more complex portfolios, rebalancing can also be achieved through new contributions or withdrawals—adding to underweighted assets rather than selling existing holdings. This method maintains balance without triggering unnecessary tax events and is especially effective during the accumulation or decumulation phases of an investor's life.

As individuals approach retirement, the importance of rebalancing becomes even more pronounced. Portfolios typically shift from growth-oriented to more defensive allocations, reducing exposure to equities and increasing stability through bonds or cash equivalents. Failing to rebalance during this stage could leave an investor overexposed to risk at precisely the time they need greater certainty. Conversely, being too conservative too early may impair growth and erode purchasing power over a retirement that could last decades. Thoughtful rebalancing ensures that these transitions happen gradually and purposefully, rather than reactively.

Ultimately, rebalancing is a powerful expression of long-term thinking. It represents the ability to look beyond recent performance, resist emotional reactions, and make decisions based on enduring principles. It demands patience, humility, and trust in process—qualities that are increasingly rare in an investment culture obsessed with short-term results and constant novelty.

When practised consistently, rebalancing strengthens every part of your financial plan. It protects your downside, supports disciplined behaviour, and maintains the integrity of your strategy in both good times and bad. It does not promise outperformance, nor does it shield you from all risk. But it does ensure that your portfolio reflects your values, your goals, and your tolerance for risk—not the market's ever-changing narrative.

By keeping your investments aligned, you give yourself the best chance of reaching your financial objectives with clarity and confidence. Rebalancing is not an interruption to progress—it is the mechanism that keeps progress steady. And over decades, this steadiness becomes your greatest asset.

Using Technology for Smart Investing

The world of investing has undergone a quiet revolution. What was once the exclusive domain of stockbrokers, fund managers, and those fluent in financial jargon has now become accessible to almost anyone with a smartphone and a bank account. Technology has dismantled many of the traditional barriers to entry, bringing tools of extraordinary power and precision into the hands of everyday investors. Whether it's a mobile app that tracks spending and recommends investment amounts, a robo-advisor that builds and maintains a diversified portfolio, or a platform offering real-time insights and automated rebalancing, technology is reshaping how people engage with their financial futures. More than a convenience, these innovations represent a profound shift towards smarter, more inclusive, and more consistent investing.

The rise of investing apps marks one of the most visible transformations in the financial landscape. These applications, often elegantly designed and intuitively navigated, have introduced a generation to the world of investing through simplicity and accessibility. No longer do investors need to navigate clunky interfaces, speak to advisers during limited hours, or wait days for trades to settle. With a few taps, users can allocate funds, adjust portfolios, and review performance metrics. Apps such as Freetrade, Nutmeg, and Moneybox in the UK have gained popularity for their ease of use, cost transparency, and educational content that demystifies financial concepts. They allow investors to begin with small amounts, reducing the psychological and financial threshold that once made investing feel intimidating or exclusive.

These tools also encourage consistency, a cornerstone of wealth-building. Regular investing, enabled through direct debits or scheduled top-ups, is effortlessly built into the functionality of modern apps. Users can set monthly contributions, automate their investment choices, and review their financial goals without needing to speak to a human intermediary. This fosters a sense of autonomy and agency while reducing the temptation to time the market or react to short-term volatility. By integrating saving and investing into the rhythm of everyday life, these platforms help transform wealth accumulation into a habit rather than a series of sporadic decisions.

Robo-advisors have taken this automation and intelligence even further. These algorithm-driven platforms assess an individual's financial goals, risk tolerance, and time horizon to create personalised investment portfolios. Unlike traditional financial advisers, robo-advisors deliver this service at a fraction of the cost, making tailored investment guidance available to a wider audience. Services like Wealthify, Vanguard's Digital Adviser, and Scalable Capital in the UK exemplify how automation can offer high-quality asset allocation, diversification, and rebalancing, all without requiring the investor to become a portfolio manager.

The algorithms underpinning robo-advisors are grounded in modern portfolio theory and decades of empirical research. Once a portfolio is constructed, the platform continuously monitors its composition, automatically rebalancing when asset weightings drift too far from the original targets. This ensures the investor's exposure remains aligned with their risk profile and long-term objectives. Crucially, it removes the behavioural interference that often causes investors to make poor decisions—panic-selling during downturns, chasing trends during rallies, or overreacting to headlines. The robo-advisor doesn't flinch. It acts according to rules, not emotions, and in doing so often delivers outcomes that rival, or even surpass, those of actively managed alternatives.

Critics sometimes argue that such automation lacks the human touch. While this may hold in highly complex financial situations—such as estate planning or tax structuring—for the vast majority of investors, the value of consistent, rules-based investing far outweighs the need for bespoke advice. Moreover, many platforms now offer hybrid models, combining algorithmic management with the option to consult a human adviser when needed. This approach blends the efficiency of technology with the reassurance of personal interaction, delivering both affordability and support.

Beyond execution and management, technology is also transforming financial planning itself. Digital tools now enable individuals to model retirement projections, test investment scenarios, and track progress towards savings goals. These platforms use sophisticated analytics to present data in ways that are easy to interpret, even for those without a background in finance. Visual dashboards, scenario modelling, and alerts for underperformance or missed contributions empower users to make informed decisions. Apps such as PensionBee or Plum not only consolidate pension pots but also provide clarity on projected retirement income, enabling users to see the future impact of their current contributions. This kind of forward-looking insight was once the domain of high-cost advisory services; now it is available at the fingertips of everyday savers.

Technology is also democratising access to market information and investment research. Whereas once investors relied on newspaper columns or high-fee advisory firms for insights, today's investors can access up-to-date data, expert commentary, and performance analysis from reputable platforms and aggregators. This information, delivered in accessible formats and often supplemented by educational content, helps users understand the context behind their investments. However, this democratisation also requires discernment. Not all sources are equal, and the flood of online opinions can be overwhelming or misleading. Smart investing is not only about using technology to act, but also about learning to interpret information with critical awareness.

Another vital area where technology adds value is in reducing costs. Traditional investing was often laden with fees—adviser commissions, fund charges, trading costs—that significantly eroded long-term returns. Digital platforms, through economies of scale and technological efficiency, have drastically lowered these expenses. Robo-advisors typically charge total annual fees (including fund costs) that are well below 1%, and often much lower. Low-cost index fund providers like Vanguard and iShares have brought institutional-grade products to individual investors, while many trading apps now offer commission-free trading. These cost savings, while seemingly small annually, compound powerfully over decades, contributing meaningfully to portfolio growth.

Despite these benefits, it is essential to recognise that technology is a tool, not a panacea. While apps and algorithms can streamline the investing process, they are most effective when paired with a clear strategy and thoughtful goals. Investors must still define what they are investing for—retirement, a home, financial independence—and understand the principles of asset allocation, risk, and time horizon. The danger of frictionless investing is that it can encourage activity without purpose. Platforms that make it easy to invest must also encourage education and reflection.

Fortunately, many do. The best investing apps and platforms have begun to integrate financial literacy into their user experience. From explainers on equity risk to interactive modules on pension planning, these features help bridge the gap between action and understanding. Investors are not only empowered to execute decisions, but to make them with growing confidence and competence. This educational shift is crucial. It ensures that as access expands, so does the quality of engagement.

Technology is also reshaping the investor's mindset. It encourages a shift from reactive, performance-chasing behaviours towards process-driven, goal-focused discipline. Investors who once checked prices daily now receive nudges about staying the course. Alerts are designed not to trigger panic but to reinforce long-term thinking. The medium shapes the message, and the best digital investing tools promote resilience, patience, and consistency.

In a world where the average person will need to take greater responsibility for their financial future, technology is a powerful ally. Defined benefit pensions are rare, state support is limited, and economic uncertainty is persistent. Against this backdrop, the ability to start investing early, consistently, and intelligently is more important than ever. Technology makes this possible. It provides the infrastructure, the guidance, and the motivation to act—quietly transforming users from passive savers into confident, goal-oriented investors.

Smart investing today is less about beating the market and more about building a process that works over time. Technology enables this process to be automated, scalable, and behaviourally robust. It simplifies the complex, makes the inaccessible available, and turns sporadic decisions into consistent habits. When used thoughtfully, it doesn't just make investing easier—it makes it better. And for those who embrace it with clarity and discipline, it can quietly support a lifetime of financial growth.

Chapter 10
Creating a Personalised Wealth Plan

When people think about building wealth, their minds often drift towards complicated spreadsheets, cryptic financial jargon, or lofty targets so distant they hardly seem real. Yet, if you strip away the noise, wealth is far less about complexity or sudden windfalls and much more about clarity, discipline, and a commitment rooted in your own values. At its heart, effective wealth planning is the deliberate process of aligning your financial affairs with what truly matters to you. It's the journey from intention, through strategy, and ultimately into consistent action. A personalised wealth plan isn't merely a cold, numeric exercise or an allocation chart—it's more akin to a blueprint for living a life marked by purpose, security, and, yes, a growing sense of freedom.

Everything begins with setting clear financial goals. Without them, investing risks becoming a purposeless activity—accumulating assets without a compass to guide them. Goals inject meaning into the numbers; they explain the "why" behind your decisions and establish the boundaries within which you're willing to take risks. These targets might be immediate and concrete—like saving for a house deposit, clearing debts, or building an emergency fund. Alternatively, they could stretch decades into the future: paying for a child's education, achieving true financial independence, or securing a retirement lifestyle that fulfils your dreams. The devil is in the detail here. A vague ambition to "grow wealth" doesn't stand up well against the urge to spend or the jitters of a volatile market. But a clearly defined aim, such as "retire at 60 with £1.2 million in investable assets," acts as a steadfast compass, keeping decisions grounded and discipline intact.

Once goals are clear, the next step is to chart a practical investment roadmap—one that starts with a candid appraisal of your current financial situation. This means taking stock of income, outgoings, existing savings, debts, and other commitments. It's about confronting the facts honestly, without self-recrimination. From this foundation, the plan carves a path forward, balancing your aspirations against real-world constraints. The objective is not to shoehorn your life into a rigid formula, but to design a strategy that supports your unique circumstances.

Consider, for example, a thirty-something with a modest income. Their focus might be on maximising ISA contributions and employer pension matches while steadily reducing student debt. Given a long time horizon, they might lean more heavily towards equities to harness growth potential. Contrast this with someone in their fifties, approaching retirement: preservation of capital becomes paramount, portfolios shift towards bonds, and income-generating investments are structured to maintain lifestyle standards. Both plans are personalised; they reflect market realities, yes—but equally, they honour individual context.

Yet no plan is fixed in stone. Life moves, often unpredictably. Careers evolve, families expand, markets fluctuate. A wealth plan that cannot adapt soon becomes obsolete. That's why regular check-ins—whether quarterly or twice yearly—are vital. These reviews are moments to assess progress, rebalance portfolios, refine goals, and course-correct where necessary. Importantly, these sessions don't demand sophisticated modelling or expert advice (though professionals can certainly add value). What they do require is attention, reflection, and an openness to update assumptions in response to new information.

Thanks to technology, this process is far less daunting than it once was. Many platforms now offer personalised dashboards that map progress towards your goals, flag shifts in asset allocation, and project future outcomes based on current behaviours. Suddenly, abstract numbers become a narrative you can follow—showing not only where you stand today but what might lie ahead. Yet these tools, useful as they are, are not substitutes for mindset. A review only bears fruit when it informs measured action rather than reactive knee-jerk moves. Staying the course during market dips can feel deeply uncomfortable but often proves the wisest choice. Remember: a plan isn't a crystal ball; it's a framework for navigating uncertainty.

One of the great virtues of long-term planning lies in avoiding familiar pitfalls. Even seasoned investors slip up—overreacting to fleeting noise, neglecting diversification, underestimating retirement costs, or failing to factor in inflation. A personalised plan guards against these errors by embedding prudent habits and sound risk management into your financial fabric. For example, keeping a cash reserve means you're not forced to sell investments in a downturn. Rebalancing keeps your portfolio aligned with your risk profile and goals. Matching investment horizons to your objectives prevents the need to liquidate long-term holdings prematurely.

There's a common cognitive trap worth mentioning: we tend to overestimate short-term gains and underestimate long-term potential. This skew often breeds impatience—prompting rash switches in strategy or chasing the latest market trend. A disciplined plan gently steers focus away from fleeting results and towards enduring patterns. It nurtures confidence in process rather than prediction and rewards steady, consistent action over spectacular but risky gambits.

Most crucially, a personalised wealth plan redefines success itself. Wealth is no longer a mere figure on a statement or a balance sheet. Instead, it becomes the power to make choices that resonate with your values. Financial freedom is not about extreme austerity or reckless risk-taking; it's the gradual accumulation of assets coupled with careful stewardship of resources. It is the liberty to live free from money worries, to pursue work out of passion rather than necessity, to support those you love, and to contribute meaningfully to causes that matter.

The fruits of patience and discipline don't always show immediately. In those early years, growth is often subtle—a slightly larger portfolio, a slowly growing pension, a small but steady financial cushion. Yet over time, these modest gains compound. Momentum builds. What once was a plan confined to paper unfolds into reality. The distant visions of financial independence, early retirement, or legacy creation begin to take tangible shape.

Take, for example, a couple now in their forties who started investing regularly in their late twenties. They prioritised tax-efficient accounts, automated contributions monthly, and gradually upped their savings as their earnings grew. They reviewed their plan yearly, adjusted allocations thoughtfully every few years, and resisted the temptation to chase hot tips or panic during downturns. Now, as they approach mid-life, they find themselves with options—not because of luck or spectacular returns, but because of steady structure, consistency, and clear purpose.

Creating a personalised wealth plan is not a one-off event. It is an ongoing conversation between your values, resources, and ambitions. It is part art, part science, and entirely unique to you. What works for one may falter for another. The aim is not perfection but alignment; not certainty but preparedness.

While no plan can guarantee outcomes, a well-considered approach greatly improves the odds of success—measured not solely in pounds and pence but in a life supported, enriched, and freed by financial confidence. By defining goals clearly, building a flexible yet structured strategy, and keeping a watchful eye on both progress and priorities, you set yourself up not just to amass wealth, but to truly live well. And in the end, isn't that what financial planning should be about?

Setting Clear Financial Goals

Wealth, for all its associations with numbers and spreadsheets, is ultimately a human concept—deeply personal, value-laden, and intimately connected to our hopes for the future. At the centre of any meaningful financial strategy lies a deceptively simple act: setting clear financial goals. These goals are the bridge between your present circumstances and your desired future. Without them, even the most sophisticated investment plan is little more than a shot in the dark. With them, financial decisions acquire focus, investments are aligned with purpose, and progress becomes measurable rather than speculative.

Identifying financial goals is not about conjuring arbitrary targets or mirroring someone else's aspirations. It is a reflective process grounded in personal priorities and life circumstances. The first step is not to ask, "How much should I save?" but rather, "What do I want money to do for me?" For one person, that might mean owning a home in the next five years. For another, it might be about supporting ageing parents, building a charitable foundation, or retiring comfortably at 55. These aspirations provide shape to your financial life and determine how resources should be directed.

The distinction between short-term and long-term goals is critical. Short-term goals are typically immediate or near-future objectives—saving for a holiday, paying off credit card debt, building an emergency fund, or funding a professional qualification. These goals often come with specific deadlines and defined amounts, making them relatively straightforward to plan around. Long-term goals, on the other hand, tend to be broader and more aspirational. Retirement, financial independence, paying off a mortgage, or leaving a legacy are examples of goals that require sustained effort, disciplined investing, and regular recalibration.

Clarity in goal-setting serves multiple functions. It enables prioritisation, ensuring that limited resources are allocated where they will have the greatest impact. It also brings a sense of accountability. When goals are specific—such as "accumulate £50,000 for a house deposit in five years" rather than "save more"—they create a framework for measuring progress. This specificity enhances motivation and allows for early course correction if the strategy proves insufficient.

A clear financial goal should meet three essential criteria: it should be measurable, time-bound, and personally meaningful. This is not just a technical guideline; it's a psychological imperative. Vague goals lack the emotional and cognitive resonance required to drive consistent action. When a goal is framed in precise, personal terms—such as "I want to pay for my child's university education without taking on debt"—it becomes emotionally salient. It ties the abstraction of money to a tangible, values-based outcome, increasing the likelihood of follow-through.

It is also vital to distinguish between goals that are aspirational and those that are foundational. Aspirational goals are exciting—they capture your vision for the future and push you to think ambitiously.

Foundational goals, by contrast, form the bedrock of financial stability. They include building a contingency fund, eliminating high-interest debt, or securing adequate insurance. While they may lack glamour, these goals are essential because they safeguard your ability to pursue the more inspiring ones. Ignoring them can lead to setbacks that derail even the most meticulously crafted plans.

A good financial plan includes a hierarchy of goals. For instance, a young professional might simultaneously aim to pay off student loans (short-term), save for a home deposit (medium-term), and invest for retirement (long-term). These goals will compete for limited resources, requiring choices and trade-offs. The value of clarity here cannot be overstated. If the goal is to buy a house within five years, it may be necessary to defer maximum pension contributions for a period, despite the long-term advantages of early retirement investing. Alternatively, one might choose to live in more modest accommodation or take on a side income stream to meet both objectives concurrently.

Real-world examples often highlight the power of clearly defined goals. Consider two individuals earning similar incomes. One takes a reactive approach to finances—saving whatever is left over after expenses, investing sporadically, and focusing only on the present. The other sets specific objectives: to save £10,000 for travel over two years, to build an emergency fund of £6,000, and to invest £400 monthly towards retirement. Over time, the second individual experiences not only better financial outcomes but greater peace of mind. They know what they are working towards, and every action—however small—feels purposeful.

Goal clarity also provides a buffer against emotional decision-making. When markets are volatile or economic news is unsettling, the investor without defined goals is more likely to panic. Their sense of progress is vague, and so too is their sense of loss. By contrast, an investor who knows that their primary objective is to generate £30,000 per year in passive income within 20 years will be more inclined to stay the course. They understand that short-term volatility is irrelevant to their long-term plan. This detachment is not apathy; it is alignment.

That said, financial goals are not static. They evolve with life stages, responsibilities, and personal growth. A person's goals in their twenties—such as travel, skills development, or debt repayment—may give way to goals in their thirties or forties, including homeownership, children's education, or entrepreneurial pursuits. Retirement, once a distant idea, eventually becomes a priority requiring increasingly detailed planning. Reviewing and adjusting financial goals should therefore be a recurring practice. It ensures that the plan reflects your current reality, not your past assumptions.

Technology can aid this process by offering platforms that help visualise goals, track progress, and project outcomes. Budgeting apps, investment dashboards, and financial planning tools can demystify the connection between today's decisions and tomorrow's outcomes. But these tools are only as effective as the goals they serve. Without a well-articulated objective, the most elegant graph or projection means little. The technology is the scaffolding; the vision must come from the investor.

Importantly, goal-setting is not just a rational exercise. It is deeply connected to meaning and motivation. What you want your money to do for you reflects what you value most. Financial goals are, in essence, life goals translated into economic terms. They can reflect a desire for freedom, security, generosity, or legacy. And when set with care, they infuse your financial life with intention. They ensure that your wealth-building efforts are not just about accumulation but about alignment—with your values, your responsibilities, and your aspirations.

As you move forward with building your personalised wealth plan, treat goal-setting as both a strategic and reflective exercise. Don't simply ask what you want to achieve—ask why it matters. Think not only about the numbers but about the life those numbers will support. Anchor your goals in specificity, revisit them regularly, and let them guide your actions. When your financial goals are clear, everything else—your savings rate, your investment strategy, your time horizon—flows with greater ease. Clarity doesn't eliminate uncertainty, but it empowers you to act within it. And that clarity, more than any single financial decision, is what makes sustained wealth-building possible.

Developing a Step-by-Step Plan

Creating wealth is often viewed through the lens of outcomes—retirement figures, property portfolios, or passive income targets. Yet behind every successful financial outcome lies something far less glamorous but infinitely more essential: a structured plan. Building wealth is not a single event or dramatic leap forward; it is the accumulation of small, deliberate steps, repeated consistently over time. A well-crafted, step-by-step plan offers the scaffolding for this process. It transforms vague intentions into tangible actions and breaks down long-term aspirations into manageable stages. Without it, even the most ambitious goals remain aspirational rather than achievable.

Structuring an investment roadmap begins with clarity of purpose. The first question to ask is not, "Where should I invest?" but "What am I investing for?" This clarity must precede every other decision. Once your financial objectives—be they home ownership, early retirement, or funding a child's education—are clearly articulated, the plan becomes a tool for reverse engineering: you begin with the end in mind and work backward to determine the steps required to reach it.

For example, if your goal is to accumulate £500,000 for financial independence by age 55, you must understand what level of annual contributions, expected rate of return, and asset allocation would likely get you there. This goal can then be broken down into annual savings targets, monthly contributions, and regular investment reviews. What begins as an abstract figure becomes a living strategy, one that evolves in alignment with income growth, market fluctuations, and personal circumstances.

A sound investment roadmap begins with building the right foundation. This includes clearing high-interest debt, establishing an emergency fund, and protecting income through insurance. These preparatory steps are not optional—they provide the financial stability necessary for long-term investing. Without them, every market dip or life disruption threatens to derail progress. Once this base is secure, the focus can shift towards investment, which must be structured according to time horizon, risk tolerance, and financial capacity.

The time horizon dictates not only what you invest in but how you invest. Short-term goals—such as saving for a wedding or house deposit in the next three years—require capital preservation and lower volatility. Cash savings or short-duration bonds are often suitable here. Medium-term goals, typically spanning three to ten years, might involve a blend of equities and fixed income to balance growth with stability. Long-term goals—retirement, for instance—allow for a higher allocation to equities and other growth-oriented assets, as they can weather short-term volatility in exchange for superior long-term returns.

Aligning risk tolerance with strategy is equally critical. Many investors misjudge their ability to handle losses, only to react emotionally during market downturns. A robust plan takes into account not only theoretical risk tolerance but behavioural patterns. Would you remain invested during a 20% market drop, or would you be tempted to sell? Would you continue contributing to your portfolio during a bear market, or would fear paralyse you? By designing a plan that reflects your actual behaviour rather than your idealised self, you significantly improve the odds of staying invested and reaping the rewards of compounding over time.

The next component is contribution strategy. Your roadmap must identify not just how much to invest, but how often. Consistency, as countless examples illustrate, is more powerful than intensity. A monthly contribution of £300 over twenty years will yield far greater results than occasional lump sums driven by surplus income or market timing. Automating these contributions ensures they are treated as financial non-negotiables, just like rent or utilities. This removes emotion from the equation and builds financial discipline into your routine.

Asset allocation is the engine of long-term investment success. The structure of your portfolio—how much you allocate to equities, bonds, property, or alternatives—has a greater impact on your long-term results than the individual securities you choose. A well-diversified allocation spreads risk across asset classes and regions, smoothing returns and reducing the impact of any one market event. The investment plan should identify a target allocation based on your risk tolerance and investment horizon, and it should include provisions for rebalancing to maintain that structure over time.

Rebalancing is not merely a technical exercise—it is a behavioural safeguard. It ensures that you do not let market euphoria or despair distort your original plan. If equities surge and begin to dominate your portfolio, rebalancing forces you to trim back and reallocate to underrepresented areas. If equities fall and bonds rise, rebalancing pushes you to buy more risk assets at a discount. This automatic correction prevents you from being overexposed to risk or overly conservative, both of which can undermine long-term growth.

Tax efficiency must also be embedded in the plan. Making use of tax-advantaged accounts, such as ISAs or pensions, can enhance net returns by sheltering gains from income or capital gains taxes. These accounts also encourage long-term thinking by restricting access or offering incentives to stay invested. A personalised investment roadmap considers the tax implications of contributions, withdrawals, and asset location to ensure that your money works as effectively as possible.

No investment plan, however well-designed, exists in a vacuum. Life changes, sometimes unpredictably. A promotion, career break, illness, relocation, or new family member can all alter your financial landscape. That's why your investment plan must be a living document—reviewed regularly, adjusted prudently, and always aligned with your evolving reality. An annual check-in is typically sufficient for most individuals, though major life events may warrant more immediate updates.

Take, for instance, a couple in their thirties with a goal of achieving financial independence by fifty. Their step-by-step plan might include: maximising pension contributions, saving a fixed percentage of their income in ISAs, investing in a globally diversified mix of index funds, rebalancing annually, and increasing their savings rate with each salary increase. Along the way, they may decide to start a business, buy a second property, or take time off to travel with their children. Each of these developments would require an adjustment to the plan—not an abandonment of it. Their roadmap is resilient not because it is rigid, but because it is structured.

It is also worth noting that the most effective investment plans are often the simplest. Complexity can be alluring—it offers the illusion of sophistication—but it rarely delivers better results. A straightforward, consistent strategy executed with discipline often outperforms elaborate portfolios that require constant oversight. Complexity increases the likelihood of error, distraction, and overconfidence. Simplicity, on the other hand, fosters clarity, repeatability, and peace of mind.

Developing a step-by-step investment plan is not a task to be completed in one sitting. It is a process that requires honest self-assessment, thoughtful design, and regular engagement. But the rewards are substantial. A well-structured plan provides direction amid uncertainty, consistency in the face of noise, and confidence through market cycles. It transforms investing from a reactive activity into a deliberate practice. It helps you act, not out of fear or impulse, but out of intention.

By building a plan that reflects your goals, your behaviour, and your resources, you put yourself in control of your financial future. The markets may remain unpredictable. Interest rates may fluctuate. Economies may stall or surge. But your strategy—anchored in thoughtful design and executed with quiet persistence—becomes your compass. It is this structured yet flexible approach that ultimately separates the hopeful from the successful, and the passive spectator from the active steward of their wealth.

Monitoring and Adjusting Your Plan

Creating a personal wealth plan is a foundational step in securing long-term financial stability, but its true value lies not in the act of planning itself, but in the ongoing process of refinement. The most successful investors are not those who draft a plan and then file it away, never to revisit it. They are those who understand that life, markets, and personal priorities change—and that effective financial planning must be a living, adaptive exercise. Monitoring and adjusting your plan at regular intervals ensures that it continues to serve its purpose: helping you move steadily towards your defined financial objectives, whatever shifts may occur along the way.

Regularly reviewing progress is not about obsessing over daily market fluctuations or micro-managing every line of your investment statement. Rather, it is about stepping back periodically to assess whether your plan remains aligned with your goals, whether those goals are still relevant, and whether your actions are producing the intended outcomes. Without this rhythm of review and recalibration, even a well-constructed plan can drift off course. The risk is not simply underperformance, but disconnection—from your strategy, your purpose, and your financial reality.

A review should begin with a clear reference point: your original objectives. Are you on track to meet them? Are the assumptions you made still valid? Has your income changed? Have your spending habits evolved? Has your risk tolerance shifted due to life events, personal experience, or new responsibilities? These are not questions to be asked only once, at the beginning of your financial journey—they are questions to return to, again and again, with honesty and curiosity.

Take, for example, an investor in her early forties who set a goal a decade ago to retire at sixty with a pension fund of £800,000. Her plan assumed a consistent savings rate, annualised returns of 6%, and steady income growth. Over time, she experienced a few career transitions, some years with lower savings, and perhaps a shift in her view of what retirement should look like. A review at age forty-two might reveal that while her investments have performed reasonably well, her contributions fell short during a few critical years. Without panic or drastic overhaul, she might adjust her plan—either by increasing her monthly contributions, extending her target retirement age slightly, or reassessing her expected lifestyle in retirement. The key is that she sees the trend early, not when she is fifty-nine and her window for change has narrowed.

Monitoring your progress is also about identifying behavioural patterns. Are you sticking to your savings and investment commitments? Have you consistently rebalanced your portfolio, or have emotional reactions led you to deviate from your strategy? These behavioural audits are just as vital as any numerical analysis. They reveal whether the plan is not only financially viable but also psychologically sustainable. If you find yourself frequently tempted to react to short-term market noise, it may be worth revisiting your risk exposure or incorporating more automation into your strategy.

Practical tools can make this review process more efficient and insightful. Modern investment platforms increasingly provide dashboards that track portfolio performance relative to your goals, show projected outcomes, and flag deviations in allocation. These tools offer a visual narrative of your progress, making it easier to see whether you are heading in the right direction. But while technology facilitates measurement, the human side of financial planning—your intentions, values, and life context—requires reflection and sometimes difficult conversations with yourself or a trusted adviser.

Adjustments to your plan should be approached thoughtfully, not reactively. It is natural to feel tempted to overhaul your investments after a market downturn or when comparing your progress to others. But short-term underperformance does not necessarily indicate a flawed strategy, just as temporary outperformance may not signal that your plan is ahead of schedule. The goal of monitoring is not to tinker for its own sake, but to ensure continued alignment. Changes should be rooted in substantive developments: a shift in income, a change in goals, an updated outlook on risk, or new financial responsibilities.

For instance, a couple who originally planned to retire early may decide to delay that timeline after the birth of a second child, prioritising education funding over aggressive accumulation. Their plan might shift from high-growth investments to a more balanced approach with dedicated savings for school fees. These are not failures of planning but validations of its flexibility. The plan adapts because their life has changed, not because the market has disappointed them.

One of the most common traps investors fall into during reviews is allowing hindsight to distort their judgment. It is easy to look back at missed opportunities or underperforming assets and think, "I should have done X instead." But financial planning is forward-looking. The role of review is not to punish past decisions but to inform future ones. Hindsight bias can erode confidence and promote impulsive shifts that do more harm than good. A disciplined review process focuses on what is within your control—your contributions, your allocation, your spending, your behaviour—not what you could have predicted.

Monitoring also extends beyond investment accounts. A comprehensive review includes income trends, spending patterns, debt levels, insurance coverage, estate plans, and tax strategies. These elements interact with your investments in complex ways. For instance, rising income may allow for increased pension contributions, while higher expenses might necessitate a temporary pause in discretionary investing. A rise in interest rates might make it sensible to accelerate debt repayment, while tax policy changes could alter the balance between pension and ISA contributions. Your wealth plan should not be a siloed exercise—it should integrate with every aspect of your financial life.

Real-life examples illustrate the value of regular adjustment. During the COVID-19 pandemic, many individuals who had previously maintained high contribution rates had to reduce or pause them due to furloughs, redundancies, or business closures. Some dipped into emergency funds or postponed investing altogether. Those who had reviewed and reinforced their emergency savings in earlier years found themselves in a better position. Others realised, during this period, that their goals had changed—not just due to financial constraints, but because their definition of a meaningful life had shifted. Travel became less central. Community and flexibility became more important. Their wealth plans, updated with these new insights, took on a different shape.

The review process should not be feared or treated as an onerous obligation. It is an opportunity to reaffirm your autonomy over your financial life. It reminds you that you are not merely subject to the whims of the market or the economy. You are an active participant, capable of adapting, course-correcting, and continuing forward. Monitoring provides clarity. Adjustment provides agency.

There is no perfect frequency for these reviews, though many financial professionals recommend a thorough check at least once a year. Significant life events—marriage, the birth of a child, a career move, or inheritance—warrant additional reviews. What matters is not how often you review, but the quality of the engagement when you do. A rushed glance at your portfolio statement or a perfunctory update to your savings rate will not suffice. A meaningful review takes time, attention, and honesty. It is an invitation to step outside your day-to-day financial habits and look at the bigger picture.

Monitoring and adjusting your wealth plan is where strategy meets reality. It is the ongoing act of ensuring that your financial architecture supports not only where you thought you wanted to go, but where you now understand you want to be. It is where discipline meets flexibility, where analytics meet introspection, and where progress—however incremental—is affirmed and advanced. A plan that is regularly revisited is not a sign of indecision; it is a mark of maturity. It acknowledges that change is inevitable and that resilience lies not in rigidity, but in readiness to adapt with clarity and intention.

By building a habit of review and adjustment, you transform your wealth plan from a static document into a dynamic practice—one that evolves with you, supports your ambitions, and strengthens your ability to weather uncertainty. The review does not merely measure what has happened. It reaffirms what still matters. And in doing so, it ensures that your financial future remains not just an aspiration, but a direction you are continually moving towards, one informed choice at a time.

Avoiding Common Mistakes

Even the most carefully constructed wealth plan can falter if it falls prey to common investment pitfalls. While financial theory offers clarity, real-world behaviour often diverges from rational models. Emotions, biases, overconfidence, and misaligned incentives can all lead investors to decisions that, over time, undermine their long-term objectives. Yet by examining the missteps of experienced investors—those who have weathered both success and setbacks—we gain insight not only into what to avoid, but also into how to recover, adapt, and grow wiser. The most instructive mistakes are not the ones made in obscurity, but the ones reflected upon and shared.

One of the most frequent and costly errors is performance-chasing—shifting investments based on recent returns rather than underlying fundamentals. This mistake often stems from the illusion that what has done well recently will continue to do so. Investors may rush into sectors, funds, or assets that have posted stellar short-term performance, assuming this momentum will persist. Yet data consistently show that yesterday's winners often fail to sustain their outperformance. Chasing them usually means buying high, only to see them underperform once the tide turns.

This behaviour was particularly evident during the dot-com boom of the late 1990s. Many individual investors flocked to technology stocks, convinced by their meteoric rise and the hype surrounding a new digital economy. When the bubble burst, vast amounts of capital were wiped out. Those who had built portfolios around long-term principles—diversification, valuation discipline, and realistic growth assumptions—were better positioned to withstand the downturn. Those who chased returns at the expense of strategy found themselves exposed, sometimes irreparably.

Closely related is the tendency to panic during downturns and abandon a well-constructed plan. Emotional responses to market declines are understandable; watching the value of one's investments fall can provoke anxiety and self-doubt. But reacting to that emotion by selling in a downturn crystallises losses and often locks in the worst possible outcome. History shows that markets, while volatile in the short term, have recovered over the long term. Investors who stayed the course through events like the 2008 financial crisis or the COVID-19 crash were typically rewarded for their patience. Those who exited during the worst days often missed the initial stages of recovery—an error that can significantly reduce long-term returns.

This underscores the importance of understanding and aligning with one's true risk tolerance. Many investors overestimate their comfort with volatility when markets are rising, only to discover their limit during a sharp correction. Learning from experienced investors reveals that setting a risk level one can realistically maintain—not just theoretically endure—is crucial. It is better to earn slightly lower returns within a plan one can stick to, than to pursue aggressive gains through a strategy that will be abandoned at the first sign of trouble.

Another recurrent mistake is neglecting the impact of fees and expenses. While individual charges may seem small—a one percent annual fee, a few pounds per trade—their cumulative effect over decades is profound. High fees erode compounding. A portfolio growing at 7 percent annually, minus a one percent fee, yields far less than one growing at the full rate. Many experienced investors have spoken candidly about learning, sometimes late in their careers, how much they had unknowingly sacrificed to unnecessary or opaque costs. Today's investors, benefiting from increased transparency and low-cost investment options, can learn from these lessons by prioritising cost efficiency as a non-negotiable feature of their strategy.

Over-diversification, sometimes described as "diworsification," is another trap. Diversification is fundamental to managing risk, but taken to an extreme, it can dilute returns and complicate oversight. Investors may hold dozens of funds or accounts, believing more is better, only to discover overlapping exposure, increased fees, and minimal differentiation. The most experienced investors refine their portfolios for clarity and intentionality. Each asset has a role—whether for growth, income, or protection—and excessive overlap is seen as an inefficiency, not a virtue.

A subtler, yet widespread, mistake is failing to define clear financial goals before constructing an investment plan. Without specific objectives, investing becomes reactive, driven by market trends, social influence, or fear of missing out. Many investors, particularly early in their financial journeys, make contributions to pension schemes, ISAs, or brokerage accounts without connecting those contributions to concrete outcomes. Over time, this lack of intentionality creates dissonance—a disconnect between the portfolio's structure and the investor's actual needs. The antidote, as seasoned investors consistently advise, is to begin with the end in mind. Whether saving for a child's education, building a home deposit, or creating a retirement income, the goal defines the process, not the other way around.

Underestimating the power of regular, modest contributions is another mistake that has cost countless investors meaningful long-term wealth. Many individuals postpone investing until they feel they have "enough" to make it worthwhile. In doing so, they sacrifice one of the most potent forces in wealth-building: time. Small, consistent investments—particularly when automated—accumulate meaningfully over decades. Experienced investors often reflect that their most powerful financial habit was not an impressive trade or strategic insight, but the simple act of setting aside money regularly, regardless of market conditions.

Neglecting to plan for taxes is also a common oversight. Taxes can quietly consume a significant portion of returns if not managed proactively. Capital gains, dividends, and withdrawals from non-tax-advantaged accounts can trigger liabilities that reduce net income. Experienced investors build tax awareness into their plans—using ISAs, pensions, and appropriate account structures to maximise after-tax returns. More importantly, they recognise that tax planning is not a once-a-year exercise but a continuous consideration. This awareness, coupled with thoughtful structuring, often distinguishes the merely successful investor from the highly efficient one.

A particularly poignant mistake is failing to factor in personal life changes. An investment plan that made sense as a single, early-career professional may require substantial revision after marriage, children, or career changes. Many experienced investors look back on missed opportunities to adapt their strategy to new responsibilities or ambitions. The most resilient plans are those that are periodically reviewed and rebalanced—not just in terms of asset allocation, but in terms of alignment with evolving personal values and goals.

Perhaps the most understated mistake, yet one that has derailed many investors, is overconfidence. Initial success—especially when driven by favourable market conditions—can lead to inflated expectations and unnecessary risk-taking. Believing that one has "figured out the market" often precedes costly misjudgements. Humility, as hard-won investors will attest, is a more reliable companion than hubris. Markets are complex, influenced by innumerable variables, and often behave irrationally. The wise investor does not attempt to predict their every move but instead builds a plan resilient enough to weather them.

Finally, the mistake of going it alone should not be underestimated. Financial independence is admirable, but isolation can breed blind spots. Many experienced investors credit their growth to mentorship, collaboration, or the willingness to seek advice. Whether through a trusted adviser, peer network, or financial education, surrounding oneself with insight and accountability enhances decision-making and guards against avoidable error.

Avoiding mistakes is not about achieving perfection. Every investor, regardless of experience or knowledge, will misstep at times. But the difference between those who succeed and those who falter lies in response. Mistakes, if acknowledged and reflected upon, become learning moments—stepping stones to better judgement and more refined strategies. Ignored or repeated, they become barriers to progress.

By studying the patterns and reflections of experienced investors, we gain not just tactical guidance, but deeper understanding. The path to wealth is less about dazzling moves and more about steady discipline, thoughtful structure, and the humility to adapt. Learning from others' missteps allows us to navigate more confidently—not with the illusion of certainty, but with the wisdom to avoid the obvious traps and stay focused on what truly matters.

Achieving Financial Freedom

Few concepts inspire more aspiration or ambiguity than financial freedom. For some, it conjures the image of early retirement—sun-soaked days without alarm clocks or obligations. For others, it means the ability to choose work based on passion rather than necessity, or to weather financial storms without anxiety. At its core, however, financial freedom is not about a specific lifestyle or a singular monetary target. It is about optionality—the freedom to make choices without being constrained by financial limitations. And while the goal is universal, the path is often misunderstood. It is not a sprint towards high returns or a gamble on the next big opportunity.

It is the patient accumulation of assets, paired with disciplined investing, thoughtful planning, and quiet consistency.

The notion of financial freedom must begin with a sober recognition of time. Most people dramatically overestimate what can be achieved in a year, yet severely underestimate what is possible over twenty or thirty. The compounding effect—the mechanism by which small gains on capital snowball into significant wealth over time—requires not just mathematical understanding, but behavioural fortitude. The paradox is that the longer the time horizon, the less dependent success becomes on finding the perfect investment, and the more it hinges on simply staying invested.

This was exemplified by the case of Grace Groner, an unassuming secretary who invested $180 in the 1930s and, through decades of disciplined reinvestment and patience, accumulated over $7 million. She did not trade frequently. She did not chase trends. She remained invested. Her story is instructive because it strips wealth-building of complexity. It reminds us that the structure of behaviour often matters more than the brilliance of strategy.

To achieve financial freedom, patience is not merely a virtue—it is a precondition. Investing, particularly for long-term objectives, demands a tolerance for boredom, volatility, and deferred gratification. There will be years when markets underperform, when portfolios stagnate, or when progress feels slow. Those who succeed are not those who avoid these periods, but those who persist through them.

Discipline, too, plays an indispensable role. It is not the dramatic act of saving half one's income for a year, only to regress the next. It is the habit of consistent contributions, automatic reinvestment, and prudent risk-taking. Discipline shows itself not just in investing decisions, but in lifestyle choices: spending less than one earns, avoiding debt traps, and aligning consumption with values rather than social pressure. These habits, repeated over years, become the infrastructure of financial independence.

A particularly illuminating insight from behavioural finance is the concept of "loss aversion"—the idea that people feel the pain of losses more acutely than the pleasure of gains. This tendency often causes investors to abandon strategies during temporary downturns, thereby forfeiting future returns. Financial freedom requires the ability to tolerate short-term discomfort in service of long-term security. It is about resisting the instinct to act when inaction is more profitable.

Moreover, financial freedom is inherently personal. It does not require the same capital for everyone. A person with low fixed expenses, modest lifestyle aspirations, and high savings discipline may achieve freedom with far less capital than someone whose expenses scale with every pay rise. This underscores the importance of defining freedom not in terms of numbers alone, but in terms of what those numbers allow you to do—or not do. For some, it is the ability to stop working. For others, it is the ability to start something new. For many, it is the peace of mind that comes from knowing they are not dependent on any one income stream, employer, or government scheme.

Consider the story of a couple who began saving and investing in their late twenties. Their income was modest, and their lifestyle frugal. Each year, they increased their pension contributions slightly, invested in low-cost index funds, and avoided unnecessary spending. They did not make dramatic financial moves, nor did they boast of short-term gains. Yet by their mid-fifties, they had accumulated enough to comfortably reduce their working hours and pursue interests that brought fulfilment rather than income. Their success lay not in exceptional earnings or market timing, but in consistency, clarity, and patience.

An important dimension of financial freedom is the psychological shift it creates. It allows individuals to think beyond the present, to take calculated risks, and to make choices aligned with personal values. It reduces financial anxiety and creates space for reflection, generosity, and creativity. People often imagine freedom as the absence of obligation, but more often it manifests as the presence of agency—the ability to say no, to walk away, or to design a life based on preference rather than pressure.

This agency extends to relationships, health, and even moral decision-making. When financial concerns do not dominate mental bandwidth, individuals are better positioned to act with integrity, to give generously, and to invest in relationships that matter. Financial freedom, then, is not merely a state of accounts—it is a state of mind.

That said, it is important not to romanticise the process. The path to financial freedom is often unglamorous. It involves saying no when others say yes, delaying rewards that are immediately available, and sometimes living below one's perceived means. It requires a long view in a culture that celebrates immediacy. Yet those who internalise its logic—and who personalise it to their circumstances—often describe not just material gains, but a profound shift in perspective.

Technology can support this path but cannot replace discipline. Apps can automate contributions, track net worth, and project retirement dates. Robo-advisors can manage portfolios and reduce emotional interference. But tools alone do not confer freedom. They are only effective when combined with clear goals, behavioural insight, and financial literacy. The role of technology is to reduce friction. The role of the individual is to stay the course.

A subtle, yet powerful, realisation among those who attain financial freedom is that the destination is not static. Needs evolve. Interests change. The number once imagined as the finish line often becomes irrelevant. What matters more is the capability to adapt—to downsize, to upskill, to relocate, or to pause—without financial constraint. This fluidity is the hallmark of real wealth: not the ability to purchase, but the ability to pivot.

It is worth noting that freedom is not synonymous with never working again. For many, it means working differently—choosing projects based on passion, not necessity; engaging part-time or seasonally; mentoring others; or contributing to communities without requiring financial compensation. In this sense, financial freedom is not an end, but an enabler. It makes room for meaningful work, not just paid work.

Ultimately, achieving financial freedom is not a matter of chance. It is the cumulative result of thousands of small, intentional decisions—each one reinforcing the next. It requires resilience in the face of setbacks, clarity in the face of distraction, and humility in the face of complexity. It rewards not speed, but steadiness; not brilliance, but commitment.

The rewards are not just quantitative. They include the confidence that comes from knowing you are prepared. The self-respect that grows from having lived in alignment with your values. The calm that comes from financial stability, and the joy of choices unburdened by fear.

Financial freedom is neither easy nor instantaneous. But it is profoundly attainable. Not through windfalls, shortcuts, or flawless execution, but through patience and discipline—qualities within reach of anyone willing to commit to the long game. And that commitment, modest as it may seem at first, can yield a life of freedom that far exceeds what any figure on a bank statement could ever represent.

Conclusion
Playing the Long Game in Life and Wealth

As we turn the final page on this journey into the art of building lasting wealth, it becomes ever more apparent that long-term investing transcends mere strategy—it is, in essence, a mindset, a philosophy, and quite often, a way of life. The themes woven through this discussion haven't been about chasing financial landmarks simply for the thrill of ticking boxes. Instead, they have centred on cultivating resilience, consistency, and a deeper sense of purpose. Embracing the long game means marrying your financial decisions to values that stretch beyond the allure of immediate gain. It is an approach that places patience above performance, sustainability above speculation, and clear intention well before fleeting gratification.

True wealth, as those with experience and reflection will affirm, reaches far beyond the confines of balance sheets or brokerage accounts. Financial assets serve as tools—means to an end, not the end themselves. They offer choice, underpin security, and carve out space for what truly matters: relationships, freedom, contribution, and, ultimately, peace of mind. If amassing money breeds anxiety, envy, or a relentless hunger for more, then one might question whether it qualifies as wealth in any meaningful sense at all. At its most profound, wealth is the quiet confidence that springs from standing on firm ground, living a life both sustainable and deliberate.

This expansive view of wealth is no accident; it echoes through the wisdom of some of the world's most esteemed investors. Each has charted their own course, no doubt, yet their enduring lessons converge on a handful of core principles: simplicity, discipline, a long-term outlook, and emotional self-control.

Take Warren Buffett, whose investment career spans over seventy years. His fortune wasn't forged by quick trades or speculative gambles, but through a philosophy anchored in value, patience, and the magic of compounding. He is renowned not merely for his sharp analytical mind but for his temperament—a deep understanding that "time in the market" beats "timing the market," and that volatility only becomes risk if you allow it to. His oft-quoted observation—that the stock market is essentially a mechanism for transferring wealth from the impatient to the patient—captures the very essence of enduring wealth-building. It rewards not the boldest or the cleverest, but the most steadfast.

Then there is John Bogle, founder of Vanguard and a trailblazer in index investing. His push for low-cost, diversified portfolios broke down barriers, bringing wealth-building tools once reserved for the elite into the hands of everyday investors. Bogle's philosophy eschewed prediction and timing, favouring evidence and principle instead. He recognised that the real adversary for investors is often themselves—their impulses, reactions, and insatiable hunger for outperformance that comes at the expense of a coherent strategy. His counsel? Stay the course, ignore the noise, and trust in the slow, steady mathematics of compounding over time.

These aren't just lofty ideals. They are practical, actionable principles—but only effective when truly internalised and applied with regularity. Consistency, whether in investing or in life, is most rigorously tested in times of uncertainty. We do not operate in a vacuum; investments unfold against a backdrop of economic shocks, political upheaval, pandemics, technological change, and personal trials. The world remains—and will always be—unpredictable.

The investor who thrives is not one who attempts to predict every crisis or seize every fleeting opportunity. Rather, they are the individual who constructs a plan resilient enough to absorb shocks and flexible enough to evolve. They understand that short-term turbulence is a feature, not a flaw, of long-term investing. They prepare rather than predict, rebalance instead of react, and concentrate on what lies within their control—their savings rate, asset allocation, and behaviour—rather than wrestling with forces beyond their grasp.

It is precisely during these turbulent moments that the emotional virtues of a long-term strategy come into sharp relief. When markets wobble, those with clearly defined goals, well-diversified portfolios, and a steadfast time horizon can afford to remain calm. They recognise that a poor quarter—or even a poor year—is no indictment of their plan. They know downturns are fleeting, and panic invariably costly. In this sense, patience is not merely a virtue; it is armour against self-inflicted damage.

Moreover, the long game stretches beyond the span of one's own life. A thoughtful approach to wealth encompasses legacy—not simply in terms of inheritance, but through the values, habits, and frameworks passed down. Many investors see their financial journey as an opportunity to foster generational stability. This is not about fostering dependence, but about equipping the next generation with the mindset, knowledge, and tools necessary for wise financial decision-making.

Imagine the profound effect of teaching children the worth of saving, the rudiments of investing, and the merits of delayed gratification. These lessons, reinforced through example, often carry more weight than the assets themselves. They sow continuity—not just of capital, but of wisdom. In a world where financial literacy cannot be taken for granted, such deliberate legacy-building is as much an act of generosity as it is of responsibility.

Estate planning, naturally, forms part of this mindset. It ensures assets pass according to your wishes, minimising confusion and unnecessary costs. Yet beyond the paperwork, your true legacy is shaped by the narrative of your life—how you earned, saved, invested, gave, and lived. This story can inspire gratitude, confidence, and stewardship in those who follow.

As we close this chapter, it is worth reiterating the fundamental truth running through every page: financial success is not a single event but a process. It is built not on flashes of brilliance but on the cumulative power of disciplined behaviour maintained over decades. It rewards those willing to forgo the quick thrill of short-term wins in favour of the quiet satisfaction found in steady progress.

The long game is no easy path. It demands resisting distraction, delaying gratification, and staying focused when others succumb to noise. But it is deeply rewarding. It offers not just financial gain but personal growth—sharpening judgement, strengthening character, and deepening appreciation for the power of intention. It teaches that "enough" is often better than "more," that resilience outweighs returns, and that true freedom is the richest dividend of all.

As you move forward, remember: your wealth reflects the sum of your choices—not merely financial, but behavioural, emotional, and ethical. Every decision—to save, invest, spend, or give—shapes not only your portfolio but the very fabric of your life. There will be setbacks, and there will be surprises. Yet with a clear plan, a steady mindset, and a view set firmly on the long term, you will navigate them with confidence.

Playing the long game is not about arriving at some fixed endpoint. It's about building a life of stability, purpose, and freedom—brick by brick, year by year. And in doing so, it reveals a truth often drowned out by the clamour of financial media and market speculation: wealth is not a number. It is the capacity to live without fear, to act without compromise, and to shape your future with intention.

That, in the end, is the promise of the long game. Available to anyone willing to begin, persist, and trust that patience and discipline, quietly applied over time, will do their profound work.

Why True Wealth is More Than Money

When most people speak of wealth, they're referring to monetary assets—bank balances, investment portfolios, properties, and material possessions. Yet, as countless individuals have discovered through experience rather than theory, the mere accumulation of money does not necessarily lead to a richer, more fulfilling life. True wealth encompasses far more than financial capital. It includes emotional well-being, personal freedom, meaningful relationships, a sense of purpose, and the ability to live in alignment with one's values. Money, though powerful, is only one ingredient in the broader composition of a life well-lived.

To understand the limits of financial wealth, it is helpful to consider what people actually desire when they seek money. Rarely is the goal the paper itself. What they truly want is what money can represent—security, autonomy, comfort, status, or the freedom to make choices. Yet these desires are not guaranteed by financial success. One can be financially secure and still feel anxious. One can be asset-rich but time-poor. There are countless examples of individuals who possess more wealth than they could ever spend, yet find themselves grappling with dissatisfaction, strained relationships, or a loss of identity.

This paradox—of having everything and still feeling empty—has long intrigued psychologists, economists, and philosophers. The field of behavioural economics has consistently shown that once basic needs are met, the marginal happiness derived from additional income diminishes. A widely cited study by Princeton researchers Daniel Kahneman and Angus Deaton found that day-to-day emotional well-being does not significantly increase beyond a certain income threshold. People might report greater life satisfaction with higher incomes, but their levels of happiness, stress, or sadness remain largely unchanged. This suggests that financial wealth, while essential up to a point, eventually reaches a plateau in its ability to improve quality of life.

One explanation lies in the adaptability of human desires. As income grows, so too do expectations. A lifestyle once considered luxurious becomes the new baseline. The car, the house, the holidays—all once aspirational—are quickly normalised. This phenomenon, known as the hedonic treadmill, keeps individuals striving for more, even as the satisfaction they derive remains static or fleeting. Without an internal compass rooted in purpose or contentment, this pursuit can become a relentless cycle.

Financial security, however, remains a foundational pillar of well-being. Its importance should not be understated. The ability to cover basic needs without fear—housing, healthcare, education, and emergency support—is indispensable. It reduces stress, enhances personal agency, and creates the mental space necessary for creative, relational, and reflective pursuits. In that sense, money does buy freedom, but only up to the point that it alleviates scarcity and vulnerability. Beyond that, the relationship between wealth and happiness becomes less direct and more dependent on how that wealth is understood and used.

A practical application of this understanding is the concept of intentional spending. Rather than chasing status symbols or impulsive consumption, financially mindful individuals allocate resources towards experiences, personal growth, or activities that reinforce their values. Research suggests that spending on experiences—such as travel, learning, or shared meals—brings more sustained happiness than spending on possessions. Experiences are relational and narrative-driven; they form memories, create stories, and foster connection. Possessions, by contrast, often lose their emotional value quickly and can even become sources of stress due to maintenance, storage, or comparison with others.

Real-world examples further illustrate this point. Consider the case of a successful entrepreneur who sells her company for millions and buys everything she once thought would bring happiness—properties, cars, luxury goods—only to find herself disoriented and unfulfilled. Eventually, she shifts focus to mentoring young entrepreneurs, supporting social causes, and spending quality time with her family. In interviews, she reflects that it wasn't the financial windfall that changed her life, but what she chose to do with it once she realised that true satisfaction wasn't for sale.

This pattern repeats across many accounts of financially successful individuals. Once the novelty of wealth wears off, those who thrive are often those who reorient their lives around purpose. They invest in health, community, learning, or legacy. They cultivate relationships and design lifestyles that reflect who they are, not what others expect of them. These choices are not available to everyone, but the principles behind them are. You do not need extraordinary wealth to prioritise meaning, connection, or generosity. These can be pursued at any income level, often with greater intentionality and impact.

Another vital component of true wealth is time. Financial independence is often defined not just by how much one has, but by how one spends each day. Time wealth—the freedom to choose how your hours are allocated—is frequently cited by those who have achieved financial stability as the most valuable dividend. Whether it's the ability to pursue a passion, care for a loved one, or simply rest without guilt, time autonomy transforms the experience of daily life.

Yet many high earners find themselves with the inverse: abundant money but no time. Careers that demand long hours, high stress, and perpetual connectivity can crowd out the very things money is meant to support—health, family, recreation, reflection. This misalignment is often rationalised as temporary: "just until I've saved enough" or "just until the next promotion." But without clear boundaries or a reset of priorities, this temporary sacrifice can become a permanent way of life. Recognising this, some choose to downshift—opting for part-time work, career changes, or simpler lifestyles. They trade excess income for flexibility and well-being, redefining wealth not by net worth but by quality of life.

A further dimension is emotional and psychological health. Chronic anxiety about money—regardless of actual wealth—undermines well-being. This is especially true for those who grew up in financially unstable environments. Even after achieving material success, they may carry deep-seated fears of scarcity or loss. For such individuals, the work of building true wealth involves not only financial planning, but also emotional processing and mindset shifts. This highlights the importance of financial education that includes behavioural insight. Understanding why we think and act the way we do with money is as important as knowing where to invest it.

Community, too, is integral to genuine wealth. Financial independence without social connection can lead to isolation. People are fundamentally relational, and the richness of life is often measured not by possessions, but by shared experiences, mutual support, and the sense of belonging. Philanthropy, volunteering, and mentorship are ways in which financially secure individuals often reconnect with community and find renewed purpose. Giving, in this sense, is not an act of sacrifice but one of integration—it reinforces the interconnectedness of financial and social well-being.

As one ages, the definition of wealth continues to evolve. Health takes precedence. Relationships deepen in importance. The desire to contribute, to leave a legacy, or to impart wisdom becomes more prominent. A lifetime of disciplined investing, budgeting, and planning may result in significant financial assets, but it is the values, habits, and impact that endure. Legacy, then, is not about what is left behind materially, but what is passed on intellectually, emotionally, and ethically.

Ultimately, true wealth is a mosaic. It combines financial security with time, purpose, health, autonomy, and relationship. It is measured not by numerical thresholds but by the ability to live authentically and with intention. While financial literacy and investment acumen are essential tools in building this life, they must be paired with deeper reflection about what money is for and how it serves the broader aims of happiness and fulfilment.

Recognising that wealth is more than money reframes how we approach our finances. It encourages us to view money not as the goal, but as a tool—one that can support a life of meaning if used wisely. In doing so, we shift from accumulation for its own sake to a form of stewardship that enriches not only our own lives, but those around us. This, in the end, is what defines true wealth: not what we have, but what we create with what we have.

Lessons from Legendary Investors

In a financial landscape saturated with information, conflicting opinions, and ever-evolving trends, the wisdom of legendary investors stands as a beacon of enduring clarity. These are not individuals who merely rode market cycles or benefited from luck. Rather, they are thinkers and strategists who cultivated principles that withstood decades of uncertainty, disruption, and technological change. Their success was not born of complexity but of insight, discipline, and a profound understanding of human behaviour. By studying their approaches, modern investors can extract principles that go far beyond asset selection or market timing—they can learn how to think, act, and endure with purpose.

Warren Buffett is perhaps the most frequently cited figure in investing history, and for good reason. Over more than seventy years, he transformed Berkshire Hathaway into a global powerhouse by adhering to a philosophy that combines deep value investing with behavioural restraint. Central to Buffett's approach is the idea of buying quality businesses at fair prices and holding them indefinitely. He is less concerned with the fluctuations of the market and more interested in the intrinsic value of the companies he owns. This long-term orientation runs counter to much of the noise in modern markets, where short-termism dominates headlines and quarterly earnings often dictate decisions.

Buffett's strategy is underpinned by two powerful ideas. First, that patience is a competitive advantage in a world addicted to immediacy. Second, that understanding one's own temperament is more important than possessing advanced technical skills. His famous remark—that the stock market is a device for transferring money from the impatient to the patient—captures a truth that many investors overlook: behaviour trumps brilliance. His ability to remain calm during periods of market turmoil, to resist herd mentality, and to make decisions rooted in fundamental analysis has created compounding effects that few can rival.

Similarly, Charlie Munger, Buffett's long-time business partner, offers equally profound wisdom. Known for his sharp wit and multidisciplinary thinking, Munger has repeatedly stressed the importance of mental models—ways of understanding the world that draw not only from economics, but from psychology, history, biology, and engineering. His belief that investors should seek to understand a latticework of disciplines reinforces a broader view of investing as an intellectual and behavioural endeavour. For Munger, success is not about predicting the future, but about preparing for it using timeless principles.

One of Munger's most enduring lessons is the importance of avoiding stupidity over seeking brilliance. He believes that consistently avoiding major mistakes—overconfidence, leverage, poor diversification, or investing in businesses one does not understand—is more impactful than chasing clever wins. This approach encourages humility, a quality often in short supply in financial circles. Munger's idea that knowing what you don't know is more important than pretending to know everything serves as a reminder that risk often stems from ignorance disguised as insight.

Another influential figure is John Bogle, the founder of Vanguard and a pioneer of index fund investing. Bogle's legacy is rooted not in complex strategies, but in his steadfast belief that simplicity and low costs yield superior long-term results. He recognised that most actively managed funds fail to outperform their benchmarks, especially after fees are taken into account. His response was revolutionary: create low-cost, passively managed funds that track broad market indices. The simplicity of this approach belies its power. By eliminating the need to predict market movements or pick individual stocks, Bogle empowered millions of investors to access market returns without unnecessary expense or stress.

Bogle's philosophy is not just about efficiency—it is about integrity. He viewed investing as a fiduciary relationship and believed the industry should serve the interests of the end investor, not intermediaries. His writings reflect a deep ethical commitment to fairness, transparency, and stewardship. In an age where financial products are often sold with opacity and complexity, Bogle's insistence on clarity and simplicity has left an indelible mark on the investment world.

Then there is Peter Lynch, who managed the Fidelity Magellan Fund from 1977 to 1990 and achieved an average annual return of 29%, making it one of the most successful mutual funds in history. Lynch's approach was refreshingly grounded: invest in what you understand. He believed that ordinary investors often had an edge because they observed consumer trends and business developments in everyday life before institutional analysts did. His advice to "buy what you know" was not an endorsement of blind familiarity but a call to stay within one's circle of competence and to conduct thorough research on businesses that one could grasp intuitively.

Lynch also emphasised the importance of discipline and long-term thinking. He warned against reacting to headlines or market dips and encouraged investors to focus on company fundamentals and growth potential. His success was not predicated on exotic strategies but on the consistent application of clear, rational criteria and a willingness to hold investments through volatility.

Ray Dalio, founder of Bridgewater Associates, offers a different lens—one that blends macroeconomic analysis with a systems-thinking approach. Dalio's principles, as outlined in his book *Principles: Life and Work*, reflect a deep commitment to radical transparency, rigorous process, and reflection. His investing style incorporates an understanding of cycles, debt, inflation, and human behaviour on a macro scale. While his strategies may not be easily replicated by individual investors, his philosophy offers critical insights: the value of intellectual humility, the need to stress-test ideas, and the importance of developing a repeatable process.

Dalio also underscores the role of pain in learning. Mistakes, he argues, are valuable data points if one is willing to confront them honestly and make systematic changes. His emphasis on feedback loops, process-driven decision-making, and understanding one's emotional triggers enhances the broader conversation about investing as a behavioural discipline, not just an analytical one.

One common thread running through these diverse voices is the rejection of short-termism. Legendary investors are rarely those who made a single windfall or correctly timed a market cycle. They are those who developed a coherent philosophy, applied it consistently, and maintained discipline in the face of temptation, panic, or euphoria. Their lessons reveal that successful investing is as much about temperament as it is about technique.

Another shared characteristic is the prioritisation of capital preservation. These investors understand that avoiding large losses is more critical to long-term wealth creation than achieving extraordinary gains. They focus on asymmetric risk-reward profiles, diversification, and margin of safety—principles that protect portfolios during downturns and allow compounding to work over time.

For today's investor, these lessons offer both inspiration and caution. The strategies used by legendary investors are not locked in the past. They are enduring because they are grounded in principles that transcend market cycles and economic regimes. Yet they require discipline, humility, and patience—qualities that are often undermined by the fast-paced, reactive nature of modern financial culture.

Applying these insights does not require millions of pounds or insider access. It requires a clear understanding of one's goals, a commitment to process, and a willingness to learn from those who have walked the path before. Whether you invest through index funds, build a dividend portfolio, or explore real estate, the essential qualities of long-term success remain the same: clarity, consistency, restraint, and an orientation towards the future.

The voices of Buffett, Munger, Bogle, Lynch, and Dalio—while distinct—harmonise around a single truth: investing is not about brilliance or prediction, but about preparation and behaviour. Their lives and legacies remind us that building wealth is not a game of chance or charisma. It is a practice of thoughtfulness, patience, and purpose. In embracing their lessons, investors can anchor themselves in a framework that resists fads, withstands uncertainty, and ultimately delivers more than financial returns—it delivers a way to live and invest with conviction.

Staying the Course in an Uncertain World

Financial markets have never been predictable. From the Great Depression to the global financial crisis, from Black Monday to Brexit, and more recently, the COVID-19 pandemic and geopolitical unrest, history is replete with periods of volatility that have tested the resilience and resolve of investors. Yet throughout these turbulent times, one consistent truth has emerged: those who remain committed to a long-term strategy fare significantly better than those who panic, pivot, or abandon their plans entirely. Staying the course in an uncertain world is neither passive nor simplistic. It is an active, disciplined choice to remain anchored to a well-constructed investment philosophy amid the noise of unpredictability.

Uncertainty is the default setting of markets. It is not an anomaly to be eliminated but a feature to be managed. The future is always unknowable, no matter how sophisticated our models or how persuasive the latest analyst commentary may seem. This is why investing requires not just intellect but fortitude. It asks individuals to make decisions today with incomplete information about tomorrow. That discomfort is the price of admission to long-term wealth.

The psychology of uncertainty is such that it amplifies fear and short-term thinking. In times of market stress, even seasoned investors can feel compelled to act—to sell off positions, shift to cash, or chase the latest defensive asset. Yet the evidence is overwhelmingly clear: frequent trading and emotional reactions typically lead to underperformance. A study by DALBAR, which tracks investor behaviour, has repeatedly shown that the average individual investor significantly underperforms the market, primarily due to poor timing decisions fuelled by fear and impatience.

Consider the 2008 global financial crisis. Markets fell precipitously, wiping out years of gains in a matter of months. Investors who exited during the downturn locked in losses and missed the early stages of recovery. Those who remained invested, however, saw their portfolios not only recover but grow substantially in the ensuing decade. The market did not reward those who tried to avoid pain; it rewarded those who endured it.

Consistency in investing is not about ignoring the world's complexities. It is about building a strategy that anticipates them. A well-diversified portfolio, calibrated to your risk tolerance and time horizon, is not a static artefact—it is a dynamic shield against the vagaries of uncertainty. It allows you to stay invested without needing to predict the next crisis or economic shift. When markets fall, you are not forced to sell. When headlines turn bleak, you are not paralysed by fear. Your strategy absorbs the shock, allowing compounding to continue its quiet, relentless work.

There is also a philosophical dimension to staying the course. It is an expression of belief—not blind optimism, but reasoned confidence in the progress of markets, innovation, and human endeavour. History has shown that despite wars, recessions, pandemics, and political upheaval, economies recover, businesses adapt, and new industries emerge. The long-term trajectory of equity markets has been upward not because the world is free of crisis, but because it is resilient to crisis. This belief is what undergirds the discipline of long-term investing. It is the conviction that the future, while uncertain, is still worth investing in.

Practical steps help reinforce this commitment. Automation is one such tool. By setting up automatic contributions and reinvestments, you reduce the temptation to time the market. This approach, often referred to as dollar-cost averaging, ensures that you invest consistently regardless of market conditions. Over time, this has a powerful effect—not just financially, but psychologically. It shifts the focus from reacting to market movements to cultivating a habit of steady progress.

Another important element is reframing volatility. Too often, volatility is equated with risk, when in fact, it is the price paid for higher long-term returns. Cash and bonds may feel safer during downturns, but they carry the risk of inflation erosion and opportunity cost. Equities are volatile precisely because they offer a share in the growth of enterprise. Viewing temporary declines as part of the process rather than as aberrations can help reduce anxiety and promote composure.

Communication also plays a role in maintaining consistency, especially for those investing on behalf of others—family members, clients, or trustees. Setting expectations clearly from the outset helps prevent panic during inevitable drawdowns. When everyone understands that markets fluctuate, that portfolios are designed to weather those fluctuations, and that time, not timing, is the key determinant of success, it becomes easier to hold the line when fear threatens to take over.

A useful metaphor is that of aviation. Pilots expect turbulence—not because they can predict its exact timing, but because it is a natural part of flying. They do not abandon course at the first sign of rough air. They rely on their training, their instruments, and the knowledge that turbulence, while uncomfortable, is rarely dangerous when the aircraft is sound. In much the same way, investors must trust the architecture of their financial plan and resist the urge to make drastic changes mid-flight.

The challenge, of course, is that staying the course can feel like doing nothing. And in a culture that prizes reactivity, movement, and optimisation, restraint is counterintuitive. But doing nothing is often the hardest work of all. It takes discipline to resist selling during downturns, to ignore sensational headlines, and to continue contributing even when markets seem hostile. Yet this is precisely where the edge lies—not in superior stock-picking or economic forecasting, but in consistent behaviour across time.

Real-world examples underscore this point. Consider the investor who stayed invested through the dot-com crash, the 2008 financial crisis, and the pandemic-induced sell-off in 2020. Their portfolio would have experienced gut-wrenching drawdowns, yet also substantial recoveries. If they had sold at any of those points and failed to re-enter swiftly, they would have missed much of the rebound. Missing just a few of the best market days can dramatically impact long-term returns. These days often occur during periods of high volatility, making them difficult to time. Hence, being invested consistently is statistically more effective than trying to avoid downturns.

Moreover, the act of staying the course builds psychological resilience. It reinforces the idea that setbacks are temporary and that progress is cumulative. Each time you resist the urge to panic, you strengthen your ability to stay composed during the next test. Over time, this becomes a form of financial maturity—an internal compass that steadies you when the external environment becomes unpredictable.

This is not to say that one should never make changes to a portfolio. Life circumstances change, goals evolve, and strategies may need adjustment. But these changes should be proactive and intentional, not reactive and impulsive. The distinction lies in whether you are steering your course or being thrown off it. The former reflects strategy; the latter, emotion.

The capacity to stay the course in an uncertain world is increasingly valuable in an age of information overload. With financial news available in real time, social media amplifying fear and speculation, and algorithms designed to provoke emotional engagement, the challenge is no longer just external volatility—it is internal disquiet. The antidote is a clear, principled investment plan and a commitment to follow it with humility, patience, and discipline.

Ultimately, staying the course is about trust. Trust in your plan, your process, and the historical resilience of markets. It is a quiet but powerful form of agency. It frees you from the tyranny of reacting to every headline and allows you to participate in the deeper, more rewarding process of long-term wealth creation.

The investor who commits to consistency does not eliminate uncertainty—but they transcend it. They acknowledge its presence without surrendering to it. They understand that while the world may be unpredictable, their approach need not be. And in that steadiness lies the essence of financial success.

Your Financial Legacy

A well-structured investment plan, when sustained over time, does more than compound returns—it builds a legacy. While wealth accumulation is often viewed through the lens of individual success, its true potential lies in the impact it can have across generations. Your financial legacy is not merely the assets you leave behind, but the values, knowledge, and opportunities you provide to those who follow. Long-term investing, when approached with clarity and purpose, becomes a quiet act of stewardship. It reflects a mindset that looks beyond immediate needs and imagines a future where one's decisions shape the security and freedom of others.

Leaving a financial legacy is not about opulence. It is about continuity. It ensures that future generations are not just beneficiaries of capital, but inheritors of stability, responsibility, and choice. In a world increasingly characterised by economic uncertainty, inequality, and rapid change, the ability to provide for one's family beyond one's lifetime is a profound gift. It allows children and grandchildren to pursue education without debt, take entrepreneurial risks without crippling fear of failure, and weather life's inevitable setbacks with a measure of resilience.

One of the most powerful arguments for long-term investing lies in its time-transcending nature. The power of compounding—when allowed to run uninterrupted—creates exponential growth that dramatically favours those who think in decades rather than years. A portfolio built with generational intent can expand far beyond its original scale. Consider an investor who begins allocating funds in their thirties and continues steadily until retirement. Even moderate contributions, left invested and allowed to grow, can result in substantial sums by the time the next generation is ready to inherit. Add another 20 or 30 years of growth, and that same capital—if properly managed—can double or triple in size.

This is why many of the world's most enduring family fortunes were not built on windfalls but on the disciplined application of long-term investing principles. They reflect a belief not just in markets, but in stewardship—a responsibility to preserve and expand wealth with intention and foresight. Crucially, these legacies are not successful merely because of financial strategy; they are anchored by structure, education, and communication.

The structural elements of legacy planning include trusts, wills, tax-advantaged accounts, and succession frameworks. These tools, when correctly employed, ensure that wealth is passed on efficiently and according to the benefactor's values. They protect against fragmentation, minimise tax exposure, and provide clarity in moments that are often emotionally charged. Yet even the most meticulous legal structures are insufficient on their own. The real work lies in preparing the recipients—financially, emotionally, and philosophically—for what they will inherit.

Too often, wealth is lost within a generation or two. The reasons are well-documented: lack of financial literacy, poor communication, conflicting values, or simply an absence of preparedness. This is where legacy shifts from a financial to a behavioural concept. Teaching future generations the principles of delayed gratification, thoughtful risk-taking, budgeting, and investing is as important as the capital itself. Legacy is not the transmission of money—it is the transfer of mindset.

This is why families who succeed at legacy-building invest in education as fervently as they invest in equities. They normalise conversations about money, not in a way that breeds entitlement, but in a manner that fosters understanding. Children are introduced to the basics of saving, compound interest, and giving. Teenagers may be included in discussions about charitable giving, budgeting, or investment decisions. Young adults are mentored through their first jobs and guided through the implications of credit, tax, and long-term planning.

These conversations create continuity. They turn financial stewardship into a family culture. They mitigate the risk that wealth will be misunderstood or squandered. More importantly, they empower the next generation to use their resources wisely—whether that means funding a start-up, pursuing higher education, or supporting social causes.

The most effective legacies also reflect personal values. They are not just about maximising returns, but about aligning wealth with purpose. For some, this may mean setting aside a portion of their portfolio for philanthropic endeavours or environmental causes. For others, it may involve investing in community infrastructure, education funds, or affordable housing. In every case, legacy becomes not just a financial question, but an ethical one: what do I stand for, and how do I express that through the wealth I leave behind?

The act of investing long-term is, at its heart, a declaration of belief in the future. It suggests that despite volatility, setbacks, and systemic challenges, progress is possible—and that it is worth participating in and contributing to that progress. It is a deeply hopeful stance, one that offers not only the possibility of material inheritance but also a philosophical one. It tells those who come next: I believed in tomorrow, and I acted accordingly.

Real-world examples illustrate this vividly. Consider the Rothschild family, whose wealth has spanned centuries, adapting to wars, financial crises, and changing economic landscapes. Their longevity is not just due to banking acumen, but to careful planning, familial education, and adaptive strategy. Or take the case of Chuck Feeney, the billionaire philanthropist who gave away the majority of his fortune while alive, leaving a different kind of legacy—one that prioritised impact over accumulation. His example shows that legacy is not always about preserving wealth; sometimes, it is about how strategically and generously it is deployed.

Even for those without vast fortunes, the principles remain relevant. A modest but well-managed pension, a home passed down, or an education fund for grandchildren can have transformative effects. What matters is not the size of the legacy, but its intentionality. The thought and care behind it, the conversations it sparks, and the confidence it provides are all part of its enduring value.

The practical application of legacy planning begins with clarity. What do you want your wealth to achieve beyond your lifetime? Who do you want to benefit, and in what way? What values do you hope to pass on? Once these questions are addressed, the mechanics—investments, trusts, insurance, and documentation—can be aligned accordingly. The process is not static; it evolves as family circumstances change, laws are updated, and perspectives shift.

A critical part of this evolution is ensuring that wealth does not become a burden. Inherited money can complicate relationships, create dependence, or trigger disputes if not managed transparently. This is why many experienced financial planners advocate for open communication and gradual involvement of heirs in the management and understanding of family wealth. The goal is not to control outcomes but to equip future stewards with the knowledge and values needed to make their own informed decisions.

In the end, your financial legacy is not a conclusion—it is a continuation. It reflects your life's work, your priorities, and your belief in what comes next. Through long-term investing, you build not just assets but options: the option for your children to choose education over debt, for your grandchildren to start businesses with less risk, and for your family to engage with the world from a place of security rather than scarcity.

Legacy, then, is not a matter of wealth alone. It is a matter of wisdom—of foresight, responsibility, and trust. It is an investment not just in markets, but in people. And when constructed with care, humility, and conviction, it is one of the most enduring forms of financial expression, offering not only material support, but a deep and lasting sense of continuity.

Final Words: Embracing the Journey

The act of building wealth over the long term is far more than a numerical exercise. It is a lived experience, one that reveals its deepest rewards not in moments of excitement or dramatic gains, but in the quiet, cumulative power of sustained effort. Patience and discipline—two principles that receive far too little attention in a world obsessed with instant gratification—stand at the heart of enduring financial success. And yet, their real value often escapes us until we look back and realise how much they've shaped the lives we've been able to lead.

Patience, when applied to investing, is not passive. It is a conscious refusal to be drawn into the distractions and temptations of short-term thinking. It means resisting the urge to react to every market fluctuation, media headline, or peer comparison. It involves trusting in a well-founded strategy even when it feels uncomfortable, boring, or out of step with the times. Patience is what allows compounding to unfold. It is the time horizon over which discipline can do its work.

Discipline, in turn, is the daily act of showing up: contributing to a pension when it would be easier to spend, rebalancing a portfolio when emotions suggest otherwise, reviewing financial goals with consistency and intention. It's not glamorous. No one receives accolades for increasing their index fund contributions or resisting lifestyle inflation. But these quiet actions—repeated, sustained, and structured—form the architecture of a financially secure and autonomous life.

When these qualities are combined, they offer a form of compounding that goes beyond money. They shape character. They develop the capacity to delay gratification, to think beyond the moment, and to prioritise what matters most. The long-term rewards of patience and discipline are not only found in wealth accumulation but in personal growth and peace of mind. They create a life that is financially stable, emotionally grounded, and strategically free.

Consider the investor who begins contributing a modest sum each month in their twenties. Over the years, they increase their contributions with each pay rise, resist the urge to chase trends, and avoid panic during downturns. By their forties, they have a portfolio that provides optionality—a buffer against redundancy, a down payment for a home, funds for their child's education. By retirement, their consistent actions have grown into a reservoir of freedom. And perhaps most importantly, they have done so without sacrificing their sanity or integrity to short-term noise.

Their counterpart, by contrast, may have made larger, more dramatic investments—bought aggressively into rising markets, traded frequently, tried to time the highs and lows. Perhaps they even had a few years of outsized returns. But without a consistent foundation, their gains were fragile. They bought high and sold low. They chased success but failed to build structure. In the end, they may have worked harder, worried more, and achieved less.

This contrast reveals a truth that is both humbling and liberating: you do not need to outsmart the market. You need to outlast it. The most successful investors are not those who predict the future, but those who prepare for it with clear-eyed realism and repeatable habits. They understand that markets will be unpredictable, that emotions will fluctuate, and that surprises are inevitable. But they build strategies that absorb those shocks and continue to function.

To embrace this mindset is to embrace a different rhythm of life. It means choosing consistency over drama, compounding over speculation, and peace of mind over performance anxiety. It is not an easy path, especially when surrounded by a culture that values novelty and speed. But it is one that delivers not only financial dividends, but emotional and psychological ones as well.

There is great power in knowing that your financial future is not dependent on external forces but on internal habits. That your progress is not at the mercy of markets but within your control. This does not mean ignoring risk, avoiding adaptation, or assuming that past trends will continue indefinitely. It means acknowledging the limits of prediction and leaning into the power of preparation.

The long game teaches humility. It reminds us that success is rarely linear and that setbacks are not failures, but part of the process. It rewards those who are willing to endure discomfort, not because they enjoy it, but because they understand its role in transformation. The wealthiest individuals—measured not just in money but in autonomy and satisfaction—are often those who learned to be comfortable being uncomfortable, to trust the unseen effects of small decisions repeated over time.

These ideas are echoed across cultures and philosophies. The Stoics spoke of self-control and endurance. Eastern traditions emphasised detachment from outcome and alignment with process. Modern behavioural finance underscores the same themes: that emotional regulation, habit formation, and long-term perspective are what truly distinguish successful investors.

As you consider your financial path, ask not just what you want to achieve, but how you want to live. What kind of relationship do you want to have with money? What trade-offs are you willing to make, and which ones are non-negotiable? What will success look like—not just on a spreadsheet, but in your day-to-day experience?

There is no single correct answer. Some will define success as early retirement. Others as the ability to travel, to support family, to give generously, or to work on their own terms. The beauty of the long game is that it accommodates all of these. It provides a platform upon which individual definitions of freedom can be built—because it is not prescriptive, but permissive.

And when the time comes to look back—to reflect on the decades of decisions made—it is not likely to be the returns alone that stand out. It will be the confidence of knowing you acted intentionally, the relief of having avoided avoidable mistakes, and the gratitude of having choices. It will be the knowledge that you lived with foresight, that you valued peace over panic, and that you created a life of sufficiency not through luck, but through deliberate action.

So let this be the final word: the long game is not about being perfect. It is about being persistent. It is not about predicting outcomes, but about shaping them through steady, informed effort. It is not about never being wrong, but about being willing to correct and continue. It is not about having more than others, but about having enough for yourself.

The rewards of patience and discipline are not just at the end of the road—they are embedded in the path itself. They are found in the quiet confidence of knowing you are aligned with your principles, acting on purpose, and building something that matters.

That is worth embracing. Not just as a strategy, but as a way of living.

About the Author

Luca Reinhardt is a European financial strategist and behavioural economics enthusiast known for his no-nonsense approach to personal finance. With over 15 years of experience studying market cycles, investor psychology, and long-term wealth planning, Luca has built a reputation for helping individuals think beyond quick wins and short-term trends.

Grounded in both data and human insight, his work focuses on empowering readers to build sustainable wealth through clarity, patience, and strategic decision-making. Luca believes the true key to financial success lies not in chasing market hype—but in cultivating emotional discipline, consistency, and purpose-driven investing.

When he's not writing or consulting, Luca speaks at international finance summits and mentors young professionals on aligning money with meaning. The Long Game distills his most powerful insights into one compelling guide for those who are ready to stop gambling and start growing.

www.ingramcontent.com/pod-product-compliance
Lightning Source LLC
Chambersburg PA
CBHW031339230926
51848CB00002B/303
9789362924803